"Just when you thought everything about the 82nd Airborne Division in World War II had been published, author Ben Powers delivers *Never a Dull Moment, The 80th Airborne Anti-Aircraft Artillery Battalion in World War II*. Excellently researched and written, this powerful book fills a critical void about a lesser known, but so very important unit in the 82nd. Simply put, while the unit's name 80th AAA makes one think about a single-mission weapon, a .50-caliber machine gun used against aircraft, the unit's 57mm gun batteries provided much-needed firepower to the lightly armed paratroopers as an anti-tank weapon. The book chronicles the fledgling birth of U.S. airborne and glider operations, but also the important challenge of converting the entire battalion to a glider-borne force and preparing the unit for combat. After landing in North Africa, the unit earned bronze campaign stars in Sicily and Italy before returning to England as part of the buildup for D-Day in Normandy. After fighting in France, the 80th AAA played a huge role in Operation *Market Garden* and the Battle of the Bulge. Finally, the battalion pushes on across the Rhine to VE Day. This book is a must read and should be included in any World War II Airborne and glider library!"
—Colonel Mark C. "Plug" Vlahos, USAF-Retired, USAAF Troop Carrier and Glider Operations historian and author

"*Never a Dull Moment* provides an intriguing insight into the WWII exploits of the 80th Airborne Anti-Aircraft Artillery Battalion. Ben Powers's book honors the legacy of these courageous WWII glidermen who fought so gallantly for our liberation, but whose contribution to winning the war has been dismally overlooked by many. The impeccable research of Powers, put together in this wonderful book, has finally given these warriors their rightful place in WWII history."
—LTC Colonel Jos Groen MSc, Royal Netherlands Army (Ret.) and author of *Three of the Last WWII Screaming Eagles*

"The 80th AAA Battalion has lacked a detailed, personalized unit history for some time. Ben Powers has filled that historical gap in fine fashion. Meticulously researched, *Never a Dull Moment* takes the reader through the development, manning and combat deployments of one of the 82nd

Airborne Division's critical subunits. In a few scant years, the 80th built up an enviable combat record, and Powers crafts that record into a highly readable, well-documented story, and does it using the words of the men that served in that fine unit."

—Joe Muccia, Marine combat veteran and co-author of *Cry Havoc: An Untold Story of Rangers at War*

NEVER A DULL MOMENT

NEVER A DULL MOMENT

The 80th Airborne Anti-Aircraft Artillery
Battalion in World War II

LTC ARTHUR "BEN" POWERS (RET.)

Pennsylvania & Yorkshire

Published in the United States of America and Great Britain in 2024 by
CASEMATE PUBLISHERS
1950 Lawrence Road, Havertown, PA 19083
and
47 Church Street, Barnsley, S70 2AS, UK

Copyright 2024 © Arthur "Ben" Powers

Hardcover Edition: ISBN 978-1-63624-006-0
Digital Edition: ISBN 978-1-63624-007-7

A CIP record for this book is available from the British Library

All rights reserved. No part of this book may be reproduced or used in any manner without written permission of the copyright owner except for the use of quotations in a book review.

Printed and bound in the United Kingdom by CPI Group (UK) Ltd, Croydon, CR0 4YY

Maps by Glenn Stover, SFC, USA (Ret.)

Typeset in India by Lapiz Digital Services, Chennai.

For a complete list of Casemate titles, please contact:

CASEMATE PUBLISHERS (US)
Telephone (610) 853-9131
Fax (610) 853-9146
Email: casemate@casematepublishers.com
www.casematepublishers.com

CASEMATE PUBLISHERS (UK)
Telephone (0)1226 734350
Email: casemate@casemateuk.com
www.casemateuk.com

Dedicated to the memory of Clifford A. Stump, E Battery, who introduced me to the history; the memory of Ray Fary, C Battery, who did more than anyone to preserve the history; and to the officers and men of the 80th Airborne Anti-Aircraft Artillery Battalion who made the history.

Contents

Preface	xi
Acknowledgments	xiii
Organization Chart and Maps	xvii

Introduction		1
1	Forming and Training the Team—Camp Claiborne, LA, Fort Bragg, NC, and Laurinburg-Maxton Air Base, NC	7
2	Learning from Experience—North Africa, Sicily, Salerno, and Naples	29
3	Adapting to the Environment—Northern Ireland, England, and Normandy	53
4	Doing Routine Things Routinely—Holland	93
5	Rising to the Occasion—The Bulge	123
6	Maintaining the Standard—Germany and VE Day	149
Afterword		177

Appendix A: 80th Airborne Anti-Aircraft Artillery Battalion Distinguished Service Cross Recipients	179
Appendix B: The Combat Infantryman's Badge	183
Endnotes	185
Bibliography	197
Index	203

Preface

In his Biennial Report for 1 July 1939 to 30 June 1941, to the Secretary of War, the Chief of Staff of the United States Army, General George C. Marshall, wrote that on 1 July 1939, "the active Army of the United States consisted of approximately 174,000 enlisted men." He went on to describe the Army at that point as ineffective, with almost no appropriation for realistic training, obsolete equipment designed to win the last war, and having "the status of that of a third-rate power."[1] By the middle of 1943, mobilization plans for that same Army called for a ground force of over 7 million soldiers, deployed worldwide and provided with the most modern arms and equipment American industry could produce.[2] This rapid expansion required officers and men from disparate backgrounds to come together into cohesive teams that could fight and win. Without training and discipline, regardless of the number of men and the quality of their equipment, these men could not achieve victory.

The story of the 80th Airborne Anti-Aircraft Artillery (AAA) Battalion is the story of the United States Army in World War II in microcosm. It consisted of men from throughout the country, most of whom would not have considered military service had their country not been attacked, brought together to learn to fight as part of a modern army and called to perform as a team under the stresses of combat. To do so successfully required leaders who could identify and articulate standards for their men so that they achieved and sustained superior performance. The men of the 80th AAA transformed from willing amateurs to seasoned professionals over two and a half years. From forming and training as a team before going overseas, through learning from experience and adapting to the environment of combat, to achieving and maintaining a high professional standard, the record established by the 80th is an example of how the U.S. Army came of age.

Acknowledgments

Writing this book has been, by turns, an international effort, a family affair, and an intensely personal journey. Authoring a book was the furthest thing from my mind when, in the spring of 2020, I saw a post on Facebook from a woman in Austria, asking for birthday cards for an 82nd Airborne Division World War II veteran. After exchanging a few messages with this woman, I learned that the veteran, Cliff Stump, shared the same birthday as me and lived about two hours from my home. Thus, I met Mr. Cliff Stump. So, thank you Dani Stöpsel for introducing me to Cliff. And thanks to Renee Davis, Lois Buford, and David Huntley for allowing me to celebrate Cliff with you.

I thought I knew a lot about the 82nd, but Cliff introduced me to the story of the 80th Airborne Anti-Aircraft Artillery Battalion, an unsung group of glider men who punched way above their weight during World War II. We lost Cliff, who served in E Battery, in 2023. I am so glad to have met him. Thank you, Cliff, for sharing your story. I can only hope I did your comrades, and you, justice.

While researching the 80th AAA, I learned that anyone interested in the World War II history of the 82nd Airborne owes an unpayable debt to Mr. Ray Fary. Ray fought as a member of C Battery and was the driving force behind preserving the memory of the battalion. I deeply regret not having the chance to meet Mr. Fary, who passed in 2014. However, I had the distinct honor and pleasure of getting to know Mr. Bob Burns, the son of Edward Burns, a veteran of D Battery, and the keeper of the 80th's history. His work on the 80th AAA Battalion Association newsletter, "The Outpost," provided a trove of anecdotes and information and is the foundation of this book. Bob is the man who

xiv • NEVER A DULL MOMENT

should have written this book. He shared so many resources with me, from primary sources and photos to his own research and notes, and most of all his time to ensure I got the story right. Anything that I got correct is due to his efforts. The mistakes are all mine.

The internet provided me the opportunity to get to know a variety of folks who are so much smarter than me and thank goodness they were willing to share the fruits of their research, and their passion for history. Foremost among them is Ms. Thulai Van Maanen. The descendant of Dutch heroes of World War II, Thulai is a 20-year veteran of the Royal Dutch Army, having deployed several times. She performs an invaluable service to the memories of 82nd veterans who fought during Operation *Market Garden*, ensuring their families receive the decoration of the Orange Lanyard of the Military Order of William bestowed on the division by Queen Wilhelmina in 1945. She is also an impressive researcher who kindly shared the fruits of her work, providing me with a great deal of primary material. Thank you so much, from one trooper to another.

One of the joys of this journey was meeting the irrepressible Micky Pratt and her husband Joe—the daughter-in-law and son of Major William Pratt, C Battery commander and battalion S3 operations officer. It has been an honor getting to know them over the last three years. Many of the illustrations in the book are the result of their generous sharing. Micky's love for her father-in-law, enthusiasm in researching and learning airborne history, and infectious energy motivated me when I was in a slump and could not envision how to see this project to fruition.

Then there are my pals in the Airborne Research Group. Moon Mullins, Glenn Stover, Mark Vlahos, and Phil Ward are true American heroes. Each is a decorated veteran and a talented historian in his own right. Moon, thanks for your friendship and example. Many of the sections of this book are the result of our discussions. I'll leave it to you to identify them. Glenn, who knew 30 years ago that we'd be the same age as old people? Thanks for the maps and the outstanding table of organization. Mark, you're an inspiration as an author and THE expert on troop carrier operations. Thanks for the support. Phil, you've been a source of motivation as an author for the last 12 years. I'm glad I can finally give you a copy of something I wrote.

I also wish to thank Ruth Sheppard and Casemate Publishers for the opportunity to tell the story of the 80th. Miss Ruth's patience and professionalism are largely responsible for this book.

To my friends Anthony Scerbo and Misty Jobe, thanks for just being there. You are the ones I rely on when I need a break from talking about airborne stuff, which admittedly is not very often. But when I DO need that break, I rely on you guys!

To John Sarno and his lovely wife Jenn. John, next to my sister you are my oldest friend and the best one a guy could ask for. It's been almost 50 years since we dug trenches in your mom's backyard, and we've lived the lives we dreamed of back then. I am so glad that, when I finally saw the church at Sainte-Mère-Église, back in 2020, you were there too. Thanks for making sure I made that trip. Jenn, thanks for taking care of John. You're the best.

To my mom, Carol Anne Libby, my dad, Arthur B. Powers Jr, and my sister, Sue Petro. Mom, you always made sure I did my best in all I attempted; success never mattered as much as a sincere attempt. You knew there was a book inside of me, and you made sure I wrote it. Dad, you motivated me to be a paratrooper, and I hope I made you proud. And to Sue, you've looked out for me from the day I was born. Your support, advice, and willingness to read this manuscript repeatedly have made this a better book than I could have produced on my own. Thank you.

To my kids, Arthur, Michaela, Emma, and Jordan. Arthur, you are the best son. Period. I don't say it enough, but you inspire me by the way you take on the challenges the world throws your way. Keep it up! To my daughters, I could say you're lovely young women, which is true, but it is more important to me to thank you for your contributions to my work. Michaela, your knowledge of the theory of vertical envelopment provided the framework for this volume. Emma, I would not have grasped the technical details of the CG-4A glider without your patient explanations. And lastly, Jordan. Our discussions about the tactical trade-offs between mobility and firepower in anti-tank weapons were both fun and informative. I love you all.

And for my wife, KC, I wish I had the words to express all I wish to say. You've endured the deployments, moves, and separations of military life, educated our wonderful kids, and did it with grace and strength of character. You're the toughest person I know and the reason I get up each day. I recall hearing somewhere that if you're going to steal, steal from the best. As Alexander Hamilton said of Eliza, you are the best of wives and best of women. I love you forever.

Organization Chart and Maps

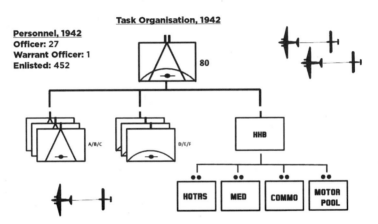

Tables of Organization and Equipment
44-275: Airborne Anti-Aircraft Battalion
44-276: Headquarters and Headquarters Battery, Airborne Anti-Aircraft Battalion
44-277: Automatic Weapons Battery, Airborne Anti-Aircraft Battalion
44-278: Machine Gun Battery, Airborne Anti-Aircraft Battalion

Assigned Weapons and Vehicles, 1942
× 353 Carbine .30 cal. M1
× 24 gun 37mm at or 40mm AA (57mm/6PDR)
× 36 MG .50 cal. HB
× 2 pistol .45 cal.
× 125 rifle 30. cal. M1903
× 43 trailer ¼-ton
× 43 truck ¼-ton
× 2 truck ¾-ton weapons carrier

Campaign Credit
× Sicily
× Naples–Foggia
× Normandy (with Arrowhead)
× Rhineland (with Arrowhead)
× Adrennes–Alsace
× Central Europe

Distinguished Unit Citation (Army), Streamer Embroidered Chiunzi Pass (Headquarters Battery, Battery D, Battery E, Battery F, Medical Detachment, 80th Airborne Anti-Aircraft Battalion Cited; WD GO 47, 1947)

Other Divisional Anti-Aircraft Battalions
11th Airborne Division, 152nd Airborne Anti-Aircraft Battalion
13th Airborne Division, 153rd Airborne Anti-Aircraft Battalion
17th Airborne Division, 155th Airborne Anti-Aircraft Battalion
101st Airborne Division, 81st Airborne Anti-Aircraft Battalion
First Airborne Task Force, Anti-Tank Company, 442nd Infantry Regiment

80th Airborne Anti-Aircraft Battalion, Table of Organization & Equipment. (Courtesy of Glenn Stover)

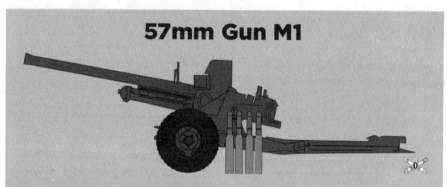

57mm Gun M1

Principal Characteristics
Crew: six
Overall length: 117in
Weight of gun and carriage: 2,810lbs
Breech mechanism: vertical sliding block, semi-automatic
Recoil mechanism: semi-automatic, hydro-spring recoil buffer

Calibre: 6PDR or 57×447mmr
Max elevation: +15 degrees
Max depression: -5 degrees
Traverse: 90 degrees (45R/45L)
Rate of fire: 12/15 rounds per minute
Armor penetration: 3.11 inches at 1,000 yards

Ammunition Types
Armor-piercing capped (APC)
Armor-piercing capped, ballistic capped (APCBC)
Armor-piercing composite rigid (APCR)
Armor-piercing discarding sabot (APDS)
High explosive (HE)
High explosive anti-tank (HEAT)
Smoke, white phosphorus (WP)
Canister
Training practice (TP)

(Courtesy of Glenn Stover)

ORGANIZATION CHART AND MAPS • xix

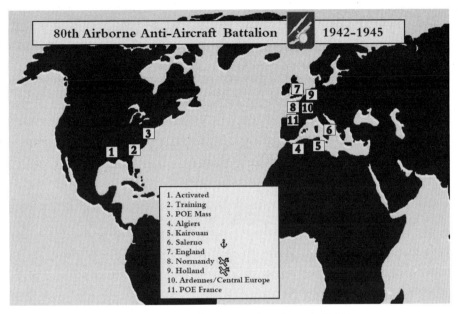

Battalion locations: from activation through VE Day.

Introduction

An American officer struggles through the unfamiliar terrain of the French countryside, looking for a place to best locate his unit's guns to support the advancing infantry—that is, if he can find any advancing infantry. All at once, a shrill buzzing overwhelms his senses, and he dives to the ground, covering his head with his arms. The earth shudders violently as the buzzing is replaced by rending, tearing noises. The Germans are bombarding suspected American concentrations, and their guesses are pretty good. The American troops have all gone to ground, and the advance is stalled.

The officer gives up on scouting gun positions and starts looking for members of his unit, the 82nd Infantry Division. As he slips, stumbles, and crawls, occasionally throwing himself down to dodge the incessant enemy barrage, he begins to come across isolated pockets of troops from his unit. Soon he has a couple of ad hoc squads with him, maybe 20 men. Not many, but enough to establish an outpost. The Germans won't be content with lobbing artillery fire. There will be a counterattack on the heels of this shellacking. The 82nd boys need to press on a little further and find a place to set up and prepare to defend against what they all know is coming.

The incoming shells aren't letting up, but the officer succeeds in locating a position with some decent fields of fire, as well as good cover. It could be better, but nothing's perfect. He starts positioning his boys, taking care not to spread them too thin. But what does that mean when you've got less than a couple of dozen guys? They must make do with what they have available. But then, things start looking up.

No, the artillery hasn't stopped. It's heavier than ever. But more troops start showing up. Attracted by the activity, and the fact that at least somebody looks like they know what they're doing, a dozen or so 82nd soldiers trickle in and place themselves under the officer's command. And then another group, and another—at least three platoons' worth. Understrength platoons, but the American officer now has maybe 50 guys under his command. They're in business. He continues moving about, giving orders, delegating tasks to junior leaders, and keeping a smile on his face. If he's upbeat, the troops won't think things are so bad.

Another enemy salvo whines through the air, the impacts ripping up the French soil. Despite the ringing in his ears, the officer can make out someone screaming in pain, along with shouts for assistance. He lifts his head and sees one of his infantrymen has been wounded by shellfire. The officer leaps to his feet and heads in that direction. After a brief sprint, he slides into the muck next to the stricken soldier and starts checking his wounds. Suddenly he feels as though he's been thrown into the air, an enormous pressure forcing all the air from his lungs. He slams back into the mud, gasping for breath. Then the pain hits.

Struggling to stay conscious, he can hear the first strains of panic begin to creep into the troops' voices. "The Old Man's down!" "The Boss got it!" The officer needs to put a stop to this. NOW. He makes some joke about how the Boche need to do better than that to keep him down. It's a weak attempt, but it does the trick. He does his best to remain in control of himself and direct the men to continue digging in, until maybe he can make it back to an aid station. But, jeez, he's starting to feel weak ...[i]

---

i   Dramatization of the Medal of Honor citation of Lieutenant Colonel Emory J. Pike, 321st Machine Gun Battalion, 82nd Infantry Division, near Vandières, France. Lieutenant Colonel Pike died of his wounds on 16 September 1918 and posthumously received the 82nd's first Medal of Honor for his actions. "Medal of Honor Citation: Emory Pike," Home of Heroes, accessed 8 March 2024, http://www.homeofheroes.com/moh/citations_1918_wwi/pike.html.

Emory Pike died over two decades before the United States entered World War II. It's unlikely that he could have imagined many of the innovations that came to fruition during World War II, such as jet engines or atomic weapons. He might not have even fathomed the idea that the inheritors of his division, by then designated the 82nd Airborne Division, would descend into battle dangling from parachutes or riding on gliders towed behind aircraft that the engineers of his day could only imagine. However, there was much about the World War II military experience that would have seemed very familiar to Pike. Taking disparate groups of individuals and forming them into a cohesive team, the need to learn from experience as well as from doctrine and theory, how to adapt to one's environment, the need to routinely perform tasks that must be done, and sometimes the need to push oneself to achieve results above and beyond the call of duty are all part of the nature of military organizations in wartime. The action for which Pike received the Medal of Honor encompassed all these tasks in a microcosm.

One recent change to the battlefield that Pike may have heard of was the introduction of mechanized armor, or tanks. The British fielded the Mark I tank in September 1915, almost one year to the day before Pike's death. At the time Pike was fighting in the vicinity of Vandières during the St. Mihiel offensive, Colonel George S. Patton was leading the first American tank attacks ever staged near the villages of Essey and Pannes, France. Once again, however, Pike probably could not have envisioned the vast armored divisions that characterized World War II. It's doubtful he ever even saw a tank in person, and if he did, he would have beheld vehicles with weaker armor, less well armed, and much slower than their successors in World War II. But the tank became prevalent on the battlefield, and thus new ways to defend against it had to be found. Much like Lieutenant Colonel Pike's 321st Machine Gun Battalion massed its firepower to support the division's infantry regiments against ground troops, the anti-tank battalions of World War II massed their firepower to assist infantry regiments against enemy armor. This book is the story of one

4 • NEVER A DULL MOMENT

such anti-tank battalion, the 80th Airborne Anti-Aircraft Battalion, 82nd Airborne Division.

The 80th AAA had to overcome several obstacles during World War II. At the beginning of the war, the officers and men had to create a new kind of unit from scratch, bringing together various skills, personalities, and prejudices. Additionally, the unit had to convert from a conventional combat unit to one transported into combat by glider. Hence, the men had to learn how to load and unload the glider properly with their cannons and other weapons, jeeps, ammunition, and supplies. In combat, the unit had to learn how to deal with German aircraft and armor and deliver maximum combat power to support the 82nd Airborne Division's infantry regiments. The men did this even though glider men did not receive the same respect as paratroopers, and the 80th lacked the status of the infantry regiments.

The 80th learned it needed heavier firepower than its original armament of 37mm anti-tank guns. They needed to obtain 57mm cannons/6-pounder cannons to deal with heavier German armor. More significant firepower would be better, but the carrying capacity of the gliders limited what the men could deliver to battle. The unit also learned they needed more anti-armor batteries and fewer anti-aircraft batteries, so they converted one of the anti-aircraft batteries to anti-armor as the war progressed.

The men initially felt forced to participate in a special unit without having the opportunity to volunteer. Men assigned to parachutist duty were volunteers, but the Army ordered men who would deploy by glider to do so without offering them a chance to volunteer. Throughout the war, the men developed pride in being glider men and airborne, although they did not initially share in the elite status enjoyed by paratroopers. As they learned lessons in combat, the men became proud of their skills and toughness but felt shortchanged compared with those in the infantry regiments. They shared the same hardships and dangers but did not receive the same respect because they were considered support troops.

The 80th AAA specifically developed an esprit de corps and a high degree of combat effectiveness while overcoming the abovementioned challenges. By the time of the Battle of the Bulge in December 1944, the unit was experienced, professional, and capable.

Despite their title, the gunners of the 80th fought more tanks than planes and went through the same processes of forming, learning, adapting, performing, and achieving characterized by Pike's World War I experiences. The payoff came during an intense 96-hour battle in December 1944, at Trois-Ponts, Belgium. But the process began two and half years earlier.

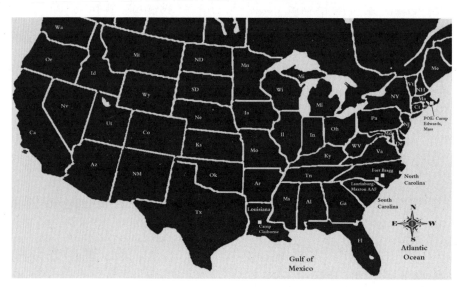

Camp Claiborne, LA, Fort Bragg, NC, and Laurinburg-Maxton Air Base, NC.

CHAPTER I

Forming and Training the Team—Camp Claiborne, LA, Fort Bragg, NC, and Laurinburg-Maxton Air Base, NC

In the summer of 1942, the 82nd Infantry Division underwent formation and basic training at Camp Claiborne, Louisiana, as part of the United States Army's buildup to fight World War II. The 82nd established a fine record during its training, and the War Department selected the division to form the nucleus of a new kind of fighting unit, the airborne division. The men and equipment of the 82nd would be divided equally, with half staying with the 82nd and half to form the nucleus of the new 101st Airborne Division. Each division would also receive one of the new parachute infantry regiments, which were then undergoing training separately as independent units. In addition to infantry, the 82nd would need special troops that could defend it from the threats of enemy aircraft and tanks; thus, it created this capability from scratch. The men assigned to be anti-aircraft and anti-tank gunners brought together various skills, personalities, and prejudices from their original companies in the infantry regiments but had to come together to learn their new mission.

The All-Americans

The Army selected the 82nd Infantry Division, which at that time was completing its formation and initial training at Camp Claiborne, Louisiana, to convert into an airborne outfit. As a standard infantry division, the 82nd was far larger than what Army Ground Forces envisioned as the correct size for an airborne division. As a result, the Army decided to divide the division in two, with each half forming the nucleus of a new airborne division. Thus, for the cost of one infantry division, the Army would receive two airborne units, the 82nd and 101st Airborne Divisions. As none of the soldiers assigned to the division were qualified parachutists, Army leaders further decided that the soldiers already assigned to the divisions' infantry regiments would be redesignated as glider infantry, and one regiment of parachutists would be assigned from airborne command to each division. The resulting structure would give the American airborne division two glider regiments, one parachute infantry regiment, and a variety of supporting arms and services to include artillery, engineers, and anti-aircraft/anti-tank battalions.

Private Edward Burns (right), D Battery, 80th AAA, with an unidentified friend during basic training. (Photo courtesy of Bob Burns)

The 82nd Infantry Division had an excellent combat reputation from World War I, when men such as Lieutenant Colonel Pike and the more famous Sergeant York of the Division's 328th Infantry Regiment earned the Medal of Honor. It performed well during its training period, led first by Major General Omar Bradley, who would rise to high command during the war, and then Mathew B. Ridgway. Ridgway was a protégé of Army Chief of Staff General George C. Marshall, and an officer with a reputation

FORMING AND TRAINING THE TEAM • 9

for high standards, efficiency, and physical fitness. While not happy that his division was to be broken up into two separate formations, he was nonetheless excited about the opportunity to engage in a new, and somewhat glamorous, form of warfare.

General William C. Lee, who had done much to bring America's nascent airborne capability from a concept to a reality, received command of the 101st Airborne Division in recognition of his contributions to the airborne concept and his expertise in parachute training. Lee had presided over the Army's Airborne Command at Fort Benning, Georgia, which was responsible for the Parachute School, two parachute regiments, and several smaller test units, including a parachute artillery battery and experimental glider units. In his role as the commander of this organization, Lee visited England to observe how the British Army organized its airborne forces and came away impressed that they had entire divisions of airborne troops, combining parachutists and glider men. Lee felt that such a unit could be organized for sustained combat and make a greater contribution in combat than independent regiments. Upon his return to the United States, Lee urged the commander of Army Ground Forces, General Lesley McNair, to organize an American airborne division. To Lee's surprise, McNair authorized two.[1] Once the matter of which units would comprise the new airborne divisions was decided, Ridgway made his way to Lee's Airborne Command at Benning to make an orientation parachute jump.[2]

The hum of aircraft engines drowned out almost any human voice, except for the loudest. The small group of men wearing plastic helmets and khaki uniforms, with parachutes strapped on their backs and across their chests, made no effort to speak. Each was absorbed in his thoughts. For most of them, this was going to be their first parachute jump. A few months earlier, none of these men would have considered doing such a thing. Jumping from an airplane was something a barnstorming daredevil would do, or the pilot of a stricken aircraft who could not save his plane—nothing professional soldiers would consider necessary as they prepared for war.

But these men are professional soldiers, and they have been earnestly preparing for war. Only now they will go to war from the air. Vertical envelopment is a new

10 • NEVER A DULL MOMENT

tactic for rapidly delivering men to the battlefield. The Italians and the Soviets were known to have experimented with parachute troops in the 1930s, but it was the Germans who seem to have made something of the idea. Their use of paratroopers and glider men during the invasion of the Low Countries back in 1940, followed by the air assault on the island of Crete in 1941, fully got the War Department's attention. The United States Army decided it was late to the party, and it was time to get into the airborne business. So, Matt Ridgway found himself getting ready to jump out of an airplane.

"STAND UP!" The officer acting as jumpmaster shouts his preliminary command. Ridgway stands and faces the rear of the aircraft.

"HOOK UP!" Ridgway snaps the metal connector attached to his parachute's woven static line to the steel anchor line cable that runs the length of the plane's fuselage. The static line will automatically deploy his chute as he falls away from the aircraft.

"CHECK STATIC LINE!" The general runs his fingers along the rolled and sewn fabric to ensure there are no rips or fraying that would cause the line to break before it can open his parachute.

"CHECK EQUIPMENT!" Now he pats the connectors that keeps his chute's harness in place across his chest and under his legs, along with the bulky reserve parachute that rests on his stomach.

"SOUND OFF FOR EQUIPMENT CHECK!"

"OK!" Ridgway replies, looking the jumpmaster in the eye.

The jumpmaster turns away from Ridgway and checks the open door. Far below, Ridgway can see the fields of Alabama stretching out toward the horizon, the ground rushing by at an impressive speed. The jumpmaster is craning his neck out the door toward the rear of the airplane. Suddenly, the plane slows.

The jumpmaster turns back into the plane and cries out, "STAND IN THE DOOR!" Ridgway shuffles his way toward the opening, keeping his left foot ahead of his right, minimizing the chance that he may stumble and fall. He turns to face the door, handing his static line off to the jumpmaster as he does so. Ridgway then slaps his hands to either side of the jump door, keeping his eyes on the horizon and trying not to look down. The jump warning light to his right glows red.

Suddenly the light flashes green, and at the same time Ridgway feels a sharp slap on his butt as the jump master calls out "GO!" Ridgway launches himself up and out and is immediately caught in the airplane's prop blast "ONE THOUSAND! TWO THOUSAND! THREE THOUSAND ...!" He's been taught to maintain a tight body position as he falls so that he won't spin and foul his parachute's shroud lines. Paratroopers count to four thousand as they await the opening shock of their main canopy No opening after four thousand, it's time to pull the reserve.

"FOUR THOU ...!!!" WHOOMP! Ridgway feels a tremendous opening shock as his main parachute deploys. Suddenly his fall is arrested and he feels himself drifting. He looks up to see the most beautiful sight imaginable—a full canopy blossoming above him.

Soon the peaceful feeling of floating is replaced by dread of the coming landing. Ridgway has several old sports injuries from his time as an athlete at West Point; a bad back is among the most concerning. Slamming into the ground at 18 feet per second is probably not the smartest thing to be doing, especially for a man in his 40s. But it's too late to reconsider that now. He prepares to land as the ground rushes to meet him. Feet and knees together, elbows tucked in, eyes on the horizon ... WHAM!!! Ridgway feels like he's just been thrown from the roof of a freight train as he tumbles across the dried dirt of the drop zone. As he comes to a stop, he takes stock. Nothing feels TOO bad. Actually, he feels pretty darn good. He's just jumped from a damn aircraft while in flight!

Airborne

The idea of American airborne forces landing behind enemy lines can be traced to Colonel (later Brigadier General) Billy Mitchell in the waning days of World War I. While serving as the Chief of Air Services for Pershing's army group, Mitchell formulated a plan to parachute infantry formations from bombers into the city of Metz in October 1918, to bypass German defenses. The plan never materialized, as the Allies already had gained the upper hand on the Western Front and the Germans signed an armistice less than a month later.[3] Subsequent development of airpower doctrine in the United States focused on using heavily laden bombers to attack a notional enemy's population centers and industrial capability, to negate large ground or naval forces and bring wars to a rapid conclusion with minimal casualties. The concept of combat parachuting faded into obscurity.[4]

The U.S. Army did not undertake a serious, systematic study of airborne infantry until the summer of 1940. As a result of reports of German military experiences and developments using glider and parachute-borne troops to cease or avoid built-up areas and fortified positions, the office of the Chief of Infantry detailed an officer to take on the project of analyzing the potential of parachute troops. An experienced infantry officer on the Army staff, Major William C. Lee, received the task. Lee was particularly suited to the role, having witnessed German airborne forces during European maneuvers while assigned as a military attaché to Paris and London in the mid-1930s.[5] Not content with conducting a mere paper drill, Lee arranged with the Infantry School at Fort Benning, Georgia, to establish a provisional test platoon consisting of two officers and 48 enlisted soldiers to undergo training as parachutists. Lee additionally coordinated with the Army Air Corps for support with aircraft, equipment, and parachute rigging. The provisional experiment proved successful, and the U.S. Army committed to rapidly expanding its capability to conduct airborne warfare.

Initial thoughts on airborne doctrine revolved around the concept that American parachute forces would be used for behind-the-lines operations involving quick strikes and sabotage of enemy installations. As such, the Army created a provisional parachute group to train a body of soldiers who, once qualified, could be assigned to independent parachute battalions and regiments that could undertake a variety of missions throughout a specific theater of operations. William Lee, promoted to colonel, assumed command of the Provisional Parachute Group in 1941. After the Japanese attacked the American naval base at Pearl Harbor, Hawaii, on 7 December 1941, the United States declared war on the Empire of Japan. Subsequently, Germany and Italy, Japan's Axis partners, declared war on the United States, and the U.S. Army faced the prospect of fighting a global war on multiple fronts.[6] The question of how airborne forces would organize and fight suddenly became far more urgent.

The War Department determined that the British Army, which began forming its disparate parachute units into division-sized units in October 1941, could offer the burgeoning American airborne some

FORMING AND TRAINING THE TEAM • 13

advice on how to deploy and sustain airborne troops in battle.[7] Once again Lee, now a general officer, found himself at the forefront of developments. He traveled to England to confer with his new allies in May 1942.[8] Lee found the British structure cumbersome, but saw a great deal of merit in combining the striking power of individual parachute battalions and regiments into a larger division and, upon returning to the United States, recommended to General Mark Clark, the Chief of Staff of Army Ground Forces (responsible for the doctrine and structure of army units) that the Americans "should organize airborne divisions of about 10–12 thousand men each, and separate parachute brigades of about 4,500 men each, each brigade to be reinforced with artillery and special units."[9] Rather than create such a division from scratch, Army Ground Forces determined to select a standard infantry division near the end of its formation and training to be designated as the United States Army's first airborne division. Any special arms or services required by the division would be created by reassigning men from within the unit wherever possible. Thus, members of the 325th and 326th Infantry Regiments would form the nucleus of the new 80th Airborne Anti-Aircraft Artillery Battalion.

The U.S. Army came late to recognize that armor would play a significant role on the battlefield after World War I. Lessons from that war identified the infantry as the supreme arm, with artillery taking a supporting role and the tank an incarnation of rolling artillery. Despite the potential that mechanization had to change the character of combat, with the promise of delivering heavy, mobile fire that could be massed against objectives, and the fact that artillery proved to be the most prolific killer on the battlefields of France, American officers chose to view the success of their infantry as proof that the individual rifleman ruled supreme. They were seen as the men who restored open warfare to its rightful place after years of stalemate and trench warfare on the Western Front. As a result, while many interwar theorists considered the potential of fast, well-armed, and protected armor formations in wars of the future, the U.S. Army consigned tanks to a supporting function, tied to the slower pace of the dismounted infantryman.

14 • NEVER A DULL MOMENT

Because of this reactionary viewpoint, defending infantry against armor was initially neglected. Dismounted infantry tactics stressed fighting against similarly armed infantry, with little thought given to fighting tanks. As time passed after the end of World War I, from 1918 to the 1930s, almost no attention was given to anti-tank weaponry. As the 1930s progressed, and war clouds began to gather over Europe once more, along with reports of German and Russian experiments with heavy armor formations, the War Department determined it was time to add some anti-armor capability to its infantry formations.

In keeping with the idea that dismounted infantry would remain the key to maneuver and offensive power in combat, the Army directed its Ordnance Department to look at anti-tank cannons that could be moved over rough terrain by small groups of men on foot. This requirement, almost by definition, removed all but the lightest cannons from consideration. Not only would the gun and its carriage need to be lightweight enough to be moved by dismounted troops, but the ammunition would also have to be carried using manpower instead of horsepower. As a result, the engineers at the Army Ordnance Department quickly settled on a variation of the 37mm gun.

From the end of the 19th century through the end of World War I and beyond, 37mm cannons had seen a spate of popularity in European armies. Initially, the round was a favorite of countries that were signatories to the Hague Convention of 1899, which limited the size and destructive capability of explosive projectiles, at a time when the idea of conducting a humane war was not considered an oxymoron. The 37mm shell was the largest type of ammunition that could be fielded and not violate the terms of the convention. As time went on, variations of the 37mm proved highly successful for the very reasons noted by American planners: its light weight, mobility, and maneuverability. At a time when armor on the battlefield was not a consideration or at least a prime consideration, such as 1916, these factors made considerable military sense. However, as tanks grew bigger and faster, with thicker armor, the advantages of the 37mm gun faded rapidly. But as the United States had won its war in 1918, the lessons of that victory became enshrined as doctrine, although the world had moved on.

By 1942, the War Department had determined the shape its anti-tank formations would take. Since anti-tank weapons were direct-fire, light cannons, the Army entrusted them with the troops who had experience with similar weapons. Anti-aircraft artillerymen, assigned to the old Coast Artillery Branch, performed an amalgam of functions that the field artillery had no interest in performing and found themselves cast in the role of anti-tank gunners. Thus, as the Army Ground Forces transformed the infantry division structure from the larger, four-regiment square divisions of World War I to the triangular three-regiment division, it assigned each airborne division an anti-aircraft battalion tasked to perform both the air-defense and anti-armor roles.

An anti-aircraft battalion consisted of six batteries: three anti-tank (AT) batteries armed with eight 37mm AT guns divided into two platoons of four, for a total of 24 cannons, and three anti-aircraft batteries armed with 12 .50-caliber machine guns, divided into three platoons of four, for a total of 36 AAA guns.

The 80th AAA Battalion of the 82nd Airborne Division was formed by assigning personnel from the machine-gun companies of the division's infantry regiments to create the nucleus of the unit. While many of these soldiers were initially infantrymen, the 80th AAA's table of organization called for the bulk of the troops to be assigned to coast artillery occupational specialties—a bureaucratic label for a job. This administrative distinction would influence how the men of the battalion were perceived and rewarded when they were subsequently deployed to combat.

The original title of the 80th was actually "80th Airborne Anti-tank Anti-aircraft Battalion." According to the unpublished unit history, this designation was not often used and was eventually forgotten. While it remains undocumented why the anti-tank designation was dropped, common sense leads one to believe that the combination of the unwieldy name and the fact that the officers and troops were assigned to the Coast Artillery Corps rather than the newly formed tank destroyer branch resulted in the use of "anti-aircraft" as the proper label.[10]

The assignment of the troops to the Coast Artillery Corps would ultimately lead to a small but significant slight to the men of the battalion.

16 • NEVER A DULL MOMENT

They had originally been infantrymen, reassigned from the heavy weapons companies of the 82nd's infantry regiments. The change of branch and collar brass may not have originally meant too much as the men prepared to go overseas. There was too much to do. Once in combat, the men performed their mission with their fellow airborne soldiers on the front lines, employing their cannons and machine guns in direct support of the parachute and glider regiments. However, when the War Department established the Combat Infantryman's Badge, awarded to recognize the unique sacrifices of front-line fighters, the men of the 80th found they were denied that honor. Their status as members of the coast artillery made them ineligible, despite the nature of their combat service. But all this was in the future. At the time of its formation, the 80th underwent its training at Camp Claiborne, Louisiana, with subsequent airborne and glider training conducted in North Carolina, between late 1942 and mid-1943. (See Appendix B for a more detailed discussion of the Combat Infantryman's Badge.)

Major (later Lieutenant Colonel) Whitfield Jack commanded the battalion throughout its time in the United States before deployment. A native of Louisiana, who went on to become a successful attorney and businessman, Jack was not tremendously popular according to the recollection of one of his lieutenants. At the time the battalion received orders for overseas movement in April 1943, Jack was assisted by Major Raymond E. Singleton in the role of battalion executive officer (XO). Once overseas, Jack received orders for reassignment to the division staff, and Singleton took command, leading the battalion throughout its combat campaigns.

The commanders of the anti-tank batteries included Captain John F. Stephens, A Battery; First Lieutenant Nock W. Russell, B Battery; and Captain William W. Pratt, C Battery. The anti-aircraft batteries were commanded by Warren C. Keith, D Battery; Captain Herald F. Jacobsen, E Battery; and Captain Choice R. Rucker, F Battery. The headquarters (HQ) established was overseen by Captain James C. Sherman. Additionally, First Lieutenant Joe S. Galatzan performed a dual role as the battalion surgeon and commander of the 80th's Medical

Detachment. All told the battalion contained a total of around 550 officers and soldiers at any given time.[11]

The administration, logistics, and training needs of such a disparate organization required competent staff work to ensure the men were properly paid, fed, equipped, trained, and looked after. While Whitfield Jack had overall responsibility for all his battalion did or failed to do, Major Singleton, as XO, oversaw the staff who planned and coordinated all the necessary activities that made the battalion a functioning military unit. Personnel functions were the purview of the S1 section under First Lieutenant Edward B. Dittmar, adjutant, with First Lieutenant Arthur Kroos acting as assistant S1. First Lieutenant Charles A. Coleman fulfilled the dual positions of intelligence officer and operations officer. Supply fell to battalion S4, Warrant Officer Junior Grade Robert F. Littlejohn. Second Lieutenant Worthington S. Telford and Second Lieutenant James E. Baugh rounded off the staff in the roles of communications officer and motor officer respectively.

The commanding general of the 82nd Infantry Division, Omar Bradley, who would subsequently rise to five stars and gain a reputation as the premier American commander in the European Theater of Operations, was determined that his division would be supremely fit, highly trained, and imbued with the spirit of the original 82nd of World War I fame. His assistant division commander, Matthew Bunker Ridgway, agreed wholeheartedly with Bradley's goals and instituted a rugged training regimen for the division once the newly inducted troops assembled at Camp Claiborne, Louisiana. The men of the 80th AAA Battalion were veterans of this program, which had a heavy emphasis on conditioning marches, obstacle courses, and weapons handling. The soldiers who passed through the 82nd's basic training course of instruction met Ridgway's goal that they be as finely conditioned as champion boxers.

As the division completed this initial training and commenced with more advanced collective training, Bradley received orders to take command of the 28th Infantry Division. The War Department considered the 28th to be struggling to complete its basic training phase and looked at

18 • NEVER A DULL MOMENT

Bradley as just the right commander to bring the division up to scratch.[12] Ridgway subsequently received command of the 82nd and was in charge when the orders arrived to assume the role of an airborne division.

Ridgway relished the challenge and announced the orders to the division with a sense of anticipation. When the troops learned that the airborne designation meant that they would ride gliders into battle—canvas and wooden aircraft with no engines, no weapons, no armor, and towed behind cargo planes like clay pigeons—they did not have the same enthusiastic reaction as their commanding general. Many went absent without leave soon after hearing the news. Ridgway was horrified but was told by his staff that the unexpected news had been a shock to the troops, and most of them would return when their shame at being AWOL overcame their fear of gliders. This prediction proved accurate, and all those except a small number who most likely were primed to desert in any event returned to the division and prepared to undergo the transition to airborne duty.[13] General Ridgway demonstrated the same dedication to leading by example he exhibited when he made his first parachute jump back at Fort Benning by coordinating with Army Ground Forces to detail a glider and an experienced pilot, Mike Murphy, to put on a demonstration of glider aerobatics, with Ridgway accompanying Murphy as a passenger. While the performance did not convert the men of the 82nd into rabid glider enthusiasts, it did prove that flying in one was not an automatic death sentence.[14]

Despite initial assumptions by Army Ground Forces that riding a glider into combat would be analogous to sitting in the back of a truck, the men assigned to glider units needed to develop specific skills for loading and securing their equipment and themselves onto the aircraft. Even though their duties required the men to acquire specialist knowledge and participate in regular flights, they did not receive the flight pay associated with being an aircraft crewmember or the hazardous duty money paid to parachutists. The men rightly perceived that they had to endure the hazards of special service with none of the perquisites. It would take two years for Army leadership to address this issue.

A young glider man sits in his bunk in a wood-frame, temporary barracks glaring at the floor. He's fed up with running around the boondocks playing war, he's

FORMING AND TRAINING THE TEAM • 19

fed up with the idea of puking his guts out riding in a glider of all things, but most of all he's fed up with the paratroopers he's had to deal with since coming to Fort Bragg. He knows he signed up to fight, and that he needs to be trained so the war games have a point, even if they feel like make-believe. Though he hated the glider familiarization ride he took, he does feel a small pride being in an airborne outfit, but he can't let go of his dislike of the jumping boys. That smug look they have on their face whenever they see a glider rider, talking about how tough jump school was and how they volunteered to take that punishment. Not to mention they get 50 extra bucks a month to jump. And those special boots they wear, tucking their trousers into the tops so they bunch up around the calves and show off that shiny leather. And calling glider troops "straight legs" or just "legs" because glider men just wear regular old low quarters. He's airborne too! And those gliders crack up on landing kind of regularly. It's dangerous, and it takes a lot of know-how to rig a glider for combat, but they don't receive any recognition for their skills or the hazards they face. Even the glider pilots get flight pay! He looks up at the mock recruiting poster some wise guy posted on the wall. It's illustrated with photos of crumpled, crashed gliders and features bold print proclaiming, "Join the Glider Troops! No Flight Pay, No Jump Pay, But NEVER A DULL MOMENT!"

Glider Operations

One of the significant challenges to be met by the 80th AAA was determining how to load and configure troops and equipment for glider operations. The glider manual produced by the War Department, Army Air Force Manual No. 50-17, specified that the various carrying capacities for the Waco CG-4A glider included 13 dismounted troops, a 37mm gun, or a jeep, among other combinations of men and equipment. The practical experience acquired during glider familiarization and training at the Laurinburg-Maxton Army Airfield in North Carolina taught the gunners of the 80th that "the glider arrangement was [to be] the gun, jeep or trailer with ammo. There would be the pilot, someone in the copilot's seat who knew a little about the glider, and four men."[15] As each gun required a gunner and assistant gunner for firing, along with a third soldier as ammunition handler, it was possible to get one cannon with its crew, or prime mover, or ammunition supply into one glider.

20 • NEVER A DULL MOMENT

Hence, multiple Waco CG-4As were necessary to deliver one gun with the crew and associated supplies and equipment into combat. Multiply that by 24 guns for the whole battalion, and the 80th needed something on the order of 66 gliders just to get its anti-tank capability into the fight.[i] This number did not include the gliders necessary for moving the anti-aircraft batteries, medical detachment, battalion staff, or other supporting elements.[16]

Subsequent events would show that the battalion would rarely bring all its combat power into battle by glider, and never would it do so in one large lift. The United States military would simply never field enough aircrews or aircraft to make such a course of action a possibility. The lack of available gliders hampered initial training in the United States before deployment. One officer in the 325th Glider Infantry described glider drills as when the men "marked off an 8x12 area and designated a door. We glider men loaded through this door and squatted opposite each other, then unloaded and fanned out in simulated combat." Accordingly, he described the troops as taking the pantomime "with a dry grin" and stated that his men eventually saw actual gliders and had the opportunity to fly in them.[17] The construction of the gliders themselves did little to inspire confidence in those tasked to ride them into the fight. T4 Leonard Lebenson of the division headquarters remarked that none of his comrades were impressed with the combination of "metal tubing, plywood, and canvas" and exposed guidewires running the length of the fuselage. Lebenson took advantage of the glider shortage to avoid participating in a familiarization flight. The lightweight gliders experienced buffeting from the prop blast from the propellers of the towing aircraft, which created a sensation for the glider passengers akin to being the last in line during a game of crack the whip. The potential for rough flights and the accompanying airsickness further exacerbated the unpleasantness.[18] Despite these drawbacks, another glider infantry officer stated that he

---

i   IX Troop Carrier Group allotted each anti-tank battery of the 80th 22 gliders to move its equipment into Holland during Operation *Market Garden* in September 1944.

had no recollection of any of his troops ever asking to transfer away from glider duty.[19]

The glider played a significant role in delivering combat power behind enemy lines during World War II. Before the advent of reliable helicopters that had the carrying capacity to move large numbers of men or heavy equipment, gliders were the only practical means of landing vehicles and larger weapons systems such as howitzers and anti-tank guns into combat, along with the crewmen who manned them. Additionally, the gliders had the advantage of delivering small units of infantrymen to their objective as a cohesive unit. When paratroopers exited an aircraft, they were on their own. Once they landed, their top priority was linking up with comrades to assemble enough strength to assault their objectives. Darkness, high winds, poor navigation, and rookie airmanship could all combine to widely scatter paratroopers during a drop. When gliders landed, the men they carried arrived together, organized and ready to fight. At least that was the concept.

Glider landings could be fraught with danger, and the landings were nothing more than controlled crashes. Riding in the back of a glider could be a hazardous duty, and the men assigned to the role did not have the option of volunteering, nor did they receive any additional compensation or marks of distinction such as the jump pay and parachutist insignia awarded to their paratrooper comrades. This created a situation where glider men were considered second-class citizens within the division—the unit with which they were supposed to identify with a sense of pride and belonging. The distinction between parachute troops and glider men especially grated on the glider troops because while paratroopers chose to volunteer for hazardous duty, glider men had no option but to follow their orders and make the best of it.

The rivalry between paratroopers and glider men has its origin in how the U.S. Army fielded its initial parachute capability. As noted earlier, the War Department did not grow interested in deploying an airborne arm until the undeniable success of Germany's use of vertical envelopment led planners to believe in its utility in warfare. Consequently, calls went out for volunteers for the airborne test platoon at Fort Benning, Georgia, in June 1940. The experiment was considered successful enough to warrant establishing a standing airborne capability. The tasks, conditions, and standards established by the test platoon set the tone for the recruitment and training of American paratroopers for the remainder of World War II. The idea was not just to train men to exit safely from aircraft and land by parachute, but to create a specially selected group of elite infantrymen who would fight behind enemy lines. As a result, the men were to be volunteers, put through a rigorous selection process, and trained to be self-sufficient and to display individual initiative.

Given this mindset, Army planners initially envisioned that airborne forces would consist of independent battalions that would conduct "behind-the-lines" missions of limited duration, more akin to special operations than conventional infantry attacks. As an increasing number of parachute battalions were formed, the Army began establishing parachute regiments of three battalions each to provide command and control, and administrative functions, rather than allow an unlimited number of battalions to operate without support. Ultimately, the idea of employing entire divisions of airborne troops and supporting arms, by a combination of parachute drops and glider landings, took root, fueled by the German success in Crete in May 1941. These divisions would consist of one of the newly formed parachute infantry regiments and two glider-borne regiments, converted over from infantry regiments either undergoing training or yet to be activated. Rather than land a small force on top of the enemy to achieve limited objectives, the idea now was to drop overwhelming combat power on him in combination with a ground assault to create an unsolvable dilemma about the direction in which to defend.

While the War Department grappled with how to best field an airborne force, Bill Lee's newly established Airborne Command at Fort Benning, Georgia, continued to train paratroopers. As weeks and months passed, the cadre at the Parachute School got the process down to a science. Aspiring parachutists went through four phases of training, designated A through D. In A phase they conducted concentrated physical training to develop the strength and stamina necessary for parachuting. Phases B through D became increasingly technically and tactically oriented, although the

FORMING AND TRAINING THE TEAM • 23

emphasis on fitness never abated. The men learned to don a parachute harness, land properly, "steer" a parachute by pulling on the risers (straps connecting the harness to the actual chute), pack a parachute, and they conducted practice jumps from increasingly higher towers. Ultimately, the students completed a total of five actual parachute descents to earn the right to be called paratroopers. The fact that each man was a "double volunteer," for both the Army and demanding paratrooper service, made the graduates feel they were something special.[20]

Converting from a conventional combat unit to one that was transported into combat by glider required that the men learn how to load and unload gliders properly with their cannons and other weapons, jeeps, ammunition, and supplies. This involved a great deal of time learning how to tie knots and secure lashings to ensure the extensive amounts of equipment required by the battalion to perform its anti-aircraft and anti-tank roles did not come loose in flight or during landings. An unsecured jeep or cannon could cause an extensive number of casualties in the glider before the men ever met an enemy on the ground.

As previously discussed, the conversion of the battalion to a glider-borne organization required creative configurations to move the men and materiel into combat. The issue was compounded by the fact that the battalion had a dual role as anti-tank and anti-aircraft protection for the division. The 1942 Table of Organization and Equipment for the Airborne Anti-Aircraft Battalion, T/O&E 4-275, dated 5 May 1942, called for a total of 18 CG-4A Waco gliders to move just one anti-aircraft battery or anti-tank battery by air. Multiplying that number by six batteries created a requirement for over 100 gliders to conduct the operations.

Additionally, the command and control, administrative, and medical elements of the battalion needed their own allocation of Wacos to conduct an airborne operation. In practice, not all elements would arrive by glider for any combat operation conducted by the 80th AAA. As the battalion was not designed to fight as a consolidated unit but distributed to support the division's infantry regiments as necessary, the actual number of gliders allocated to transport the batteries varied by operation.

Captain William Pratt, Commander C Battery, 80th AAA Battalion, Christmas 1942. (Photo courtesy of Micky and Joe Pratt)

The practice of properly loading and securing equipment in the gliders was a significant part of the 80th AAA's training. As one officer in the battalion observed, when a glider landed with "an abrupt stop ... in many instances, the glider would tilt, and the front would be crushed by the weaponry and vehicle."[21] Such landings could injure passengers and crew, damage the glider, and potentially damage the equipment on the aircraft. In training, this had the associated costs of limiting scarce resources needed to train other units on glider operations, degrading the strength of the unit, and causing material shortages that needed to be made up before the unit could proceed overseas. In combat, the consequences of unsecured loads could be more devastating, and the result would be a lack of combat power and the airborne force failing to achieve its objectives. Thus, proper preparation of loads became of paramount importance.

The experience of C Battery, 80th AAA, bears this out. Captain William Pratt, commanding officer (CO) of the unit, observed in a letter home that while he was conducting field training at the tank destroyer officer's advanced orientation course at Camp Hood, Texas, in February 1943, he was alerted to return to the cantonment area. Once he came in from the field, Pratt immediately received orders to pack up his kit and start movement that night for North Carolina, where he would rejoin his battery, which would then undergo initial glider training. The orders came on a Tuesday, and by the following Wednesday, the battery had relocated all its equipment and personnel and was at Laurinburg-Maxton Army Airfield. Pratt noted that training

FORMING AND TRAINING THE TEAM • 25

at Laurinburg-Maxton focused on proper loading procedures, with an emphasis on night operations.[22]

Laurinburg-Maxton Air Base is where the troops of the 80th AAA practiced the techniques to deploy their equipment by glider. They memorized the weight and dimensions of cannons and vehicles and learned to calculate how much space was required to transport personnel, as well as ammunition and supplies. The glider men focused on aircraft loading, weight and balance calculations, and even the strength of a glider's floor to ensure proper distribution of load. They received training on the following factors:

1. Limiting the gross weight to that for which the glider is designed.
2. Placing the load so that the center of gravity (CG) is within the designed stability limits of the glider.
3. Distributing the load to avoid excess weight concentration on the floor structure.
4. Securing the cargo to prevent it from shifting in flight or on landing.

Any deviation from the specified cargo capacity of the glider could result in a stall during landing, rendering the craft uncontrollable and resulting in a crash. Additionally, overloading lowered structural safety margins, which could cause the glider to break apart on landing.

Army Air Force Manual 50-17 contained detailed instructions for determining centers of gravity and other factors affecting airworthiness, but also provided more practical instructions in the form of simplified loading plans. Aircrews and troops could adopt the simplified plans and be assured that weight and balance standards would not be exceeded. These tables formed the basis of almost all load training conducted at Laurinburg-Maxton.[23]

The U.S. Army's infantry-centric approach to arming its formations led to the selection of the 37mm as the primary anti-tank gun for divisional anti-tank battalions. By 1942, there was ample evidence collected as lessons learned from Allied countries fighting Axis forces that the 37mm cannon was already outmoded.[24] Despite these reports from the field, the airborne community continued to focus on mobility and air transportability as primary considerations. The Army Ordnance Corps conducted a series of experiments at Aberdeen Proving Ground, Maryland, using 75mm cannons from World War I modified for direct fire, mounted on anti-tank (AT) gun carriages, to provide a quickly available source of heavier firepower. This experiment failed to generate much interest from the operational Army.[25] However, the potential of a 75mm airborne AT gun is an interesting what-if. The airborne field artillery had success with glider-borne and parachute-delivered 75mm pack howitzers during World War II. A similarly armed anti-tank battalion could have been a significant force multiplier for an airborne division. An advantage of the 37mm cannon, however, was the fact that it could be transported by Army Air Force gliders. This was not true of the larger, more powerful anti-tank cannons then available to the 80th AAA.

A lack of gliders, tow aircraft, and trained pilots negatively affected the 80th's ability to train and to develop standard operating procedures to safely transport men and equipment. To conduct even minimal training, around-the-clock operations became a hallmark of training at Laurinburg-Maxton.[26] On the face of it, learning to operate at night made sense, as crews and troops could expect to be called upon to deploy and fight under a variety of conditions, including darkness. However, there was a more prosaic reason for the 24-hour training schedule: the availability of aircraft. Glider production proceeded in fits and starts, hampered by management, contracting, and procurement issues. As a result, insufficient numbers of gliders were available for training glider pilots as well as the troops whom the pilots would deliver to combat.[27]

The leaders of the 80th AAA faced a series of challenges preparing their men for combat. They had to mold men from different regiments within the 82nd into a cohesive team, while also dealing with their new role as airborne troops. This assignment entailed taking on the hazards of riding gliders into combat, an additional danger the men did not volunteer to face. Glider operations also entailed training the men in a new set of technical and tactical skills, to prepare their equipment for aerial delivery and fighting while surrounded behind enemy lines.

The glider troops also found themselves treated with benign contempt by the parachute troops assigned to the airborne. They had to maintain their morale while the Army denied them the special distinctions and additional pay provided to the parachutists. Despite these challenges, the 80th's leaders ensured the men were ready to deploy overseas in the spring of 1943.

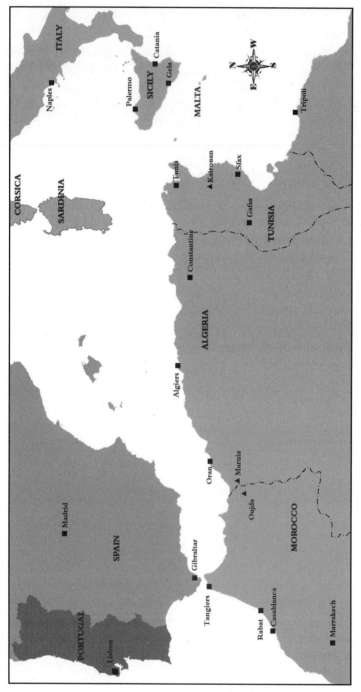

North Africa, Sicily, Salerno, and Naples.

CHAPTER 2

Learning from Experience—North Africa, Sicily, Salerno, and Naples

North Africa

Once the 80th deployed overseas to North Africa, they began to learn more about German armor from veteran units, including British AT troops. The 80th's leaders discovered they needed heavier firepower than its original armament of 37mm anti-tank guns. To deal with heavier German armor they needed to obtain 57mm cannons; however, they knew the standard American 57mm could not be configured for glider transport. After a lot of trial and error, the 80th discovered that British 6-pounder cannons fit the bill between air transportability and combat power.

The 82nd Airborne Division departed for war from Fort Bragg, North Carolina, on 17 April 1943. The men initially moved to Camp Edwards, Massachusetts, ultimately embarking for North Africa on 29 April 1943. Given the battalion's capabilities, the men of F Battery participated in the anti-aircraft protection of the troopship, the SS *George Washington*. The battalion historian notes the crossing proved uneventful, despite the ship being called to General Quarters on more than one occasion. After 12 days at sea, the battalion reached its port of debarkation at Casablanca, French Morocco. Immediately upon debarkation, the battalion experienced a situation that would become all too familiar; it was divided up to send its assets where they were most needed. The three anti-aircraft batteries moved by rail, via the Moroccan city of Ouijda, to the 325th Glider Infantry's cantonment at Camp Marnia, Algeria. For the time being, the anti-tank batteries remained in Morocco with Major Singleton.[1]

One man from the battalion was at the docks to meet his comrades, First Lieutenant Kroos. Kroos had departed Fort Bragg a week before the rest of the division as a member of the advanced party. He recollected that "we had to prepare everything for the 82nd Airborne Division. We had a week or 10 days to get everything ready for the guys before they arrived from the States. Things like a place to sleep, rations, etc."[2]

Ultimately, the battalion reunited in Algeria by 15 June, but the gunners soon found themselves on the move once more, as plans were afoot to relocate to Kairouan, Tunisia, where there was sufficient space for ranges and training grounds. The troops arrived at their new home by the end of June 1943. As the men and equipment made their way to Tunisia, Lieutenant Colonel Jack preceded them, arriving at Kairouan to assume duties as the division AA officer, in addition to his responsibilities as a battalion commander.

Jack's role was far from administrative, as the division had the task of integrating its anti-aircraft defenses with those established by British units to protect American and British airfields in the area. These fields were the home of bombers that staged out of North Africa to strike targets in the Mediterranean, as well as the troop carrier units that were to carry the Allied airborne forces into combat. Captains Keith, Jacobsen, and Rucker found their batteries dispatched to protect various fields throughout the region, with Captain Keith acting as a de facto battalion commander of the separated batteries due to his seniority. The anti-tank gunners co-located with the 325th Glider Infantry. The 325th provided an administrative home for the batteries during this period, taking care of logistics needs, but the anti-tank batteries conducted their own training independently.

Whitfield Jack retained command of the 80th AAA but focused on his role as the senior anti-aircraft officer in the division. Major Singleton handled the day-to-day administrative functions of managing the battalion. Jack performed his duties well, as evidenced by the fact that the division commander, General Ridgway, moved him to the division staff as G-3,

An example of the .50-caliber machine guns used by Batteries D, E, and F of the 80th AAA Battalion, North Africa, 1943. (Photo courtesy of Bob Burns)

operations officer, a position that is first among equals on a division staff. This move took place on 20 August 1943, during the closing days of the Sicily campaign. With Jack's departure, Major Singleton assumed command of the 80th. Captain Jacobsen moved into the now-vacated XO role, and adjutant Lieutenant Dittmar assumed command of E Battery.

Exceedingly few men of the battalion lamented Jack's departure. His discipline philosophy centered around ideas more appropriate for a garrison force than a combat outfit preparing for battle. Sergeant Charles Ianni stated that Jack had disciplined him for emptying trash rather than delegating the task to a private soldier. Other tales of Jack's priorities include insisting that the 80th's officers' dining tent in North Africa be cleared of flies, or requiring that a sick lieutenant attempting to make it to the latrine to relieve himself first stop to render appropriate courtesies to the battalion colors posted in front of Jack's office tent. In that instance, the emphasis on rendering honors resulted in the young lieutenant not completing his run to the sinks before succumbing to the urgency of the moment and then retreating to his tent, embarrassed.[3] In one sense, Jack's notions of discipline could be viewed favorably. Flies spread disease, and not controlling their presence in the mess facilities could seriously impact the battalion's health. However, an insistence on eliminating flies in the middle of a camp in the North African desert indicates a level of unreasonableness that makes soldiers' lives difficult rather than a focus on their welfare.

During this time, Arthur Kroos found himself bitten by the paratrooper bug. The fact that officers received an incentive pay, colloquially called "jump pay," motivated him to volunteer, as he would be able to send most of his base pay home to his family as an allotment and meet his own needs with the extra funds he received for parachute duty.[4] But if the fight was in Europe, what led to the 82nd's deployment to North Africa in the first place?

American troops first entered combat against Germany and Italy in a surprising location, North Africa. The Chief of Staff of the United States Army, General George C. Marshall, was a proponent of a direct invasion of Northwest Europe by an assault across the English Channel, utilizing the British Isles as an intermediary staging base for training, stockpiling supplies and equipment, and preparing combat divisions for a return to the European continent. Marshall's fixation on attacking Europe head-on reflected American military doctrine, which stressed the offensive and striking against the main source of enemy strength to obtain a decisive result. The administration of American President Franklin Roosevelt pursued a strategy of "Germany First," reflecting the fact that the United States faced enemies in both Germany, supported by Italy, in the West and Japan in the East. Many American military commanders, especially in the naval service, felt Japan should be dealt with first, as Japan had directly attacked American warships and facilities at Pearl Harbor, Hawaii, on 7 December 1941. Roosevelt pursued the European-centric strategy, however, because of the pressing danger that German hegemony presented to Great Britain. Were the British to be knocked out of the war, it would be nearly impossible for the United States to mount an invasion of Europe because there would be no friendly country from which to prepare for the assault. Additionally, Hitler would be able to turn his focus exclusively to the East to deal with the Soviet Union.

British planners, whose troops had been fighting Germany for three years by 1942, felt that it was premature to attempt a cross-channel invasion in 1942. British military leaders shared this assessment with their

American counterparts in a series of strategic conferences throughout the first half of the year. Britain suggested an invasion of North Africa instead, to place an Allied force in the rear of the German and Italian troops who had fought the British Army since 1940 to overrun Egypt and cut Allied access to the Suez Canal and the Far East. Marshall and his subordinates were against the North African invasion, which prompted President Roosevelt to declare he was willing to abandon the Germany First strategy to focus on defeating Imperial Japan. British Prime Minister Winston Churchill prevailed upon Roosevelt to see the strengths of a North African invasion (an offensive action in the enemy's rear, an operation that would consume some level of enemy resources to take pressure from the Soviets bearing the brunt of the war against Germany, and an opportunity for American forces to gain combat experience before the attack on Europe). Roosevelt, convinced by Churchill's arguments, ordered Marshall to prepare an attack on North Africa, to be mounted before the end of 1942.

The result was Operation *Torch*, a multi-pronged amphibious assault against positions in French Morocco and Algeria. The initial Axis resistance faced by the invaders came in the form of Vichy French troops, ostensible allies of the Germans since the fall of France in the spring of 1940, when a provisional government formed under World War I hero Marshal Pétain signed an armistice with Hitler. Attacking on 8 November 1942, the invading Allied troops met with varying levels of resistance from the Vichy troops; however, the landings were broadly successful. Additionally, Allied leaders negotiated with the senior Vichy officer in North Africa, Admiral Darlan, who agreed to order his forces to cease hostilities against the Allies. Soon, American units were moving east into Tunisia to engage German and Italian troops fighting against British and Commonwealth forces. What followed was a six-month campaign, which saw much hard fighting, but by 10 May 1943, the Axis forces were ejected from North Africa, and the Allies had a significant area in which to stage an attack across the Mediterranean against Axis positions in southern Europe.

Once the 82nd arrived in North Africa, their training continued unabated. For the 80th AAA, being in what was still considered a combat zone resulted in an emphasis on placing the anti-aircraft batteries in positions to protect critical locations and conducting outpost duty to acclimate the men to combat conditions.

Major Singleton took advantage of the 80th's proximity to veteran troops and met with British officers who had experience fighting against German Mark IV and Tiger I Panzers. Both tanks had frontal armor between 3 and 4 inches thick, and the British confirmed that the 80th's anti-tank batteries were seriously under-gunned. Even though Singleton's gunners did not yet have access to heavier cannons, the new battalion commander had his operations officer, First Lieutenant Nelson, arrange for an informal training program with the British. Each week the 80th AAA would exchange non-commissioned officers (NCOs) with the British, to work with their 6pdr anti-tank gun. The 6-pounder was the British version of the 57mm cannon and, with the correct types of armor-piercing ammunition, capable of penetrating 2.9 to 3.9 inches of armor at 1,000 meters. The training program provided Singleton's NCOs with familiarization with the technical aspects of the weapon and introduced them to effective tactics for dealing with enemy tanks.

The British soldiers proved to be excellent hosts in addition to a source of much sought-after information about fighting the Germans. The 80th found itself encamped in proximity to a crack British unit, the motorized infantry of the 6th Battalion of the Grenadier Guards. The 6th Battalion had relocated from Syria to North Africa in March 1943 and joined the British Eighth Army under General Bernard Law Montgomery. As

An example of 6-pounder anti-tank gun introduced to the 80th AAA Battalion in North Africa, 1943. (Photos courtesy of Matthew Moss and The Armourer's Bench)

LEARNING FROM EXPERIENCE • 35

part of the 201st Guards Brigade, the 6th Battalion Grenadier Guards endured high casualties during the Eighth Army's successful flanking of the Mareth Line, their valor sustaining the Grenadier Guards' reputation as an elite regiment. Batteries A, B, and C of the 80th all spent a week at the 6th Battalion's beachside encampment at Sousse where, according to the battalion history, the Americans experienced all the hospitality the Guardsmen could provide.[5]

Although each battery enjoyed its beachside interlude, Major Singleton continued his efforts to up-gun the anti-tank batteries. Unable to employ U.S. Ordnance Department M1 57mm guns, Singleton once again turned to the British. With the assistance of the 82nd Airborne Division staff, the 80th AAA Battalion received 18 6-pounder cannons from the British. The batteries divested themselves of the obsolete 37mm guns to take possession of the new cannons. This created a situation where each battery had two fewer guns, although they now had significantly greater firepower. The standard AT battery organization no longer worked in the 80th, as it was predicated on being equipped with eight cannons. Major Singleton gave his AT battery commanders significant leeway in reorganizing their units to adapt to the changes in weapons. The results varied, with Battery A fielding two platoons armed with three cannons each, and Battery B using three two-gun sections. Captain Pratt's C Battery came up with the most creative solution, organizing into a large platoon of four 6-pounders, supported by a two-gun section.[6] Pratt's organization provided a combination of concentrated stopping power backed by a more mobile capability that could be deployed to crisis points quickly.

Even though the 80th's Table of Organization and Equipment called for the more mobile, less powerful 37mm cannon, Major Singleton sought to acquire more firepower for the battalion by obtaining British 6-pounder cannons. American units fighting in the North African campaign learned that their 37mm anti-tank guns, identical to those issued to the 80th, were ineffective against modern German armor. The United States Army Ordnance Corps developed a more powerful, 57mm AT gun with greater penetrating power, but Airborne Command continued to equip its AT units with 37mm cannons because the larger carriage on the 57mm gun could not fit properly in a glider for use in air assaults.[7] The British guns also utilized 57mm shells but fired high explosives (HE), which proved more effective against enemy armor, and, more importantly, the 6pdr's carriage possessed a narrower wheelbase, which facilitated loading the weapon onto a glider. The fact that the British gun could be easily transported by air eliminated the only advantage the 37mm cannon provided to airborne forces.

Despite all the information gleaned from the British, it would take actual combat for the 80th's leadership to begin to analyze what worked and what did not in combat. Experience in Sicily and Italy would teach lessons on the importance of massing the combat power of the AT batteries. While more firepower would be better, the 80th AAA was still limited by the carrying capacity of the gliders that supported them and the limited number of 6-pounders provided by their British allies.

Sicily

In early summer 1942, the 82nd Airborne Division began preparing Operation *Husky*, for the invasion of Sicily. With the conclusion of the North African campaign, the Combined Joint Chiefs of Staff, at the urging of British Prime Minister Winston Churchill, sought the invasion of southern Europe as the next phase in the campaign to push back the German armies. While the Americans, led by Marshall, continued to press for a cross-channel invasion directly into France, Churchill believed that an assault into what he termed "the soft underbelly of Europe" would allow Allied forces to outflank German defenses along the Atlantic coast. The reality at this time was that the strength of German coastal positions in France was more apparent than real during this phase of the war; however, Churchill firmly believed that attacking Europe across the Mediterranean rather than along the Channel coast would achieve decisive results while avoiding unnecessarily high casualties. Once again, the British point of view prevailed, and the Allies commenced planning for an amphibious invasion of the island of Sicily as a precursor to an attack on the Italian mainland.

The invasion called for a combined British and American effort using amphibious landing craft and airborne troops. The British would seize objectives inland of the beaches using the glider-borne First Air Landing Brigade, while the 82nd Airborne Division's role was to seize the high ground beyond the American landing areas to prevent the Germans' mobile armored force, the Hermann Göring Division, from counterattacking the beaches. General Ridgway selected the 505th Parachute Infantry Regiment under Colonel James Gavin to spearhead the division's effort, jumping in on 9 July 1943, known in military terms as "D-Day." While D-Day would be popularly associated with Operation *Overlord* in 1944, the first day of any American military operation is termed "D-Day" for planning purposes. Days after a D-Day are labeled D+1, D+2, sequentially. The 82nd's plan called for the 505th Parachute Infantry Regiment (PIR) to be reinforced by Colonel Reuben Tucker's 504th PIR on D+1, and the 325th Glider Infantry Regiment led by Colonel Harry Lewis on D+2.

The 80th AAA also received orders to be prepared for movement by glider to Sicily on D+3. The new 6-pounder cannons of the AT batteries would be necessary to provide fire support to the infantry staving off anticipated German counterattacks. In the event, the 82nd Airborne Division's combat debut would be marred by confusion, mistakes, and tragedy but also marked by incredible valor on the part of the soldiers themselves. However, the air movement plan was ultimately scrapped, and no elements of the 80th AAA went into Sicily via glider.

The 505th PIR's parachute drop was in no way a textbook demonstration of vertical envelopment. The troop transport crews, despite their best efforts, suffered from a lack of training in nighttime navigation, especially over water. Taking off from airfields in Tunisia, the 505th flew across the Mediterranean in a series of doglegs before making landfall over Sicily. The troop transports were widely dispersed, resulting in paratroopers dropping all across the island. None of the assembly drills the men practiced in the States or while in North Africa proved of any use. The troops were left to band together into small teams with whomever they came across and set out toward the objectives. If they did not know the direction in which the objective lay, they caused whatever mayhem they could.

38 • NEVER A DULL MOMENT

This phenomenon would be known by later generations of American paratroopers as "The Rule of LGOPs," or Little Groups of Paratroopers.[i]

Ultimately, Colonel Gavin and elements of his regiment made it to the vicinity of Biazza Ridge, where the regiment set up the best defense it could, although it lacked any significant anti-armor capability, as the 80th's gun batteries remained across the sea, awaiting their turn in the air movement order. The anticipated German counterattack materialized, and Gavin led his men in a tenacious defense that saw the 505th take significant casualties but successfully stave off the German armor driving toward the beaches where the U.S. 45th Infantry Division was coming ashore. Despite the navigational problems that plagued the drop, the airborne plan was working sufficiently well for the 504th PIR to receive the go-ahead to jump to reinforce the 505th on the night of D+1. Sadly, many of Tucker's men suffered a tragic fate.

A vast armada of warships sat off the coast of southern Sicily, supporting the invasion. Tucker's regiment was due to fly near this fleet on the night of 10 July 1943, en route to their drop zones. The Allied plan called for the air defenses of these ships to hold their fire when they heard aircraft approach during the specific hours of the 504th Parachute Infantry inbound flight, to preclude the chance that nervous gunners might mistake the friendly transports for German aircraft and open fire. Unfortunately, that is precisely what occurred. The 504th PIR and the associated troop carrier squadron took significant casualties from the ensuing fusillade.

Battalion motor officer Second Lieutenant James Baugh found it difficult to get any sense of what was occurring once the parachute infantry left for Sicily. According to Baugh:

---

i   The author first learned the Rule of LGOPs at Fort Bragg, North Carolina, in 1993. The rule is explained thus: "After the demise of the best Airborne plan, a most terrifying effect occurs on the battlefield. This effect is known as the rule of the LGOPs. This is, in its purest form, small groups of pissed-off 19-year-old American paratroopers. They are well-trained, armed to the teeth, and lack serious adult supervision. They collectively remember the Commander's intent as 'March to the sound of the guns and kill anyone who is not dressed like you ...' or something like that. Happily, they go about the day's work."

> We stayed glued to our radios; we were glued to the broadcasts from Rome, Berlin and especially London. The broadcasts from Berlin announced there had been attempted landings on the southern coast of Sicily, but the operation was not a success, and the airborne attempts were shot down with most of the troopers killed or captured. We always discounted anything from Berlin. The strange thing about the initial phase of the operation was that the propagandist from Berlin was more accurate than we had dared to believed.[8]

The number of casualties inflicted by both friendly fire and enemy action caused Baugh to reflect, "from the very high price paid for the results attained, it would require an extreme degree of optimism and a staunch supporter of the airborne concept to say it was a resounding success."[9]

On the ground, Gavin's 505th Parachute Infantry Regiment continued to deal with the problem of enemy tanks. The actions of the commander of 1st Battalion, 505th PIR, Lieutenant Colonel Arthur Gorham, illustrate the consequences of not having sufficient anti-tank guns committed to the Sicily fight. On 11 July 1943, Gorham's battalion was fighting in conjunction with the 1st Infantry Division's 2nd Battalion, 16th Infantry, which had conducted a successful amphibious landing and moved off the beaches to link up with the paratroopers. The 1st Infantry Division was in the process of unloading its anti-tank guns from ships at the beachhead and were rushing to get this firepower to its regiments in combat.[10] The paratroopers had only the light weapons they had jumped in with previously. After the two battalions had completed their linkup, armor-equipped German troops attacked the American position. Gorham led a force of roughly 50 men in conducting an ad hoc anti-tank defense.

According to the citation for the Distinguished Service Cross Gorham received for this action, the attacking Germans' strength consisted of an estimated 10 tanks supported by a battalion of infantry.[11] This force surrounded Gorham's position and took it under tank cannon fire at close range. Gorham was reduced to moving "from point to point, firing at the eye-slit of tanks, shouting encouragement to his men and directing their fire." Gorham's efforts to fight off this attack succeeded; however, he lost his life three days later in a second engagement with enemy armor. On 14 July 1944, again leading by example, "Lieutenant

40 • NEVER A DULL MOMENT

Colonel Gorham personally manned a rocket launcher and destroyed one tank. While attempting to destroy another with hand grenades and a rifle, Lieutenant Colonel Gorham was killed."[12] Had the 80th AAA Battalion been able to get its anti-tank weapons on the ground in Sicily as part of the initial airborne assault, the paratroopers on the ground might not have been reduced to engaging tanks with rifles and grenades. This lesson was not lost on the 80th AAA Battalion's commander, Major Singleton.

The All-Americans were not the only soldiers facing a rough introduction to the world of airborne combat. The British 1st Air Landing Brigade had orders to take a critical bridge, the Ponte Grande, in the vicinity of Syracuse, on Sicily's southeastern coast. The operation involved almost 150 gliders, piloted by members of the British Glider Regiment. These men had trained primarily in the Horsa glider; however, limited quantities of that aircraft were available in Tunisia. With no other option, the 1st Air Landing Brigade received a significant number of American CG-4A Waco gliders. The British pilots were unfamiliar with the Waco, so 26 American pilots volunteered to train their counterparts and to accompany them on the combat assault.[13] There was insufficient time for a thorough training program, so the Glider Regiment pilots received a handful of familiarization hours, with very limited night flying, and then flew their combat debut. The results were similar to the 504th PIR's experience and equally tragic. Although the men of the 1st Air Landing Brigade did not face friendly anti-aircraft fire, enemy anti-aircraft batteries decimated their formations. Of the 144 gliders launched on Ladbroke, a mere 12 reached their assigned target. Of the remainder, 90 ditched into the waters off Sicily, 32 were lost in crashes once they made landfall, and the remaining 10 failed to find the landing zones. Amazingly, the glider-borne troops succeeded in taking and holding the Ponte Grande bridge until late in the afternoon of 10 July. With only 15 men remaining, the British troops defending the bridge surrendered to Italian troops; however, British infantry who had made the amphibious landing the preceding day succeeded in making their counterattack and retaking the bridge.

General Ridgway canceled the subsequent glider missions scheduled for D+2 after the fiasco involving the 504th PIR. Elements of the 80th AAA scheduled to fly via glider into Sicily instead loaded their weapons onto cargo transport aircraft, made a non-combat flight, and joined their comrades on or around 16 July 1943.[14] Singleton established a command post by Mount Etna,[15] midway up the eastern coast of Sicily. By then the 82nd Airborne Division was supporting Patton's Seventh Army in its drive to the west. Patton sought to clear the western part of Sicily of enemy forces, before moving north and taking the city of Palermo. By this point, German forces defending the island recognized there was no strategic advantage in holding the island, and thus focused on evacuating men and materiel across the Strait of Messina to mainland Italy. The happy result of this retrograde movement is that Patton, and thus Ridgway, made rapid progress. The anti-tank guns of the battalion faced little organized enemy armor, although the battalion received reports that the 6-pounders proved useful in mountainous terrain.[16]

Sicily nearly proved to be the death knell of the American airborne division. General Eisenhower, then acting as the Supreme Commander of the Allied Expeditionary Force in the North African Theater of Operations, felt that the airborne division lacked the capacity for large-scale combat operations, due to its limited firepower and reliance on scarce air transport. It could not overwhelmingly mass combat power and thus was vulnerable to being overwhelmed itself by the enemy until friendly ground forces could achieve a linkup to relieve them. Eisenhower believed after Sicily that no unit larger than a regiment should be employed for an airborne operation and then only for a very limited objective of short duration.[17]

Despite General Eisenhower's misgivings regarding large-scale airborne operations, the Chief of Staff of the United States Army was not yet ready to abandon the concept of the airborne division. General Marshall had been an avid supporter of the airborne concept since the time of the test platoon back in 1940. Marshall had great respect for Eisenhower and was prepared to give his recommendations serious consideration, but the Chief of Staff also wanted a thorough examination of airborne operations in Sicily and recommendations on what worked, what needed improvement, and whether those improvements could make the airborne division a viable instrument of war.

Major General Joseph Swing, a career artillery officer and West Point classmate of Eisenhower, received the task of leading a board of officers to conduct the review of Operation *Husky*. Swing commanded the 11th Airborne Division, then training in the United States, and had acted as Eisenhower's airborne advisor during the lead-up to invading Sicily. His investigation, known colloquially as "The Swing Board," looked at both the American and British airborne operations, interviewed aircrews, commanders, and staff officers in both parachute and glider units, and considered all aspects of airborne combat, reviewing both friendly and enemy use of vertical envelopment from the start of the war.

The board found many areas requiring improvement, including the need for better aerial navigation training for aircrews, more thorough coordination between air and ground units during the planning phase, deploying airborne phases in delayed stages rather than in overwhelming force, and the need to revise procedures for employing gliders. The board specifically recommended not releasing gliders from tow aircraft over water, which had caused an overwhelming number of losses during the Ladbroke operation.[18] The board's recommendations were summarized in Training Circular Number 113, "Employment of Airborne and Troop Carrier Forces." Swing's findings concluded that the airborne division was a viable concept if the recommendations contained in the training circular were implemented by operational forces.

Lieutenant General Lesley McNair, Chief of Army Ground Forces, despite his original endorsement of the airborne division, had come to disagree with the concept of specialized divisions. He preferred the idea of general-purpose light infantry divisions that could be adapted to a wide variety of special circumstances. McNair wanted to see the Swing Board's recommendations validated in a field test, resulting in what became known as the Knollwood Maneuvers, in which Swing's 11th Airborne Division executed a variety of exercises against the defending 17th Airborne Division, which convinced Army leadership that the concept of the airborne division was functionally sound.[19]

While the Swing Board went about its work, the 82nd Airborne examined its performance, to correct flaws exposed in combat. The division's baptism of fire resulted in several lessons learned. First and foremost, as much combat power as possible had to be delivered to the objective area immediately. The plan to introduce the division's three regiments and supporting elements into Sicily over three days left the troopers of the 505th Parachute Infantry in a precarious position for the first 36 hours of the battle. Not only did Gavin, as senior commander on the ground, face a manpower shortage as he sought to assemble his regiment and carry out his assignment, but he also had to deal with a serious lack of firepower. The regiment's handheld 2.36-inch rocket launchers, colloquially known as bazookas, were completely ineffective against enemy tanks in all but the most favorable circumstances. Gavin insisted that future operations needed to include a mixture of parachute and glider landing to ensure critical support weapons, including the 80th AAA's anti-tank guns, arrived on the landing zones in time to assist in the initial assault.

The division also learned about the significance of properly reconnoitered and prepared drop zones. The pilots who delivered the 505th PIR into Sicily could not recognize landmarks or ensure they were in the vicinity of assigned drop zones except for dead reckoning, traveling for such a distance and such a speed for a specified period. To rectify this issue, American airborne commanders begin adopting the pathfinder concept, to provide navigation assistance and visual aids to support the pilots in identifying where to deliver their cargoes of paratroopers. Pathfinders were specially selected and trained jumpers, equipped with beacons and lights, who would insert into the objective area before the main body to ensure the drop zones were correctly marked, to maximize the number of troopers who would land in the vicinity of their assigned drop zone. The pathfinders would jump with radio transponders that receivers located on the transport aircraft could use as beacons to home in on the drop zones and glider landing areas, as well as a variety of lights for short-distance recognition.

The 509th Parachute Infantry Battalion, an independent unit that had made the first American combat jumps in North Africa as part of

Operation *Torch* the previous year, had been exposed to British pathfinder techniques after the initial combat in North Africa.[20] The British had refined their doctrine and organization for such operations and dropped the 21st Independent Parachute Company ahead of the British 1st Parachute Brigade on 13 July 1943, whose objective was the Primosole Bridge, needed to facilitate the inland advance of the Eighth Army on the eastern end of Sicily. In a situation reminiscent of Ladbroke, the paras initially took their objective but could not hold it, and the Germans retook the bridge. Eventually, ground forces from the Eighth Army broke through from the beaches and seized the bridge.[21]

American airmen also learned that they needed to increase the amount of time invested in preparing transport pilots to conduct parachute and glider operations—specifically, training transport crews in coordinating with airborne units, nighttime navigation, and navigation over water. Little time was available for intensive training, because of the high demand for cargo aircraft to move materiel throughout the theater.

Major Singleton determined that he needed not only to get his weapons and his people into the fight earlier, but also the means to command and control his assets once they arrived. While each battery would be assigned to support a different line regiment, the anti-tank battalion commander needed to maintain visibility of the location of his guns throughout the battlefield, their ammunition requirements, and the enemy armor threat. This was critical to keep the division commander and his operations officer informed on how best to use the division's tank-killing weapons. Arriving on the battlefield well after the assault commenced relegated the anti-tank commander to near irrelevance as he did not understand the current situation as well as the commanders already in the fight and thus could contribute little to decision-making.

Salerno

Once the island of Sicily was secure, the 82nd Airborne Division found itself earmarked for Operation *Giant II*, an invasion of mainland Italy. Even while the soldiers of the division fought through Operation *Husky*, Allied planners were looking toward the next step in the effort to retake Europe from the Axis. A quick drive across the Straits of Messina, into Italy, appeared to be the logical move. At first, to capitalize on the momentum created by the victory in Sicily, the 82nd was tasked to move the 504th and 505th PIRs—then concluding combat operations in Sicily—directly into Italy along with whatever division assets were also on the island. The remainder of the division that had not yet departed Tunisia would move directly to Italy so that the entire division would once again be whole. This course of action was not well received by General Ridgway. He intended to return his regiments to North Africa for retraining, refitting, and to absorb replacements for the casualties sustained during *Husky*. At this time, Ridgway was constantly on the move, coordinating between two different command posts in Sicily and Tunisia, as well as dealing with orders from an operational headquarters for the ongoing campaign and a separate higher headquarters for planning the Italy mission. By early August, the elements of the division on Sicily received orders to return to Tunisia. It was too late for the retraining program that Ridgway had envisioned, but now his division was in one place and could resupply the *Husky* veterans and get newly arrived troops assigned to units that needed them. The division staff could now also focus on planning for what came next.[22] Operation *Giant II* involved a planned airborne drop on Rome, and the 82nd's assistant division commander, Brigadier General Maxwell Taylor (later to command the 101st Airborne Division), performed a feat worthy of a spy novel when he conducted a reconnaissance of drop zones and met with Italian leaders eager to surrender, but determined that German resistance would be too great. *Giant II* did not materialize and the 82nd Airborne was designated as the strategic reserve for Operation *Avalanche*, the amphibious invasion of Italy at Salerno.

A new mission was not long in coming. The 82nd received orders to proceed to Italy in support of Operation *Avalanche*. The anti-aircraft batteries of the 80th AAA Battalion were alerted for movement to an assembly area 5 miles from Bizerte, along with a headquarters element and medical detachment. The glider artillerymen were to go into combat by sea. These elements were assigned to travel via vessels known by the pragmatic name Landing Craft–Infantry (LCI). These ships had hull numbers, but no names. The men of the 80th embarked on LCIs 180, 266, and 270 of the 1st Canadian LCI Flotilla (Royal Navy LC Flotilla 260), heading for Salerno.[23]

Operation *Avalanche* was conceived as a lightning strike to seize the city of Naples and cut defending German troops off from retreating north up the Italian peninsula. Simultaneously, the king of Italy, Victor Emmanuel III, supported a coup to remove Italian dictator and Axis supporter Mussolini from power in favor of Marshal Badoglio. The invasion of the Italian mainland was believed to be an opportunity to force Italy out of the war while simultaneously capturing a large amount of German assets in southern Italy.[24]

The ships carrying the seaborne elements of the 80th AAA arrived off Salerno on 10 September 1943. The batteries disembarked in the early morning, and found themselves attached to Task Force Ranger, under Colonel William O. Darby. The Rangers had made a name for themselves in North Africa as an American version of the commandos, with the original members of the 1st Ranger Battalion undergoing the same training as their British counterparts at the commando training depot in Scotland. However, as a provisional strike force, the Rangers lacked supporting weapons and fielded even less heavy firepower than the airborne forces. Batteries D, E, and F would provide the Rangers with much-needed support by fire.

The Rangers had the mission to take and hold a key piece of terrain called Chiunzi Pass, which facilitated movement between the coast and locations further inland. The initial task of holding the pass to prevent counterattack by German forces against the Allied landing force eventually shifted to ensuring the pass remained open for American troops, most significantly the 36th Infantry Division, to pursue withdrawing enemy units as they fell back under the weight of the Allied attack.[25] Battery D immediately assumed outpost duty near the town of Maiori, previously the responsibility of Task Force Ranger, while Battery F set upon the right flank of Colonel Darby's lines and took over local security for a village called Capo d'Orso. Battery E established anti-aircraft positions on the landing beaches to assist in providing air defense to the growing beachhead.

Joe Galatzan, 80th AAA Battalion surgeon, set up medical operations in the vicinity of Paestum, operating a casualty evacuation point in an available church, the Chiesa de San Dominico, augmenting a small detachment of Ranger medics. Battery F supported Ranger operations along the forward line of troops, using their .50-caliber machine guns as indirect fire support. The gunners accomplished this by employing plunging fire, which could be directed by a spotter who communicated the location of enemy targets to gun crews, who often could not directly observe the targets themselves.[26]

Throughout this period, the anti-aircraft batteries accompanied the Rangers in combat around the towns of Minori, Maiori, Castellammare, and Paestum. For his tireless work providing lifesaving care, Captain Galatzan received a Bronze Star medal for meritorious achievement in ground operations against hostile forces. This award marked the first combat decoration for a member of the 80th AAA Battalion.[27]

Battery E received an unusual assignment on 19 September 1943. A detachment under the command of Lieutenant James Ison set out to light signal fires on a mountain range north of Tremonte. The purpose of the fires was to provide visual navigation for bombers that were striking targets deeper inside Italy. Ison received serious burn injuries during the mission, and he was evacuated, ultimately back to the United States. Meanwhile, Lieutenant Floyd Dixon, of 3rd Platoon, E Battery, successfully saw the task through to completion.

While the anti-aircraft gunners and medics made their combat debut, the anti-tank batteries faced a challenge just getting to the fight. As the coup against Mussolini developed, the 82nd Airborne received a series of orders for various missions to jump into Italy to take advantage of the situation to force an Italian surrender, including an ill-advised coup de main against Rome itself. B and C Batteries found themselves emplaned on gliders preparing for takeoff for that assault when word came that an armistice had been signed. The gliders were 17 minutes from takeoff.

Naples

Battery A received orders for movement by Landing Ship–Tank (LST-T) to support landings at Red Beach during the initial stages of *Giant II* but no sooner had completed loading at the harbor at Bizerte when word came that this mission too had been canceled. Eventually, all three batteries relocated to Castelvetrano airfield, Sicily, where they staged for movement to the Salerno beachhead, arriving at the beginning of

October. The ubiquitous Captain Pratt of C Battery took charge of all three batteries to conduct a motor march from the assembly area in the vicinity of Battipaglia to rejoin the remainder of the 80th in Naples. Once again, however, the reunion of all elements was short-lived, as A Battery found itself detached in support of the 325th Glider Infantry, B Battery working with the 504th Parachute Infantry, and C Battery operating with Gavin's now veteran 505th PIR.

Post-combat operations in Naples provided a much-needed break, and by 4 October the battalion was performing more routine duties in the city and its surrounding environs. Missions included a variety of security tasks, from mounted and dismounted patrols to providing a guard force for critical infrastructure. One of the more unique roles assigned to Battery F included providing a five-man detachment, under the command of an NCO, to secure Major General Ridgway's quarters. Otherwise, the troops of F Battery had the more routine duty of guarding an ammunition depot inside the city. Battery D integrated its .50-caliber anti-aircraft guns into Naples's air defenses, and Battery E took responsibility for the defense of Capodichino Airfield. They shared these duties with a British anti-aircraft group equipped with 40mm Bofors cannon. The anti-tank batteries retained their supporting relationship with the division's infantry regiments: Battery A with the 325th Glider Infantry, Battery B with the 504th PIR, and Battery C with the 505th PIR.

Despite being off the front lines, the battalion suffered its first soldier killed in action on 21 October 1943. German bombers conducted a raid on the Naples area, and eight bombs struck the 3rd Convalescent Hospital; Corporal David Williams died in the raid. Williams, assigned to Battery A, had been a patient in the hospital at the time of the attack.

The battalion's time in Naples was a return to a life of near normalcy. Although the danger of German air raids remained and the batteries supported occasional missions with the infantry, day-to-day life improved, compared with being on the line for days or even training in North Africa. B Battery's Lieutenant Edward McLean recorded that the battery bunked indoors rather than under tent canvas or the open sky for the first time since departing overseas the previous spring. His battery commander, Nock Russell, bought fresh vegetables from local vendors for his men.

And many men chose to take in the sites of Italy, including trips to see Mount Vesuvius or visit the island of Capri.[28]

After Sicily and Italy, Major Singleton still needed to determine the most effective way to deploy his battalion in combat. Sicily illustrated that the difficulties of the battlefield would derail intricate plans, and seemingly unrelated events would have unintended consequences. The division could not rely on the arrival of vital support weapons merely because a deployment timeline said they would be there. The friendly fire tragedy that cost the 504th PIR 25 percent casualties led to the cancelation of subsequent airborne missions, leaving the 80th's anti-tank batteries, along with the 325th Glider Infantry Regiment (GIR) and other division elements, stranded in North Africa.

In the future, the division would be much better off phasing the arrival of such vital equipment throughout an airborne operation, ensuring at least some anti-tank assets made it to the fight. Reinforcing this premise, the battle at Biazza Ridge revealed that even if the 80th's guns had arrived according to plan on D+2, Colonel Jim Gavin needed them far earlier. Singleton's 57mm anti-tank guns would have been invaluable for Gavin and the 505th PIR facing German armor with only the shoulder-fired 2.36-inch bazooka.

Men of the 80th AAA relax in Italy. (Photo courtesy of Bob Burns)

Italy also informed Singleton's thinking. He saw firsthand why massing combat power matters. The nature of the Salerno invasion meant that the division committed the 80th to battle piecemeal. Task Force Ranger's lack of organic supporting weapons created a situation in which the anti-aircraft batteries found themselves in a unique role rather than contributing to the air defense of the division. The batteries acquitted themselves well and received the Distinguished Unit Citation, later renamed the Presidential Unit Citation when awarded to Darby's Rangers. Despite the honor, the Task Force Ranger mission serves as an example of how the battalion's assets could be spread throughout a combat theater once attached to other units, diluting the battalion's combat power. Soon Singleton had more immediate matters to consider, however; the 80th AAA Battalion was leaving Italy.

The battalion continued to carry out its Naples assignments until 17 November, when they were notified to prepare for another movement by ship. Relieved of their security and patrol responsibilities, the men turned to packing their gear and preparing equipment to embark on the SS *Thomas Jefferson*. To preserve security, the men received orders to remove their distinctive red, white, and blue patches with the prominent "Double AAs" and airborne tab, from the shoulders of their uniforms, as well as the round glider patches from their caps. Once all passengers and cargo were aboard, the *Thomas Jefferson* set sail on 18 November. Similar to their trip across the Atlantic for North Africa the previous spring, the men of the anti-aircraft batteries once again took part in providing their ship with anti-aircraft protection.[29]

The battalion first briefly returned to North Africa, putting in at Oran, Algeria. The SS *Thomas Jefferson* then joined a convoy of ships and headed westward on 1 December 1943. After a week at sea, the battalion's leaders informed the men that their destination was Northern Ireland, where they disembarked in Belfast on 9 December, prior to going into camp near Kilrea.[30]

LEARNING FROM EXPERIENCE • 51

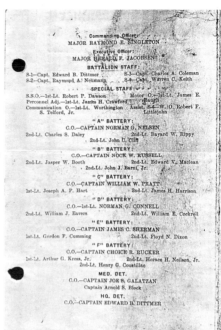

MESSAGE
from
Battalion Commander.

ON THIS CHRISTMAS DAY IN IRELAND, I speak for all the Officers. May you, each individual of the Battalion and all those at home, experience the very Merriest Christmas possible.

May the year of 1944 be your very best, and it will be if such spirit, hard work and co-operation continues as it has done during the past months. To have such spirit after doing and seeing the different things we have done and seen is a fair measure for contemplating future results.

I am proud to be your Commanding Officer.

R. E. SINGLETON.

MENU

Christmas Dinner

DECEMBER 25, 1943

Roast Turkey w/Dressing
Giblet Gravy
Mashed Potatoes
Cranberry Jelly
Creamed Corn
Sweet Pickles
Celery
Mince Pie w/Sliced Cheese
Rolls
Butter
Hard Candy
Coffee

Christmas menu for the 80th AAA Battalion, 25 December 1943. (Menu courtesy of Bob Burns; Photos courtesy of Emma Powers)

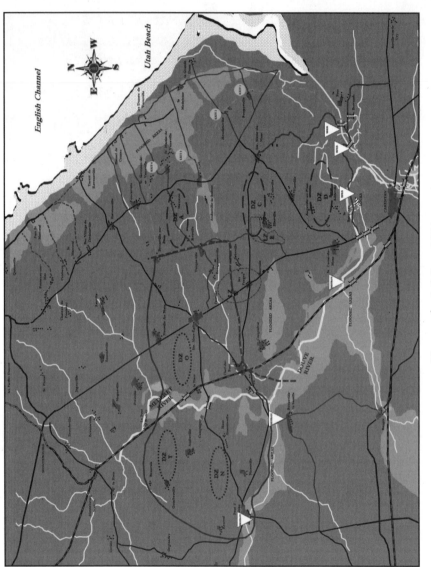

Normandy, 6–9 June 1944.

CHAPTER 3

Adapting to the Environment— Northern Ireland, England, and Normandy

Northern Ireland and England

The Allies differed on the best way to take the offensive against Nazi Germany, with the Americans urging a direct, cross-channel invasion into Northwest Europe. American strategic thought encouraged taking the fight to the enemy and engaging them in decisive battle as quickly as possible.[1] Conversely, the British favored an indirect approach, attacking German forces on the Reich's periphery to drain their combat power and exhaust the Wehrmacht through the cumulative effects of a thousand cuts. From 1942 through late 1943, the British Imperial General Staff successfully advocated for offensives in North Africa, Sicily, and Italy; however, by December 1943, increasing American troop and materiel contributions gave the U.S. Joint Chiefs a more powerful voice in strategic deliberations. They insisted that a direct attack on Fortress Europe take place in 1944, or else they would abandon the Germany First policy decided upon by the Allies in 1942 and direct their full power against the Japanese in the Pacific Theater of Operations.

A small, combined planning cell labeled COSSAC (Chief of Staff to the Supreme Allied Commander) stood up in 1943 after the North

Africa campaign to develop options for an Allied invasion of Europe, with the expectation that such an assault would take place at a time to be determined. At the time, most observers expected that the Supreme Allied Commander would be a British officer, with an American deputy, so Combined Chiefs of Staff decided to appoint a British Chief of Staff for initial planning, with an American deputy to mirror anticipated command arrangements. Lieutenant General F. E. Morgan received the Chief of Staff appointment and began studying the problems attendant with an invasion of Northwestern Europe, codenamed *Overlord*. Historian Russell Weigley referred to the preliminary planning for the operation as having a "stepchild status" because it began while the Allies mounted operations in the Mediterranean Theater.[2] As a result, the anticipated availability of resources constrained Morgan's efforts. According to the memoirs of General Dwight D. Eisenhower, the eventual Supreme Allied Commander, Morgan based his planning figures on a "fixed number of ships, landing craft, and other resources."[3] Under Morgan's leadership, COSSAC developed a plan for an assault landing by three infantry divisions on France's coast. The available sealift could not carry a larger force.

Morgan's planners considered landings in either the vicinity of Pas-de-Calais or the Normandy coast in the vicinity of Caen. Considerations included anticipated enemy defenses, access to ports for rapidly landing and building up combat power, and room to expand a lodgment quickly. Pas-de-Calais offered established port facilities; however, COSSAC reasoned that the Germans would tenaciously defend such assets, and the ports could face substantial damage during a contested landing. Alternately, Caen offered ample space for amphibious landings to establish a beachhead, and planners determined the Allies would face less initial resistance from the enemy. Once ashore, the assault units would be reinforced by an additional 15 divisions that would break out of the lodgment area and drive south and then west to secure the Cherbourg ports.[4]

General Dwight D. Eisenhower received orders appointing him Supreme Commander of Allied Forces in December 1943, reflecting the power shift in the Allied command structure. As late as July 1943,

British Prime Minister Winston Churchill backed Chief of Imperial General Staff Alan Brooke. However, as the year progressed into the fall, it became clear an American would assume the role. Chief of Staff of the U.S. Army, George C. Marshall, briefly topped the list as the presumed nominee; however, President Roosevelt insisted on retaining Marshall in that role. Eisenhower made an obvious alternative. He possessed the confidence of both British and American leadership as the Allied Forces commander during operations in the Mediterranean from November 1942, including the successful campaigns in North Africa and Sicily.

Eisenhower arrived in London to assume command in January 1944 and immediately set to work examining COSSAC's efforts to date. Before coming to London, he had studied Morgan's three-division plan and shared it with his chief subordinate for ground operations, British General Bernard Law Montgomery. Montgomery, a decorated veteran of World War I, rose through the levels of command during World War II, winning victories in North Africa and Sicily before assuming command of the 21st Army Group for the invasion of Europe. Eisenhower and Montgomery agreed that the COSSAC plan lacked sufficient scope to seize the necessary ports quickly to establish the required logistics pipeline to support an invasion, while simultaneously occupying defending Germans across a wide area. If the assault force presented too small a frontage, defenders could easily organize counterattacks before reinforcements could land.[5]

Eisenhower and Montgomery oversaw a drastic expansion of the plan, bringing the total number of assault divisions to five, rapidly reinforced by additional combat power. American, British, and Commonwealth forces would land abreast on the Normandy coast, between Ravenoville to the west and Merville to the east. The British troops would drive south to create sufficient maneuver room for follow-on forces, while the Americans would pivot north to drive for Cherbourg as rapidly as possible. The Allies revised their strategic plans and priorities to provide sufficient ships and landing craft to support this more powerful assault force. Included in this reassessment was a dramatic increase in the size and complexity of airborne operations in support of the beach landings.

COSSAC's original vision for the airborne assault utilized parachute and glider forces landing in the beachhead's vicinity to block German counterattacks. Brigadier General James Gavin, assistant division commander of the 82nd Airborne Division, believed COSSAC's concepts for the use of airborne forces to be unimaginative and a waste of a potent combat multiplier. Gavin found himself on temporary duty away from the division in the winter of 1944 after fighting in Italy. He served in the role of airborne advisor to the Supreme Headquarters Allied Expeditionary Force (SHAEF), sharing the benefits of his recent combat experience in command of paratroopers.[6]

Gavin found that Montgomery was pressing for an increased role for the airborne to support his ideas for an overall more powerful invasion force. American General Omar Bradley, also recently returned from the Mediterranean Theater, supported Montgomery's vision. Bradley believed that the landings at Utah Beach in the American sector could not succeed without paratroopers securing the causeways that led inland from the coast. Despite opposition from Air Chief Marshal Sir Trafford Leigh-Mallory, Commander in Chief of the Allied Expeditionary Air Forces, and responsible for the safe delivery of airborne troops into battle, Montgomery and Bradley fought successfully for the use of a sizeable airborne contingent in the invasion. Leigh-Mallory feared that the paratroopers and glider men would incur unacceptably high casualties in the battle's opening hours. The ground commanders insisted the attack could not succeed without airborne participation and offered to take full responsibility for the decision.[7]

As planning for the initial assault (codenamed *Neptune*) evolved, planners assigned three airborne divisions (one British and two American) various roles. They would secure key terrain beyond the shoreline to include beach exits, bridges, and crossroads; provide protection to the lodgment area's flanks; and tie up German defenders to protect the beaches from counterattacks.[8] The British 6th Airborne Division, under General Richard Gale, had the mission of securing the left flank of the landings in the vicinity of Sword Beach. The American 101st Airborne Division, under the command of Maxwell Taylor, would land behind Utah Beach to secure the causeways that served as exits from the beach and critical terrain just inland in the vicinity of Sainte-Marie-du-Mont. Ridgway's 82nd Airborne Division would jump further inland, seizing the village of Saint- Sauveur-le-Vicomte, securing river crossings, and setting up blocking positions.

When Bradley shared aerial reconnaissance photographs of the potential objective areas near the Cherbourg peninsula with Gavin, the paratrooper general found his confidence growing:

> One of the most reassuring things about them was that the Germans were beginning to flood the area—a clear indication that they did not intend to fight an offensive battle or use large amounts of armor. We would be at our best under those conditions, where we would be engaging their infantry with little armor.[9]

Despite Gavin's enthusiasm, the German defenders were beginning to seriously prepare to resist any Allied landings, after years of benign neglect of the Reich's western flank. After the fall of France in 1940, Hitler intended to build up a series of robust, mutually supporting defenses along the Atlantic coast. These measures assumed new urgency after the Allied raid on Dieppe, France, in August 1942; however, the task of developing these fortifications did not begin in earnest until the fall of 1943. Field Marshal Erwin Rommel took command of the construction effort, using his hard-won combat experiences from the battles of France and the North African campaign to design an effective barrier to an enemy offensive.[10]

German operational doctrine emphasized counterattacking an enemy offensive as soon as possible. The overall German commander in the West, Field Marshal Gerd von Rundstedt, based his defensive concept on this idea. He maintained an armored force as an operational reserve, designed to deploy to any point on the coast where the Allies landed. Rommel possessed a better sense of the balance of force between the Germans and their enemies. Any large mobile formation that attempted to maneuver against an Allied landing would be subject to withering attacks from the air.[11] The Luftwaffe would not be providing any meaningful opposition to Allied airpower in the forthcoming battle. Between the withdrawal of a majority of its aircraft to Germany to protect the homeland from the British and American strategic bombing offensive and the ensuing casualties sustained among its pilots, the lower standard of training of German replacement pilots due to the need to get them flying operationally as soon as possible, and concentrated efforts by the

Allies to decimate the German fighter inventory before D-Day, the Luftwaffe could muster few aircraft to counter enemy air superiority. In the ensuing battle, the Allies would launch over 130,000 aircraft sorties against fewer than 14,000 mounted by the Germans.[12]

Rommel determined to meet the American and Commonwealth attacks directly on the beaches to throw them back into the sea. He believed, should the enemy gain and consolidate a position on the continent, the defeat of Germany would be only a matter of time. Conversely, if the Allies could be prevented from landing, the attendant losses in men and materiel would prevent them from making any invasion attempts for a significant period. This time could be turned to German strategic advantage. But first, the Allied invasion had to be stopped.

As the more experienced American airborne division, having seen action in Sicily and Italy, the 82nd was assigned a more ambitious mission than its sister unit, the 101st. The 82nd's regiments would be fighting further inland from the beaches and have longer to wait to link up with heavier ground forces. Despite the experience of the division's senior leaders and the impeccable combat record achieved by its 505th PIR, the newly attached 508th and 507th PIRs would be making their combat debuts. As a result, the 505th PIR received the most important mission of seizing Saint-Sauveur-le-Vicomte as well as a series of crossing points over the Douve River. The other regiments would take and consolidate positions to the north and south of the 505th.[13]

The German 91st Luftlande (Air Landing) Division arrived in Normandy shortly before the anticipated invasion occurred. The division received extensive training in countering airborne forces and by coincidence received the assignment to defend the inland areas behind Utah Beach, augmenting the static 709th and 243rd Infantry Divisions who had the mission of coastal defense. Compared with the elite Panzer divisions that participated in the 1940 invasion of France and the fighting on the Eastern Front against the Soviet Union, the 91st was a second-rate formation at best; however, the German High Command still ensured that its task organization adhered to the principle of combined arms or the use of mutually reinforcing combat units under a single commander.

Two infantry regiments and an independent rifle battalion comprised the division's infantry strength, supported by an assortment of outdated artillery and armor. The armored component, Panzer Abteilung 100 (Tank Task Force 100), consisted of almost 30 assorted French tanks captured in the battles of 1940 augmented by a few obsolete German models. While the 91st lacked the maneuverability and firepower of a Panzer division, it possessed sufficient strength, backed by its small mobile reserve, to offer lightly armed paratroopers spirited resistance, and it was sitting astride the 82nd's proposed objectives.[14]

Air Chief Marshal Leigh-Mallory, upon learning that Allied intelligence had discovered the deployment of the 91st to the Cotentin area, sought to cancel the American airborne drops altogether. Already nervous about the potential for high casualties, Leigh-Mallory believed that dropping parachutists and landing gliders in the vicinity of an enemy unit specifically trained to repel them was tantamount to consigning the troopers to a death sentence. General Bradley insisted that both the 82nd and 101st needed to drop to ensure the success of the Utah Beach landings. Airborne planners resolved the issue by scrapping the proposed drops around Saint-Sauveur-le-Vicomte.[15] The 505th Parachute Infantry received the assignment to take the crossroads town of Sainte-Mère-Église, while its sister regiments were to secure river crossings over the Merderet River, in the vicinity of the towns of Amfreville and Chef-du-Pont. The regiments would drop before dawn on D-Day on drop zones in the vicinity of their objectives.[16]

Applying the lessons learned from Sicily and Italy, the 82nd's planners determined that the entire complement of the 80th's anti-tank guns needed to be delivered into Normandy as rapidly as possible to aid the parachute infantry in its mission to seize and hold key road networks and river crossing points. Batteries A and B received allocations for 16 guns to be delivered by glider as part of Mission *Detroit* in the initial aerial assault, as soon as possible behind the paratroopers. The high-velocity, flat-trajectory guns would be crucial to stopping any German armor. Battery C would reinforce the initial landings by air on the evening of D-Day, along with sections of the battalion headquarters as part of Mission *Elmira*. The remaining elements of the battalion would comprise part of the seaborne echelon of the division, to be landed at Utah Beach once the assault force secured a lodgment.[17]

General Ridgway deemed the anti-tank guns of A and B Batteries so critical that he tapped a trusted officer, Major Al Ireland, whose experience included time as the regimental S1 of the 505th PIR and as the Executive Officer of 1st Battalion, 505th, to land by glider with Mission *Detroit*. Ireland's responsibility was to personally oversee the recovery of the weapons.[18] Why Ridgway did not consider this role within Lieutenant Colonel Singleton's purview as the 80th's commanding officer, or one of the two battery commanders, is unclear. It is possible that because batteries were attached to the 505th for the initial invasion, Ridgway entrusted the delivery of the 57mm guns to an officer assigned to the regiment who was known to the battalion commanders tasked with seizing Sainte-Mère-Église, the 505th PIR's objective. Ireland, an experienced paratroop officer who made combat jumps into Sicily and Italy, would ride a glider into Normandy with the anti-tank guns.[19]

The 80th AAA Battalion relocated from Italy, first to Northern Ireland and then to England, to prepare for Operation *Overlord*. The entire division—minus the 504th PIR, which remained in combat in Italy through spring 1944—made this move between December 1943 and February 1944. The men of the 80th spent a great deal of time training on weapons familiarization and qualification and completing conditioning marches to prepare them for the upcoming campaign. As winter turned to spring, training began to emphasize airborne operations and the attendant loading, securing, and unloading of AT guns, jeeps for towing the weapons and ammunition, and other equipment. The glider men of the 80th trained on both the CG-4A Waco Glider and the British Airspeed AS.51 Horsa Glider. The Horsa carried a far bigger payload than the Waco, but most glider riders preferred the Waco, as it was considered sturdier. Both aircraft consisted of wooden materials and fabric; however, the Waco also had an internal metal frame that provided some protection to crew and passengers during rough landings.[20]

The 80th also participated in larger training exercises in support of the division's parachute infantry regiments in preparation for the attack across the English Channel. Such events highlighted the challenges the artillerymen faced when operating in support of infantry units. Lieutenant James Baugh of the 80th's Headquarters Battery recalled specific issues with command and control: "To whose authority did we operate? Could a battalion commander, [in] say the 505 Parachute Infantry, take the Antitank and 50 calibers and park them and use the specialized personnel for light infantry ... Once a specially trained individual was lost it would be awfully hard to replace him."[21]

Answering such questions before entering combat assumed great importance to the 80th AAA. To maximize the available combat power provided by the battalion's AT guns and heavy machine guns, commanders of both supported and supporting units had to understand the limits of their authority. Supported infantry commanders had ultimate responsibility for accomplishing their mission's objectives, while commanders of supporting units such as the 80th were obligated to ensure their men and equipment were employed within their capabilities. An infantry commander who wasted the advantages conferred by a special attachment through misuse squandered a scarce resource, while an attachment that insisted it be employed by strict doctrinal guidelines might wind up not

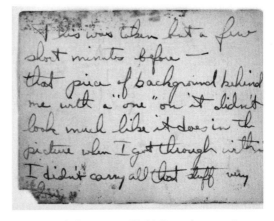

Captain William Pratt, 6 June 1944, at Royal Air Force Field Ramsbury, prior to departure for Normandy. Pratt wrote on the back, "This was taken but a few short minutes before—that piece of background with a 'one' on it didn't look much like it does in the picture when I got through with it." (Photo courtesy of Micky and Joe Pratt)

First Lieutenant Marshall Stark, 6 June 1944, at Royal Air Force Field Ramsbury, prior to departure for Normandy. (Photo courtesy of Micky and Joe Pratt)

contributing to winning a fight on the ground. Beyond the decision to send the anti-tank batteries into combat by glider and land the anti-aircraft batteries from the sea, no hard and fast rules resulted from the pre-invasion exercises, and commanders and men were left to improvise answers on the ground in Normandy.

As May 1944 ended, the men of the 80th AAA Battalion received orders to head to their embarkation stations to make final preparations for the operation. The battalion split, with half making an amphibious landing and half deploying by glider. The seaborne echelon departed for Cardiff, Wales, on 19 May to waterproof and load equipment for shipment across the Channel. This echelon consisted of elements of the Headquarters Battery, along with the .50-caliber anti-aircraft D, E, and F Batteries. Meanwhile, Batteries A, B, and C were staged at Royal Air Force Field Ramsbury in preparation for the airborne assault. The moment for the great invasion would soon be at hand.[22]

Normandy

Over the last two years, he's lost count of the number of times he's heard gliders referred to as "the silent wings." He feels the moniker is inappropriate, as this ride is anything but silent. Sure, the Waco doesn't have its own motor, but you could easily hear the drone of the two engines powering the C-47 towing them. Not to mention the buffeting the fabric stretched over the Waco's frame is taking from the turbulence. This must be what sitting inside a bass drum feels like. Other than the noise, though, this flight is going okay. The pre-flight briefing confirmed the gliders were going make the Channel crossing in a column of fours. As far as he can tell looking out the small window, they are holding a nice formation.

Suddenly they hit clouds, and he can't see anything but a milky haze. Then there's a new noise ... they're taking fire. The paratroopers went in earlier, so now the German gunners are wide awake. The Waco's really shaking now, but the pilots are pros, holding everything as steady as they can despite the heavy flak. He can feel in his belly that they're starting to descend, so they must've cut loose from the tow ship. There's light coming through the windows, and he can make out the ground rushing below, although the sun isn't up yet. The pilot tells them to brace for impact, and he tenses up, expecting the worst, but to his surprise, they land as smoothly as if they were back at Laurinburg-Maxton. Except for the gunfire. That's enough to remind him they're in occupied France. He needs to get off this bird and start finding his boys and rounding up his guns ...

The taking and defense of Sainte-Mère-Église was a major D-Day objective for the 82nd Airborne Division. The recovery and positioning of guns on major avenues of approach into the town, and the defense of Merderet River crossing points against German counterattacks at Chef-du-Pont and La Fière Causeway were the primary missions of A and B Batteries on 6 June 1944. If it controlled the crossing points, the 82nd could prevent enemy attacks across the flooded Merderet toward the American beachhead at Utah Beach.

Lieutenant Colonel Singleton (promoted effective 1 February 1944) and the 80th AAA had learned from the debacle of Operation *Husky* and made sure that they got their 57mm anti-tank guns into action as soon as possible. A and B Batteries were assigned to glider serials that departed Ramsbury Field, England at 0150, 6 June, following on the heels of the parachute infantry regiments. Both batteries were destined to land at Landing Zone "O," near the village of Sainte-Mère-Église. The batteries' cannons were critical to the division's mission of holding key crossing points of the Merderet River against the German counterattacks everyone expected. The paratroopers needed the stopping power of those 6-pounders. The troops landed soon after 0400, two hours ahead of the amphibious invasion.

64 • NEVER A DULL MOMENT

Technical Sergeant John McFadden, Headquarters, 80th AAA, was among this first group, whose efforts focused on gathering weapons, ammunition, and jeeps, and finding enough personnel to man the guns. After the campaign, Singleton would recall that manpower was the issue as soon as the men hit the ground. The gliders got the equipment to the landing zones, and even if a glider cracked up, some of the gear could still be recovered and put into action. The problem was that a standard gun squad had 10 troopers. Once a glider had a gun, jeep, or ammunition trailer loaded on it, there was only room for two or three men in addition to the pilots. Putting together gun crews on the ground proved to be problematic in the first confusing hours of the invasion.

Things began looking up once Pratt's C Battery arrived around 2100 hours that night. In short order, the battery had a two-gun section set up 3,000 yards to the southwest of Sainte-Mère-Église. A Battery had an additional cannon in place further south, covering the crossing point of the Merderet River at Chef-du-Pont. By 1500 on the 7th, the anti-tank batteries had eight cannons emplaced, either overlooking the Merderet or covering avenues of approach into Sainte-Mère-Église: less than 50 percent of their authorized combat power. The manpower situation for the battalion was not much better. Lieutenant Colonel Singleton was unaccounted for, 36 hours after landing, and Captain Nelson was acting commander. His strength report for 7 June mentions A Battery's strength as three officers and 36 enlisted men, providing the unit with almost a full complement of officers. B Battery, comprised of one officer and 45 enlisted soldiers, reported the highest strength. C Battery had no officers present at the time, and only four soldiers. Sergeant McFadden had the distinction of being the lone representative of the headquarters. Nelson's report noted A Battery destroyed an enemy armored car sometime earlier as well. Meanwhile, the seaborne element made its landing around 1730 on 8 June at Utah Beach. The battalion motor officer, Lieutenant James Baugh, gives a vivid account of his experience moving inland:

> Our landing craft eased to the shore and let down the ramp and we went on land. The very first thing I observed was the screeching of 88's that was so familiar to me. Evidently, there was some enemy not too far away. I noted as we passed the great

breastworks the Germans had so carefully placed with concrete embankments, that some were as deep as 20 feet. I shuddered when I looked into them to see dozens of German soldiers lying there killed perhaps by grenades on concussion or from the pounding given them by the Naval vessels offshore. Our column progressed along a lane in which there was a guide that had been sent from Division Headquarters, or at least that knew where Division was located ... There were chutes everywhere beginning just a few miles from Utah Beach.[23]

The battalion had struggled to establish an anti-tank defense over the previous 48 hours. Merely assembling enough men and guns proved challenging. Batteries A and B flew into Normandy as part of Mission *Detroit*, the first glider lift assigned to support the 82nd's initial assault. The 505th, 507th, and 508th Parachute Infantry Regiments faced vastly different circumstances after their drops. The 505th PIR landed on or near their assigned drop zone, designated "O," in the vicinity of Sainte-Mère-Église. The 507th PIR's paratroopers were widely scattered on both sides of the Merderet and had trouble assembling a force of sufficient size to secure its D-Day objective of Amfreville. The 508th experienced a similar drop to the 507th, but were able to form four relatively large, ad hoc formations that subsequently linked up with elements of both the 505th and 507th Parachute Infantry Regiments to attack a variety of German positions.[24]

Lieutenant Colonel Singleton's vision from a year ago had come to fruition, and each anti-tank battery was now fully equipped with eight 57mm guns. The batteries once again consisted of two platoons of two gun sections each. The 82nd's planners expected Mission *Detroit* to deliver 16 guns to support the parachute infantry, but the men of the 80th only recovered four guns by mid-morning, 6 June 1944. Engineers from the 307th Airborne Engineer Battalion recovered a fifth 57mm gun, which they deployed overlooking La Fière Causeway, the objective of 1st Battalion, 505th PIR. The 2nd and 3rd Battalions, meanwhile, set about securing the roads running in and out Sainte-Mère-Église. The 3rd Battalion, under Lieutenant Colonel Ed Krause, focused on defending the southern half of the town, while Lieutenant Colonel Ben Vandervoort's 2nd Battalion defended the northern half. Two guns deployed with 2nd Battalion, one covering the northern approaches into Sainte-Mère-Église, while a second accompanied Lieutenant Colonel Vandervoort and a

66 • NEVER A DULL MOMENT

platoon under the command of Lieutenant Turner T. Turnbull 1 mile north of Sainte-Mère-Église, to outpost the village of Neuville-au-Plain. Meanwhile, Lieutenant Colonel Krause established an additional gun position guarding the southern entrance to Sainte-Mère-Église, along Highway N-13, and sent the 4th to cover the approaches over the Merderet at Chef-du-Pont.

Historian Bob Burns and 80th AAA Battalion veteran Ray Fary recount, in a 2004 article on the taking of Sainte-Mère-Église, that during the morning of 6 June 1944, as paratroopers and glider men assembled throughout the French countryside, the leaders of the 82nd Airborne Division, particularly General Ridgway, had no means of communication beyond the use of runners. Thus, Ridgway was ignorant of the situation of much of his command and unable to influence much beyond his immediate vicinity. He knew the 505th PIR had succeeded in liberating Sainte-Mère-Église and was preparing to hold it against counterattack, along with efforts to secure the crossing points at La Fière and Chef-du-Pont; thus, he decided that whatever anti-tank assets the troops recovered would be committed to the defense of the town and its environs. As stated by Burns and Fary, Saint Mère-Église was the Alamo, the fallback position for the division that must be held. Additionally, the river crossings and Highway N-13 made the area ideal terrain to facilitate a German armored strike on the landing area of Utah Beach. Should enemy armor succeed in getting over the Merderet and past Sainte-Mère-Église, it could wreak havoc among the American troops coming ashore.[25]

The decision to retain the anti-tank assets at Sainte-Mère-Église soon paid off. A five-man crew manning a 57mm established its position on a slight elevation, with a downward sloping field of fire, south of the village. Their mission was to support the blocking position emplaced by the paratroopers of the 505th Parachute Infantry. Historians Burns and Fary surmise that the crew, under the command of Sergeant Raynor Wilson, consisted of the NCO and four privates: James Fields, Victor Allegretti, Jim Gates, and Donald Coburn, all from A Battery.[26]

A large German formation occupied a prominent terrain feature, Hill 20, and launched an attack up Highway N-13. The troops, from the German 3rd Battalion of 1058th Regiment, supported by self-propelled artillery, struck about 1000 on the morning of 6 June. Krause's roadblock, manned by George Company, 3rd Battalion, 505th, successfully stymied the initial German assault. The fire support from the 57mm gun played a pivotal role in deterring the enemy guns from advancing on the town, and the direct attack up the highway faltered. The Germans did not give up after this initial failure; instead, they maneuvered to attempt to bypass the roadblock.[27] This effort ran into I Company, 3rd Battalion, 505th, assaulting Hill 20. The German infantry ultimately withdrew in the face of this opposition.

As the day wore on, pressure from the Germans on the defending Americans grew. Enemy infantry attacks from the north and west signaled the German desire to break through the airborne troops and drive for the beaches. Sometime after noon, the troops from the 2nd Battalion, 505th, posted to Neuville-au-Plain, received word from a French civilian that a body of German infantry was approaching from the north. Battalion commander Ben Vandervoort, leading from the front despite a broken ankle from a lousy parachute landing, was forward with his men, from Lieutenant Turner Turnbull's 3rd Platoon, Dog Company.[28]

As the German formation approached the American position, it appeared at first that they were surrendering, or else already prisoners, as they were accompanied by men bearing orange air-ground recognition panels, a standard method used by the Americans as a visual identification signal. However, the battalion commander and platoon leader saw the dismounted men trailed by two German fighting vehicles—treaded, not wheeled. The officers found this strange because while it was plausible that an ad hoc force of American paratroopers could round up a sizeable number of enemy infantry, it was unlikely the lightly armed Americans could force armor to surrender or to operate it, if it fell into their hands. Vandervoort directed a nearby machine-gun team to open fire on the trailing vehicles; upon receiving fire, the Germans took cover, and the

68 • NEVER A DULL MOMENT

tracked vehicles began maneuvering forward. The paratrooper officer's instincts had proven correct. The surrendering prisoner formation was a ruse to approach the American positions.

Vandervoort had hitched a ride to Neuville-au-Plain with one of the 80th AAA's anti-tank guns. Now that the enemy armor, identified as self-propelled (SP) guns, was moving against the Dog Company outpost, the AT gunners went into action. There is some question about whether the AT gunners first took cover once the self-propelled guns began returning fire and Vandervoort had to directly order them to man their cannon. Vandervoort never made any such statement; however, a veteran of the 505th PIR reported the occurrence in a history published 40 years later.[29] The historian had been in C Company, not Neuville-au-Plain, so this report is likely based on hearsay. In any event, the crew engaged the enemy SP guns with direct fire and scored mobility kills. The Germans still possessed vastly superior combat power, even with their armor support out of the fight. Turnbull eventually had to withdraw under pressure and only escaped with 16 of his men, supported by a platoon from Easy Company, 505th PIR, sent forward to assist him.[30] The withdrawal from Neuville-au-Plain allowed the enemy to encroach further on the 505th's positions around Sainte-Mère-Église.

Meanwhile, the 1st Battalion, 505th PIR, had their hands full to the west of the town, defending against German attacks across the Merderet River, at a place soon to be renowned in 82nd Airborne Division history, La Fière Causeway. Major Frederick C. A. Kellam, commander of the 1st Battalion, 505th PIR, was responsible for taking and holding the small bridge to deny German armor a vital crossing point of the flooded Merderet. Lieutenant John Dolan, a Boston Irishman nicknamed "Red" of Able Company, 505th, led the initial movement toward the bridge. Dolan's company initially needed to seize the bridge's eastern end, which included securing La Fière Manor, a large stone building dominating the road leading from Sainte-Mère-Église to the bridge. More paratroopers from the 505th, as well as troops from the 508th and the widely scattered 507th PIRs, moved to the sound of the guns at La Fière. After a morning of firefights, in which those elements from multiple units reinforced A Company on an ad hoc basis, the bridge's eastern edge was in American hands, while German forces massed in Cauquigny, over the Merderet on the western side of the La Fière Causeway.

Sometime in the mid-morning, the Germans launched an assault from the western side of the Merderet, consisting of dismounted infantry from the 1057th Regiment, 91st Division, and two Renault medium tanks. The Renaults were captured French vehicles and assigned to the 100th Panzer Replacement Battalion.[31] Dolan's position received anti-tank support from a 57mm gun, suspected to be from B Battery, 80th AAA, that had been recovered in the early hours after the mission *Detroit's* gliders landed. Engineers from the 307th Airborne Engineers located and salvaged the gun, under the direction of General Gavin, and placed it overlooking the eastern end of La Fière Bridge. With no anti-tank gunners available, volunteers from the 307th operated the weapon.

As the Renaults began to move toward the bridge, the engineers-turned-gunners opened fire. Burns and Fary indicate that some reports state the gunners succeeded in making hits on the tanks but no disabling shots. In turn, the tanks engaged the 57mm, causing several casualties among the men operating the cannon.[32] Meanwhile, paratroopers of A Company engaged the enemy with bazookas. Two teams from the company, including Lenold Peterson and Marcus Heim, maneuvered to get close enough to fire effectively at the oncoming armor. With the anti-tank gunners out of action, the success of the bazookas became paramount to an effective defense. The bazooka men did manage to stop the onslaught, with an additional soldier chucking a grenade down the hatch of one of the enemy tanks for good measure. Members of bazooka teams would eventually receive the Distinguished Service Cross for their actions.[33] Sadly, during this engagement, Major Kellam and his battalion operations officer, Captain Dale Roysdon, were killed by mortar fire as they raced to resupply the bazooka teams with ammunition. American paratroopers refer to the bridge at La Fière as "Kellam's Bridge" in honor of the fallen battalion commander.[34] The Americans halted the German attack for now, but it would be three more days of fierce struggle before fate decided the final victors at the La Fière crossing.

HEADQUARTERS 82ND AIRBORNE DIVISION
OFFICE OF THE DIVISION COMMANDER

8 March 1946

Mrs. F. C. A. Kellam
305 Corona Avenue
San Antonio, Texas

Dear Mrs. Kellam:

    I have just talked to Colonel Ekman, the Commanding Officer of the 505th Parachute Infantry, who was Commanding Officer when Fred was assigned to the Regiment.

    Fred was not recommended for a promotion. I thought you would be interested in knowing this, and as I recall, I wrote you in January and told you as soon as the Regiment returned, I would let you know.

    The bridge over the Merderet River in Normandy was named Kellam's Bridge, and as long as the 82nd Airborne Division was in that locality, which was in excess of one month, it was always referred to as his bridge, because of the gallant fight made by his Battalion there, and the fact that he lost his life in the capture and retention of the bridge. I do not believe that it is the intention of our government to retain this name for the bridge, because it would perhaps conflict with the French Provincial and National Government. It is very likely, however, that during this post war period that the War Department will name an Airborne Installation in honor of Fred. This has been the policy in the past, and I feel that they will follow it. If any action takes place I will be sure to let you know about it.

    I trust that the post war world is treating you well, and that you and your son Michael are happy.

Sincerely,

JAMES M. GAVIN
Major General, U. S. Army
Commanding.

Letter from Major General James M. Gavin to Mrs. F. C. A. Kellam referring to the bridge at La Fière Causeway as Kellam's Bridge, 8 March 1946. (Photo courtesy of Major Kellam's granddaughter Christie Michelle Kellam)

Further south, a similar scene occurred at the Chef-du-Pont river crossing. Throughout 6 June, elements of the 505th and 507th PIRs fought to take control of the bridge at this location. The struggle was still ongoing as late as 2100 that night. Throughout the day, General Gavin monitored the fighting at both La Fière and Chef-du-Pont and, at one point, reinforced the fighters under Dolan with 75 men who had been at Chef-du-Pont. This action left the commander on the ground, Captain Roy Creek, with only a handful of troopers to hold off approximately 100 German infantry supported by artillery. Creek's men received the worst of the exchange but managed to hold on.

The tide shifted with the arrival of Mission *Elmira* on Landing Zone W shortly after 2100. C Battery, 80th AAA, spread across 14 larger British Horsa gliders of serial 30 landed, bringing badly needed anti-tank guns, jeeps ammunition, and gunners.[35]

Captain Pratt's glider, en route to Normandy, taken by First Lieutenant Marshall Stark, 6 June 1944. (Photo courtesy of Micky and Joe Pratt)

C-47 aircraft towing a glider over the English Channel, 6 June 1944. Note the tow rope extending out behind the airplane. (Photo courtesy of Micky and Joe Pratt)

Some daylight remained due to the time of year, making the landings visible to friend and foe alike. After the landing, Captain Creek found he had the support of one C Battery gun to bolster his defense. The gunners succeeded in suppressing the artillery supporting the Germans across the bridge, and soon General Gavin replaced the men he stripped from Chef-du-Pont with others from the La Fière defenses. In the battle to take the crossing sites, Gavin continuously robbed Peter to pay Paul as the scattered paratroopers struggled to mass enough combat power to be effective. But for the time being, Creek had enough men to go on the attack. Lieutenant Charles Ames, with a small squad of men, assaulted across the bridge while the remainder of Creek's troops provided supporting fire. Ames's attack drove off the German defenders, and the 507th Parachute Infantry troopers now held both ends of the bridge.[36]

To expand the lodgment, a 57mm gun from A Battery, thought to be under the command of Sergeant Lawrence Fox and crewed by Private First Class Earl Crause and Privates Ben Albin and Dent Carter, established another position further south of the Chef-du-Pont bridge to assist in guarding against a possible attack from the village of Les Forges. Author Ed Ruggero later captured Creek's summary of the taking of the Chef-du-Pont bridge: "We had done some things badly. But overall, with a hodgepodge of troops from several units who had never trained ether as a unit, [who] didn't even know one another and were engaged in their first combat, we had done OK. We captured our bridge and held it."[37]

C Battery received additional orders to position a gun behind the 57mm already in place overlooking the La Fière Causeway to bolster the defense against anticipated German attacks sometime on 7 June. Fary and Burns postulate that Corporal Walter Wilson, Sergeant William Stevens, and Sergeant Isadore Dembovitz from B Battery likely moved to the La Fière position to help operate these weapons.[38]

Normandy marked the first combat airborne operation and the first period of sustained combat experienced by the 80th AAA. The battalion largely missed the fighting in Sicily, arriving well toward the end of the campaign as the Germans withdrew to the Italian mainland. The period of fighting around the Salerno beachhead provided invaluable experience in patrolling and outpost duty, but after the move to Naples, the battalion primarily conducted sentry operations. The ferocity that marked the fighting in Normandy was noticeably absent. Thus, the battalion experienced its first heavy casualties in the fighting around Sainte-Mère-Église.[39]

During Operation *Neptune*, the battalion experienced casualties almost immediately. First Lieutenant Jasper Booth of B Battery is likely the first man of the battalion killed in the Normandy campaign. Lieutenant Booth flew into Drop Zone "O" via glider as part of Mission *Detroit*. Booth likely died on impact, as he was sitting in a jeep loaded in the rear of the glider, and the ties securing the cargo came undone, whether accidentally or by design to expedite unloading the vehicle under fire is unknown. Both the glider and jeep sustained damage, the jeep coming out of the

74 • NEVER A DULL MOMENT

glider due to the impact. Booth's body sustained gunfire wounds as well, but the lack of bleeding indicated he was already dead when shot.

The battalion records initially listed an additional three members of the battalion who participated in Mission *Detroit* as missing in action. Battery A's Corporal Paul Buel and two of his gun crew, Private First Class John Hunt and Private Cleon Wyman, flew into Normandy with a 57mm gun on Glider 42-46517. The glider missed the landing area, and as a result was not initially recovered after the battle. Eventually, the Army located the wreckage, and identified the bodies of the missing men in early 1945.

The first 80th men killed on the ground died due to the confusion inherent in the first few hours of any airborne operation. The soldiers were not killed by enemy fire but by a landmine emplaced by friendly paratroopers. Staff Sergeant Stanley Kubas and Private Joe Fisher of Battery A recovered their cannon and a jeep to haul it and made their way toward Sainte-Mère-Église.[40] At the same time, 3rd Battalion, 505th, was establishing its roadblocks to defend the town from enemy armor. Three privates from H Company manned one such position on the Chef-du-Pont road. As Kubas and Fisher sped toward Sainte-Mère-Église, they detonated the mine, killing them and destroying their vehicle and cannon.[41] Meanwhile, the fighting at La Fière Causeway continued unabated.

In a 1959 letter to General Gavin, Dolan (acting as the senior commander on the ground) wrote that the enemy fire lessened during the night of 6–7 June but resumed with intensity early on the morning of the 7th. The men of the 505th Parachute Infantry sustained heavy casualties from enemy mortar fire, which reached its peak in the early afternoon. The barrage presaged another German assault on the bridge. Dolan recounts that the 80th AAA crew operating the 57mm gun abandoned the cannon because they believed that the 505th PIR would withdraw and give up the La Fière Bridge to the Germans.[42]

Dolan stated he first learned that the 57mm had no crew when the Germans launched a combined infantry armor assault sometime in the early afternoon. The German tankers learned from the previous day's experience and did not approach within effective range of the paratrooper's bazookas.[43]

The bazooka had an advertised effective range of 150 yards, but combat experience revealed its true effective range was much shorter.[44]

Dolan looked to the supporting anti-tank cannon to engage the German tanks; however, he realized it was silent. Upon investigating, Dolan found the weapon unmanned, with the firing mechanism removed. With no effective anti-tank support available, Dolan prepared a squad of paratroopers to engage the tanks with gammon grenades, a last-ditch weapon designed for close combat against enemy personnel or armor. The Number 82 Gammon grenade was an elastic, knitted bag that the user filled with varying amounts of plastic explosives depending on the target. Invented by a British paratroop officer named Captain R. S. Gammon, the grenade detonated by use of an "always fuse." The fuse was kept safe by the use of a pin attached to a strip of linen tape. When thrown the tape unraveled, releasing the pin, and arming the grenade, which detonated on impact. Most of the troops carried one or the other of these weapons. Fortunately for Dolan and his men, two gunners returned to the 57mm with the firing mechanism before they went after the tanks and opened fire. Dolan recalled them as very young soldiers (17 or 18) and credited them with destroying both tanks. He also wrote that he recommended them both for Silver Star awards for bravery.[45]

A variety of sources both corroborate and contradict Dolan's letter. Fary and Burns speculate that the gunners had not abandoned the gun but had left to obtain additional ammunition and supplies. The mere fact that the men returned to the firing position supports this line of thought. Regarding the men destroying two tanks, the 80th AAA Battalion History entry for 7 June credits Corporal Wilson with destroying a "Mark IV across the bridge." Wilson, in fact, destroyed one Renault of the 100th Panzer Replacement Battalion. Wilson received a Bronze Star, but the date for the award is 8 June rather than the 7th.[46] By all reports, though, it is apparent that the men of the 80th AAA gave a good account of themselves at the La Fière fight on 7 June.

The Germans also continued trying to break through the Sainte-Mère-Église defenses from the north that day. The 2nd Battalion, 505th PIR, stopped an enemy armor attack with support from battery

76 • NEVER A DULL MOMENT

men under the command of Second Lieutenant John Cliff. One of Cliff's men, Private Carl Uitto, received credit for destroying a Mark IV in this engagement; however, this vehicle was likely a self-propelled gun fitted over a chassis from a Mark IV.[47]

Uitto's kill occurred within 50 yards of the 2nd Battalion, 505th PIR's command post as part of a much larger action. The self-propelled gun formed part of a heavy push by the 1058th Regiment, augmented by the German 7th Army Sturm Bataillon (assault battalion). In addition to destroying the SP gun, Cliff's men received credit for a 1,900-yard shot that stopped an armored car, as noted in Nelson's report referenced earlier. However, Uitto and his crew received severe wounds in this fight, leaving their cannon without operators. At this moment, Private John Atchley stepped into the picture.

Atchley, from H Company, 505th PIR, saw the men from Battery A go down and that the enemy vehicles continued to close in on the battalion command post. Atchley broke cover and headed for the anti-tank cannon. There is some speculation that Atchley may have undergone previous artillery training, but he had never operated an anti-tank gun. Unassisted, Atchley opened fire and destroyed a second SP gun with only his second round. This action caused the remaining German track crews to experience second thoughts about continuing the advance. Instead, they retreated from Sainte-Mère-Église. For his actions, Atchley received the Distinguished Service Cross, an award for valor just below the Medal of Honor, for "courage, daring, and complete disregard for his life."[48]

Lieutenant Cliff led the anti-armor defense under the watchful eye of Lieutenant Colonel Vandervoort, who recommended that Cliff receive the Silver Star for heroic leadership. Cliff's citation emphasizes that Cliff and his men refused to retreat in the face of the German advance and notes the destruction of the armored car and two tanks (the self-propelled guns described earlier).[49]

On 8 June, the anti-aircraft assets of D, E, and F Batteries and the remaining headquarters elements of the 80th AAA landed on Utah Beach. They proceeded inland to link up with the rest of the battalion. The anti-tank batteries had sustained a beating in the past 48 hours of combat, and it became necessary to reassign some anti-aircraft officers to the tank busters. B Battery had lost Lieutenant Booth but also lacked a commander and an additional lieutenant, as Captain Nock Russell and Second Lieutenant John Barni both sustained injuries on the initial glider assault. C Battery's First Lieutenant Marshall Stark also suffered a hard landing and was out of action.[50]

While the battalion shuffled its deck of officers, the officers at the division level recognized that the threat to Sainte-Mère-Église had abated, and Ridgway's thoughts turned to offensive action. The amphibious landings continued, and both the 4th and 90th Infantry Divisions were moving inland and prepared to turn west and begin clearing the Cotentin Peninsula.

Paratroopers from the 505th Parachute Infantry firmly held the eastern side of La Fière Causeway, while members of the 507th and 508th Parachute Infantry Regiments, recovering from the 6 June jump that had scattered them on both sides of the river, continued to try to mass sufficient combat power to overwhelm the Germans holding the western side of the causeway. By the evening, the division, reinforced on 7 June by the 325th Glider Infantry Regiment, turned its full attention to forcing the Merderet River.[51]

Elements of the 507th PIR discovered a shallow crossing of the river north of Cauquigny. They communicated this intelligence to the division commander, Major General Matthew B. Ridgway, who ordered the 325th Glider commander, Harry G. Lewis, to use this crossing site to move a battalion across the river in an attempt to flank the village from the north. Colonel Lewis gave the mission to his first battalion under the command of Major Teddy Sanford. Sanford led his force across the river and linked up with troopers from Charles Timmes's 2nd Battalion, 507th PIR, to attack the German positions. Sanford's 1st Battalion, 325th GIR, led the attack.

B Company, 1st Battalion, 325th, attacked south as the main effort in the early morning of 9 June, supported by A Company. C Company secured the battalion's rear against German positions to the northeast. By 0330, C Company moved south to link up with the bulk of the battalion.

Due to the pressure of German counterattacks from the northeast and general confusion during a night attack, C Company blundered into a German artillery battery.

Initially believing the Germans wished to surrender, the American glider men only acted once they suddenly received fire from both flanks. The company withdrew north out of the village, except for one platoon that was outflanked and unable to maneuver. The troops sought what cover they could in low ground by the road out of Cauquigny.[52]

As German infantry moved closer to their positions, Private Charles N. DeGlopper, armed with a Browning Automatic Rifle (BAR), volunteered to lay down a base of fire to provide cover for his platoon mates to make their escape. He left the shelter of the platoon position, fully exposed to the attackers, and took a position in the middle of the road. According to reports, DeGlopper "sprayed the hostile positions with assault fire. He was wounded, but he continued firing. Struck again, he started falling. The Germans could not break DeGlopper's determination and valiant fighting spirit. Kneeling in the roadway, weakened by his grievous wounds, he leveled his heavy weapon against the enemy and fired burst after burst until killed outright."[53]

DeGlopper's valor allowed his platoon to withdraw and establish a more defensible position, which became the first American bridgehead on the western end of the La Fière Causeway. General Ridgway later called the taking of Cauquigny "the hottest single incident I experienced in all my combat service." Charles N. DeGlopper stepped up to protect his comrades under such conditions and proved beyond any doubt by his actions that the glider men could fight as well as the paratroopers of the 82nd Airborne Division.

The 3rd Battalion, 325th Glider Infantry Regiment attacked across the causeway, along with the 505th PIR and elements of the 507th and 508th, later on 9 June. After a brief but very tough fight in which Ridgway and Gavin led from the front, the men defeated the German 1057th Infantry Regiment. They then expanded and held the bridgehead until elements of the American 90th Infantry Division arrived. The 90th, nicknamed "Tough 'Ombres" because of the entwined letters "T" and "O" on their shoulder patches, representing Texas and Oklahoma, supported Ridgway's troopers in securing the bridgehead on 10 June 1944. This action set conditions for follow-on American forces to continue the attack into the Cotentin Peninsula.[54]

According to the battalion history, Lieutenant James Harrison received orders on the morning of 9 June to reinforce the 505th PIR with three C Battery anti-tank guns. Given the assault was to be launched against the 1057th Regiment the following day, it is apparent that Ridgway decided to reinforce his main effort to ensure success. As more men with additional materiel made their way to the 82nd's positions around Sainte-Mère-Église, the 80th AAA Battalion could begin to mass combat power to support offensive operations. The equipment situation improved drastically over the first 96 hours of the operation. By 10 June, the battalion reported the following assets on hand: 14 57mm anti-tank cannons, including one recaptured by the 325th Glider Infantry; 23 1½-ton trucks; 17 ¼-ton trucks; and five ¼-ton trailers.

On 10 June, the battalion's anti-aircraft batteries moved out to the southwest of the 82nd's positions around Sainte-Mère-Église. The anti-aircraft gunners had the opportunity to engage enemy aircraft late that night when they opened fire on a JU88. The gunners received credit for downing one German airplane, with suspected hits scored on a second recorded as "probable." The battalion officers slated for inter-battalion assignments also took over their new jobs that day. Captain Choice Rucker took command of B Battery and brought Lieutenant Bayard Rippy along. Captain Raymond Neuman assumed command of F Battery, and Lieutenant George Barre received assignment to E Battery.[55]

The original plan, following the 82nd's seizure of the Merderet crossings and the passage of lines of the 90th Infantry Division to the west, called for the paratroopers and glider men to consolidate and refit after 48 to 72 hours of near-continuous combat. The 507th and 508th PIRs and the 325th GIR, minus its 1st Battalion, sustained high losses and conducted reorganization between 10 and 12 June. The 505th PIR and 1st Battalion, 325th Glider Infantry Regiment remained in the line in the vicinity of Le Ham until 13 June, when they were relieved by a conventional infantry regiment.[56]

80 • NEVER A DULL MOMENT

However, at this time, the 82nd's higher headquarters, the United States VII Corps, assigned the division to assist in taking the Douve River Line in response to a rocky combat debut by the 90th Infantry Division. In time, the 90th would develop into a lethal infantry division, but it required assistance during its first days of combat. No sooner had the 508th completed its reorganization than it received the mission to seize a bridgehead across the Douve River to the west and effect a linkup with elements of the 101st Airborne Division.[57] At this time, the 82nd's staff also alerted the 507th PIR and the 325th GIR to prepare for follow-on operations to the west of the Merderet. Choice Rucker's B Battery had the mission of supporting the 508th PIR with eight cannons. Rucker received two guns each from Batteries A and C to ensure he had sufficient combat power for the mission. Seven additional 57mm guns remained in reserve.[58]

The 508th PIR attacked west across the Douve between 12 and 13 June, south of Beuzeville-la-Bastille. Battery E provided fire support, using ground mounts for their .50-caliber M2 Browning machine guns, while both Batteries B and C provided anti-armor protection as the regiment advanced 5 miles. The 508th destroyed between 12 and 14 enemy vehicles with bazookas and gammon grenades.[59]

The date 13 June marked a significant day of combat for the 80th AAA. Staff Sergeant Richard E. Rider, leader of the Battery A section operating in support of the 508th PIR, encountered a significant armor threat. According to the official summary of the action, Staff Sergeant Rider faced off against five enemy tanks that were maneuvering against one of his section's guns. The Battery A gunners accompanied a patrol near the village of Baupte, Normandy, when the enemy armor attacked Rider's gun. Rider took over as gunner and destroyed three tanks despite the Germans engaging him with cannon and machine-gun fire. As the remaining German tanks withdrew, Rider and his crew pursued with their 57mm and destroyed the final two tanks for five kills. Having previously received a recommendation for a Bronze Star for his performance so far in the campaign,[60] Rider received the Distinguished Service Cross for his heroism.[61] He ultimately would earn a commission and be one of the most highly decorated officers in the battalion.

No witness statements from 80th AAA battalion soldiers or after-action reviews exist describing Rider's action at Baupte. However, Ray Fary identified a member of the 319th Glider Field Artillery Battalion who recalled seeing 57mm guns in the thick of the fight on 13 June.[62] Technician Fourth Class Edward Ryan served as part of a forward observer team under the command of an officer identified as Lieutenant John Gutshall. Ryan stated that he observed, "German tanks, Renault tanks ... Six of them shooting in every direction."[63] Ryan noted that one of the gunners was displeased that the 508th PIR continued to place his anti-tank gun team where the action was hottest and, in a display of grim humor, "taped a bayonet to the muzzle."[64] According to Fary, Ryan witnessed the team chief bore sighting directly down the barrel of his cannon and destroying two tanks.[65] While there is no confirmation that Ryan witnessed Rider's actions, the circumstances, date, and location corroborate Rider's Distinguished Service Cross Citation.

While Rider and the patrol from the 508th fought off German armor, the division staff issued Field Order No. 7 to secure the north bank of the Douve. Batteries A and B would support the 508th PIR, while Pratt's Battery C worked with the 507th Parachute Infantry, and the anti-aircraft batteries protected the division reserve. The following day, the 508th remained in heavy combat, with Battery A reporting the destruction of one Mark IV tank and one Renault.

On 14 June, Battery C experienced severe combat losses in the attack on Saint-Sauveur, Normandy. Two anti-tank teams supporting the 507th PIR entered the town, and one was almost immediately destroyed by German armor. The ambush resulted in the loss of the cannon, the jeep towing the weapon, and the crew. The gun commander, Sergeant Bernard Wilson, received severe wounds, dying on 16 June. Three of his troopers died immediately, including Corporal Anthony Apicella, Private Harold Husk, and Corporal Paul Snyder. The remaining four members of the crew—Wilbur Doughty, Keith Honeycutt, Raymond Zimdars, and Harold Richgels—survived the fight, but all were wounded.[66]

For the next week, the 82nd Airborne Division continued its attacks to the west, operating under the command of VII Corps and in harness with other infantry divisions to cut the base of the Cotentin Peninsula.

82 • NEVER A DULL MOMENT

Planners at higher headquarters believed this action would isolate the port of Cherbourg at the northern tip of the peninsula and force its defenders to surrender. Supreme Allied Headquarters sought Cherbourg to relieve stress on Allied logistics, continuing to bring supplies across the beaches seized on D-Day. The Allies succeeded in taking the port by the end of June, but the German defenders destroyed the port infrastructure, rendering the city useless as a logistics staging area. However, that outcome lay in the future; the men of the 80th AAA fought mightily to accomplish their assigned missions.

Between 15 and 20 June, the anti-tank batteries moved constantly, rotating duties between the various parachute and glider infantry regiments. Battery A, having seen significant combat in support of the 508th, received orders to pull it off the line and go into reserve, with C Battery replacing them on 15 June. On the 16th, Battery B received an unexpected "replacement" when Private Brank J. Skufea joined them. Skufea was a Battery B man who made the glider assault on D-Day but wound up behind enemy lines. C Battery shifted its support to the 505th PIR and reported destroying an enemy towed 88mm gun.

By the 17th, Battery D advanced to protect a crossing of the Douve near Saint-Sauveur-le-Vicomte. Their presence made a difference when it engaged a flight of Messerschmitts menacing the crossing area. Meanwhile, Battery A went back into action with the 508th PIR, while Battery B moved to support the 507th. The anti-tank batteries continued to suffer casualties, and eight drivers from each anti-aircraft battalion moved to the anti-tank batteries on special duty to ensure they could continue maneuvering with the infantry. The assault continued during 18 and 19 June, with Battery E providing fire support for the 325th GIR's crossing of the Douve. Battery B's commander, Choice Rucker, and Lieutenant Rippy were wounded by mortar fire during the 507th PIR's assault on the village of Vindefontaine. Captain Charles Coleman replaced Rucker, and the battalion motor officer, James Baugh, moved to Battery D, as Lieutenant William Hauptman went to B Battery as Rippy's replacement.[67]

At this time, an 80th AAA alumnus also distinguished himself. During the fighting around Baupte, Captain Art Kroos, former assistant S1, led an effort to repair a bridge over the lower Douve River under hostile fire. While serving as a liaison between the 80th and the 82nd Airborne Division staff in Sicily and Italy, Kroos had impressed General Ridgway. Once in England for the train-up prior to D-Day, Ridgway invited Kroos to join his personal staff as an aide-de-camp. He was acting in that role during the Baupte action.

Ridgway directed the 325th Glider Infantry Regiment, supported by elements of the 508th Parachute Infantry Regiment, to establish a bridgehead across the river in preparation for the drive on La Haye-du-Puits. Clay Blair writes in *Ridgway's Paratroopers* that the Germans had destroyed the bridge at Pont-l'Abbe and were defending the far bank of the Douve in force. Airborne engineers worked feverishly to repair the bridge while receiving heavy indirect fire, but the extent of the damage caused a considerable delay in the attack. In addition to the destroyed bridge, the glider men of the 325th Glider Infantry exhibited less enthusiasm for the assault than Ridgway demanded. The commanding general exposed himself to the German shellfire as an example to the glider infantrymen, but the troops did not respond immediately to this display of leadership. To get things moving, Kroos suggested creating an alternate crossing point by positioning a floating span between two damaged trestles standing in the water. He then personally led the effort to put the temporary bridge in place, in deep water at night while under bombardment. Kroos's citation for the Bronze Star medal concludes, "his suggestion and assistance materially increased the rate of reinforcement and contributed to the success of the river crossing."[68]

As the division continued its offensive, the 80th continued to discover men they had considered lost. Three more members of B Battery who had landed in German territory on D-Day rejoined the unit after nearly two weeks: Corporal Norvill Duncan, Private First Class Floyd Downs, and Private Michael Linke. The date 20 June found the entire battalion across the Douve with the battalion command post west of Étienville, and the batteries arrayed around the division defensive area, except for B Battery, which was on call in reserve and prepared to move.[69]

The division pivoted south after the capture of Saint-Sauveur-le-Vicomte and drove for La Haye-du-Puits. Between 20 June and 3 July 1944, the men of the 80th continued to provide support to the advancing infantry regiments.

84 • NEVER A DULL MOMENT

HEADQUARTERS 508th PARACHUTE INFANTRY
A.P.O. 469, U. S. ARMY

8 July 1944.

SUBJECT: Commendation.

TO : Captain William W. Pratt, O-342644, Battery C, 80th A/B A.A.
(Thru: C.O. 80th A/B A.A.)

1. The courage and resourcefulness demonstrated by you while commanding a battery of 57 mm Anti-Tank Guns attached to this regiment, during the
period of 22 June 1944 to 7 July 1944 has proved greatly effective in our
operations against the enemy. At times when roads had not been cleared of
enemy mines and it was imperative to establish road blocks against enemy
armored counter action, you have moved your guns into position quickly and
efficiently and without regard to hazards enroute. Your conduct and co-
operation have greatly assisted the security of our defenses and have been
such as to bring credit upon yourself, your organization and the service.

2. For the above I highly commend you.

ROY E. LINDQUIST
Colonel, Infantry
Commanding

201 - Pratt, William W. (Off) 1st Ind.
(8 July 44)
HEADQUARTERS 82D AIRBORNE DIVISION, APO 469, U. S. ARMY, 10 July 1944.

TO: Commanding Officer, 80th Airborne Anti-Aircraft Battalion, APO 469.

The Division Commander takes pleasure in forwarding this commendation
and requests that a copy be placed in Captain Pratt's 201 file.

By command of Major General RIDGWAY:

F. M. SCHELLHAMMER,
Lt. Col., G. S. C.,
& C of S, -- G-1.

Commendation earned by Captain Pratt for Normandy. Signed by the 508th PIR
Commander Colonel Roy Lindquist. (Photo courtesy of Micky and Joe Pratt)

Battery A deployed two two-gun sections to the Bois de Limors Forest as part of the 505th Regimental Combat Team. By this point in the campaign, the battery's anti-tank guns featured additional protection. Based on the lessons learned in combat, the 782nd Airborne Ordnance Company spot-welded double armor plating on the 57mm cannons. During this point, the battery's most dangerous scrape came from friendly aircraft when P-47 Thunderbolts misidentified the gunners and strafed their position, but without causing casualties.

Once VII Corps took Cherbourg, control of the 82nd Airborne passed from VII Corps to Troy Middleton's VIII Corps, tasked with conducting a breakout from the initial bridgehead into open country south of Cotentin.[70] VIII Corps prepared for its initial attacks with significant artillery barrages on 26 June. Still, the 80th AAA Battalion experienced a period of relative quiet for the batteries as it prepared to support a major assault on a position labeled Hill 131. The 82nd would participate in a three-division attack on La Haye-du-Puits. The 79th Infantry Division would be on the 82nd's right flank, and the 90th Division would be on its left flank. As the divisions approached their objective, the 82nd would halt on a significant terrain feature, Hill 95, while the flank divisions continued the assault. The 8th Infantry Division would then take over for the 82nd, which was to assume a defensive posture.[71]

On 1 July 1944, an enemy artillery barrage killed Battery D's First Lieutenant William J. Evers. He died of wounds inflicted by fragments from a tree burst, which sent wood slivers flying at what Battery D veterans later described as "a seemingly impossible angle."[72] Sergeant Fred Risovich also sustained wounds because of this indirect fire. By 3 July, the division once again assumed the offensive as part of VIII Corps' attempt to break out into open terrain to the south, with the 80th providing its customary superior fire support. Battery E fired over 20,000 rounds during the 505th PIR's attack on Hill 131. Battery E's work impressed the infantry commander, and he requested they remain attached to the regiment once the 505th PIR took the hill and occupied defensive positions. By 5 July, the division had achieved all its assigned objectives, including taking Hill 95, and the anti-tank batteries assumed forward defensive positions as the infantry dug in and prepared for potential counterattacks.[73] The 80th AAA retained these positions through 8 July, when the 8th Infantry Division passed through the 82nd Airborne's lines and moved further south.

VIII Corps' initial attack proved successful against local German defenses but failed to produce the decisive breakout desired by Allied commanders. Despite this failure, the 82nd Airborne Division and the men of the 80th AAA did all that the high command had asked of them. On 9 July, the 82nd stood relieved of its combat role and received orders to return to England. The 80th AAA went into a staging area near Hébert on 10 July, remaining there for three days. On the evening of 13 July, they moved back to Utah Beach, where LCT 735 waited to return them across the English Channel. The battalion landed at Southampton, England, at 0730 on 15 July. An awaiting train returned the 80th AAA to Leicester by 1700 that evening.

Normandy marked the first period of sustained combat where the 82nd fought as an integrated unit, with the division headquarters coordinating multiple regimental combat teams and their supporting arms. Sicily had been largely a regimental affair with the 505th PIR at center stage. In Italy, the division committed its forces piecemeal to bolster General Mark Clark's Fifth Army at crisis points. Normandy was different. The division fought as a division, with its objectives integrated into larger corps and army plans, and it cemented its reputation as an elite fighting force.[74]

The men of the 80th participated in the creation of the aura that surrounded the division. Where once the paratroopers saw themselves as something separate from the rest of the 82nd, and the glider men merely as just another set of "straight legs," now they were truly an integrated airborne force. Ridgway and the War Department both recognized that the glider men faced hazards as dangerous if not worse, than the those the jumpers faced. As early as May 1944, Ridgway wrote the War Department advocating for hazardous duty pay for the glider troops. Simultaneously, the War Department sought to recognize these soldiers with a distinctive insignia similar to the parachutist badge—a silver set of curved wings with a parachute in the center.

Ultimately, the War Department published War Department Circular 220 on 2 June 1944, authorizing a glider badge. The insignia resembled the

ADAPTING TO THE ENVIRONMENT • 87

parachutist badge, with the exception that a representation of a Waco glider as viewed from the front sat in the center of the wings. The 80th Airborne Anti-Aircraft Battalion did not take notice of the authorization to wear this new badge at the time the War Department made the announcement. With final preparations for Operation *Neptune* underway, the officers and men had more pragmatic concerns. It is unlikely that news of the circular even reached them prior to the beginning of the invasion.

Perhaps more important than the new glider badge, the troops received word that Congress passed a bill on 29 July 1944, authorizing hazardous duty pay for glider troops. Five days later, President Franklin D. Roosevelt signed the bill into law.[75] Al Ireland, one of the few if not the only officer in the 82nd Airborne Division to make combat parachute jumps and a combat glider landing, provided an unsolicited endorsement of this policy upon his arrival in Sainte Mère-Église on 6 June 1944. When asked by members of the division staff how his glider landing turned out, Ireland responded with a laconic, "Those guys don't get paid enough."[76] Ridgway's advocacy for his troops paid off and validated the glider troops as equals to parachutists as members of the airborne fraternity.

The battalion history records on 10 July 1944, as the batteries prepared for their return to England, "Personnel began to receive boots as standard dress."[77] This intriguing boot reference raises the point that the men of the 80th and other glider troops in the division may have received authorization to wear the distinctive jump boots, one of the most visible marks of the airborne elite. The boots, designed by William P. Yarborough in 1941 as the U.S. Army worked to build its airborne capability, featured high sides designed to protect jumpers' ankles upon landing and cutdown heels to prevent the soles from catching on parts of the aircraft upon exiting. The boots' style set the wearer apart from most soldiers who wore a more traditional "low-quarter" shoe, which would be enhanced with canvas leggings to protect ankles and calves in the field. Paratroopers took great pride in their footwear, which was polished to a high shine, and showed off by "blousing" their trousers with rubber bands around the tops of the boots. In contrast, the glider men wore the standard shoes with leggings.[78] The disparity in footwear was just one more artificial divider between the two groups. Did the

Pre- and post-Normandy photos of 80th AAA Battalion men. Note the man on the far left is wearing leggings over low quarter field shoes. Both men on the right wear newly issued boots. (Photos courtesy of Bob Burns)

glider men receive boots at the end of the campaign as a visible display that shared hardships during the campaign combat had erased the divide? Perhaps not. The 80th may have received an issue of the M43 Combat Boot on 10 July. The Army fielded the new boots in 1943 to replace both low quarters with leggings and jump boots. The new boots featured two buckles attached to a cuff that secured the boot to the wearer's calf. The boots proved unpopular with airborne troops, who preferred to retain their signature footwear.[79] However, the fact that receiving boots merited a mention in the battalion history indicates the importance the 80th attached to the event.

Normandy was a crucible that tested both the 80th AAA Battalion and the 82nd Airborne Division, but it also was a learning laboratory. Combat quickly revealed flaws in planning and execution that the battalion sought to correct before the next operation. Lieutenant Colonel Singleton participated in a commander's conference on 13 August 1944, in which every battalion-level commander and higher had the opportunity to give a frank assessment of what worked and what did not during Operation *Neptune*. Singleton identified the lack of transport to simultaneously get both guns and gunners into the fight. He stressed that the Waco carried an anti-tank cannon, jeep, or ammo to battle but lacked the room to accommodate the whole gun crew. The 82nd prioritized getting the guns into Normandy based on lessons learned from fighting in Sicily and Italy. However, not enough crewmen went with them. Singleton said, "We took in 16 guns in the dark, and the next day, we had about five out of those 16 within the Division area ... The guns were OK, but we did not have enough personnel."[80] He recommended getting the Waco CG-13, if possible, to transport the supporting arms. This Waco variant had twice the cargo capacity of the CG-4A; however, it was never used in combat to support the 82nd Airborne Division due to its late operational debut. Future operations would require new combinations of gliders, men, and materials.

Normandy also convinced Ridgway that no glider operations should take place during nighttime. Low-visibility conditions prevented glider pilots from avoiding obstacles when approaching landing zones and prevented glider troops from quickly recovering their equipment. These issues negated the value of using gliders to deliver units to combat as an integrated whole, fully equipped and ready to fight. Operation *Neptune* marked the last time the 82nd Airborne Division conducted a nighttime glider assault.[81]

Another lesson learned involved the Airspeed Horsa glider. American troop carrier groups used both the American Waco CG-4A and the British Airspeed Horsa to carry the 82nd and 101st Airborne glider troops into Normandy. The Horsa featured a larger carrying capacity, which American planners wanted to use to deliver cargo quickly. However, in the actual invasion, American glider pilots found the British glider difficult to maneuver, hard to control on landing, and vulnerable to breaking apart upon impact.[82] As a result, the Horsa would not be employed again by American forces in World War II.[83]

Beyond the discussions of how to deliver the battalion more effectively by glider, the 80th applied the lessons of Normandy to how they trained and organized for future combat. The anti-tank batteries sustained significant casualties in the opening fights of the campaign, necessitating shifting personnel from the anti-aircraft batteries to make up the losses. Battalion leaders realized the anti-aircraft batteries required cross-training on the 57mm anti-tank guns in case such a scenario occurred again. The battalion log records eight instances of anti-tank gunnery between 1 August and 29 August 1944. All six batteries of the battalion participated in the exercises.[84] Additionally, the lack of enemy air threat in France, combined with the effectiveness of German armor, led to the 80th creating an additional anti-tank battery by converting one of the anti-aircraft batteries to anti-armor before September 1944. This training and reorganization paid off during Operation *Market* in September 1944, when Battery E deployed to Holland as an anti-tank battery.[85]

General Ridgway endorsed the 80th's decision to reorganize into four anti-tank and two anti-aircraft batteries. Both the diminished effectiveness of the German air force and the nature of the 82nd's mission to hold key points such as road networks and water crossings made emphasizing anti-armor capabilities over air defenses a prudent planning consideration.[86]

Normandy settled the question Lieutenant Baugh had raised before the invasion about operational authority as well. In the two first weeks of fighting after 6 June, the question about whether a battery would be attached to a regiment or fight in support of the regiment persisted. Attachment, although a temporary designation, implied the commander of the regiment to which a battery was attached had full authority over the battery and could employ it as he saw fit. A supporting relationship allowed the battery to remain in the 80th AAA Battalion's command structure, but its priority mission would be to answer the supported regiments' requests for assistance.[87]

Clay Blair termed the 82nd Airborne Division's performance in Normandy "the stuff of instant legend." A glamour persisted around the airborne and the assault on Europe in particular. The men may not have considered themselves heroes, but the public did. This image prevailed even among Americans who experienced combat during the war, although not in France. D Battery's Private Edward Burns wrote to his sister that their brother Robert, a veteran of combat with the US Army Air Force in the Mediterranean Theater, thought Edward was a hero because he fought in Normandy. Burns provided a more pragmatic summary of his participation in Operation *Overlord*: "I would never have gone if they hadn't taken me there."[88]

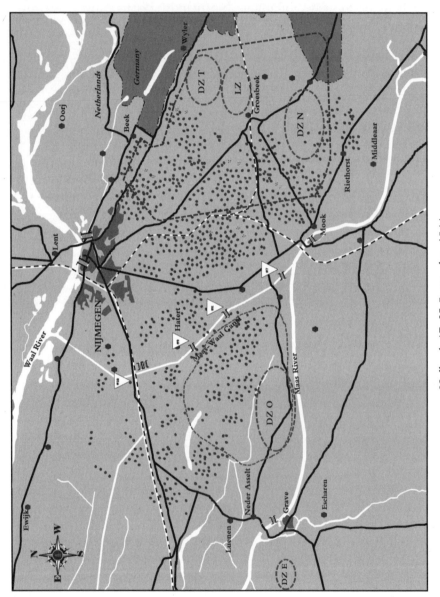

Holland, 17–25 September 1944.

CHAPTER 4

Doing Routine Things
Routinely—Holland

One hundred replacements awaited the 80th AAA Battalion upon its return to Leicester. The battalion log for the second half of July 1944 illustrates that the initial priority was to reward the men who survived Normandy. The division allowed furloughs for the troops, and they received back pay for the month spent in France. The battalion also held an awards ceremony for the men who earned valor decorations. By the end of the month, the log notes that leaves ended, and the gunners turned to training in preparation for their next battle.[1]

The strategic situation in Europe in August–September 1944 was both a cause of excitement and concern for Allied commanders. The German army was rapidly retreating eastward. The 82nd Airborne was absorbed into a larger organization titled the First Allied Airborne Army, which was assigned to participate in several operations, however, the assigned objectives of each mission were overrun by Allied ground troops before the airborne forces could launch.

As airborne leaders restructured the 80th AAA because of Normandy's lessons, the higher levels of the Allied command structure also underwent reorganization to create a more efficient and effective airborne force. Most importantly, the Allies realized that airborne assets required a unified command to eliminate the problems of coordinating between different branches of service and multiple nations. The Supreme Headquarters Allied Expeditionary Forces (SHAEF) created the First Allied Airborne Army on 2 August 1944, by order of General Eisenhower, to assume responsibility for all airborne assets assigned to the European Theater of Operations.

Previously, the aircraft assigned to drop parachutists and tow gliders into combat came from troop carrier units of the US Army Air Forces or the Royal Air Force (RAF), under the command of the Allied Expeditionary Air Forces. SHAEF intended for the First Allied Airborne Army to retain direct command and control of its own troop carrier unit to ensure unity of command. This decision resulted in the U.S. IX Troop Carrier command being placed under the command of the First Allied Airborne Army, but RAF troop carrier units were attached as required for specific operations.

In contrast to the troop carriers, both British and American airborne units fell under the First Allied Airborne Army's purview. As the war continued and more airborne units went into the field, there was a need for higher headquarters that understood how to employ and sustain airborne forces. The British understood this as early as 1943 and created the 1st British Airborne Corps to oversee the 1st and 6th Airborne Divisions. The U.S. Army did not field an airborne corps headquarters until after Operation *Neptune*. The U.S. XVIII Corps moved overseas to Europe in August 1944. Upon arrival, the corps received the "airborne" designation, and General Ridgway moved from the 82nd Airborne Division to command the new formation. General Gavin moved from his role as assistant division commander of the 82nd Airborne to the role of commanding general of the division. The 101st and 82nd Airborne Divisions fell under the XVIII Airborne Corps in this new structure.

The First Allied Airborne Army spent the first month planning for a series of airborne operations to take vital positions ahead of the advancing Allied armies that broke out from Normandy at the end of July 1944, once the 82nd had returned to England. British General Montgomery's 21st Army Group and American Omar Bradley's 12th Army Group sped westward toward Paris, while the German army fell back under the combined pressure of the Allied advance. The ground offensive made

DOING ROUTINE THINGS ROUTINELY • 95

such rapid advances that the proposed airborne operations that SHAEF tasked First Allied Airborne Army to plan never made it to the execution stage because, invariably, the ground troops overran the objectives set forth. The need for the airborne operation vanished.

The First Allied Airborne Army planned multiple operations over the last weeks of August into the first 10 days of September. According to the commanding general of the First Allied Airborne Army, Lieutenant General Lewis Brereton, "In the 40 days since the formation of the First Allied Airborne Army we have planned 18 different operations, some of which were scrubbed because our armies moved too fast and others because Troop Carriers were in engaged in air supply."[2]

The 80th Airborne Anti-Aircraft Battalion's log reflects the hectic situation during this time. Between 31 August and 5 September, the batteries underwent a series of inspections, preparing combat loads and moving from their quarters at Camp Oadby to staging airfields at Langar, Balderton, and Fulbeck. The log details how, once directed to deploy, their leaders would inform the troops that a mission higher has canceled the mission, and then the batteries received orders for a subsequent mission, only for headquarters to cancel that operation as well.[3] However, newly promoted Field Marshal Bernard Law Montgomery devised a plan that would require the full participation of the First Allied Airborne Army in September 1944 and, if successful, promised to bring a quick end to the war in Europe.

Montgomery's plan to quickly end the war in Europe called for using a "carpet" of airborne units to seize key bridges across a series of water obstacles in Holland, thus allowing a heavy armored force (XXX Corps) to advance rapidly across the Rhine River into the German industrial heartland. This was believed to be the means to get into the German rear and achieve the result of destabilizing German defenses and forcing the Nazis to surrender.

Field Marshal Montgomery's vision involved a sharp thrust deep into German lines through Holland. The purpose of this drive was to cross the Rhine River and break into the German industrial areas, thereby rendering the Germans fighting the Allied drive from the west strategically irrelevant. Montgomery's plan contrasted sharply with his boss's. General Dwight

D. Eisenhower, Supreme Commander of the Allied Expeditionary Force, favored what became known as "the broad-front strategy." Historian and World War II veteran Roland G. Ruppenthal described the broad-front concept as arraying Allied "forces along the Rhine through the whole length of the Western Front, from the North Sea to Switzerland, before launching a final drive into the heart of Germany."[4] The differing philosophies came to a head in late summer, 1944.

In the wake of Operation *Overlord*, the German forces defending France and the West disintegrated in the face of the Allied advance. The 12th and 21st Army Groups advanced far more rapidly than planners had anticipated, taking Paris 55 days ahead of schedule. Such lightning progress upset all predictions for logistical support, particularly for fuel, and by August the services of supply found themselves stretched thin. Eisenhower wanted the port of Antwerp, Belgium taken to shorten Allied supply lines, while Montgomery wanted an opportunity to show the efficacy of his "single thrust" strategy. Montgomery's proposal that airborne forces be used to seize a series of bridges through Holland and then pass a heavily armored force forward to the doorstep of Germany seemed to fit the bill for both Eisenhower and the British Field Marshal. Historian Forrest Pogue wrote that Montgomery's plan had the further advantages of outflanking German defenses on the Siegfried Line, confounding the Germans who would not expect the attack along the route chosen by the Allies, and consisting of objectives within range of the assigned airborne forces.[5]

Montgomery's vision evolved into an operation dubbed *Market Garden*. The title came from a combination of the airborne assault to seize the bridges along the 60-mile route between the Belgian–Dutch frontier and the town of Arnhem along the Lower Rhine, and the ground assault conducted by Lieutenant General Brian Horrocks's XXX Corps. Operation *Market* referred to the airborne mission, and Operation *Garden* to XXX Corps' role. First Airborne Army assigned the responsibility for the tactical conduct of *Market* to the British 1st Airborne Corps commanded by Lieutenant General "Boy" Browning. Browning's Corps consisted of the American 82nd and 101st Airborne Divisions, the British 1st Airborne Division, and the Polish 1st Independent Parachute Brigade for the initial task of taking the bridges en route to Arnhem. Additionally, the plan called for the British 52nd (Lowland) Division to airland on a captured airfield near Arnhem on the fifth day of the operation.[6]

The 101st Airborne Division received the mission of seizing bridges near the city of Eindhoven, while further to the north, the 82nd had the role of taking bridges at Grave and Nijmegen. Both missions, while challenging, placed the Americans in closer proximity to the advance of XXX Corps, with the attendant promise that they would link up with ground support within 24 to 48 hours of the start of the operation. The First Airborne Division drew the most harrowing mission, to take and hold the bridge over the Lower Rhine at Arnhem. This mission placed them furthest away from support by the XXX Corps while simultaneously fighting to force open the door into Germany. Thus, the 1st Airborne Division, under the command of Major General Roy Urquhart, would face defenders motivated to protect their soil from an invading Army.[7]

The concept for the operation involved significant risk and great reward. The forward progress of the XXX Corps depended on the airborne forces taking and holding their objectives on a strict timetable. Any delay left forces further up the road vulnerable to German counterattacks, and as more time passed, the Allied troops would lose strength, and their vulnerability would increase. Additionally, the scope of the airborne assault required all three divisions to strike their targets nearly simultaneously. The mission of dropping three airborne divisions would tax the aircraft assets of the IX Troop Carrier Group and the supporting RAF Number 38 Group. Reinforcing troops and equipment would be dropped or airlanded over subsequent days due to limited aircraft availability. If weather or enemy activity interrupted further deliveries of men and materiel, the troops already on the ground faced increasing jeopardy. However, the prospect of outflanking the Siegfried Line, defending Germany's western frontier, and striking into the German industrial Ruhr was a glittering opportunity to quickly end the war in Europe.[8] As the Supreme Commander of the Allied Expeditionary Force, Eisenhower deemed the result worthy of the risks.

Allied planners determined that the troops executing *Market Garden* had the advantage of facing a demoralized enemy in substandard units. Since breaking out from Normandy at the beginning of August, the Allies had driven eastward and scored a signal victory at the battle of the

98 • NEVER A DULL MOMENT

Falaise Pocket on 21 August.[9] The intervening weeks saw German forces continuing to retreat before the British and American armies. However, by the first week of September, the Germans exhibited remarkable resilience, reconstituting and building up forces in Holland. Units included the 719th and 176th Infantry Divisions, the 9th and 10th Panzer Divisions, the II SS Panzer Corps, and First Parachute Army elements. The Germans had the means and motivation to put up a stiff resistance.[10]

The 80th's previous combat experience in France had been mobile and chaotic, with the troops constantly advancing eastward as the Germans withdrew. Operation *Market Garden* was also very dynamic and confusing, with the race to seize bridges for the northeastward passage of XXX Corps and the ultimate failure to take and hold Arnhem Bridge. The initial glider landings and attempts to seize and hold bridges in the vicinity of the city of Nijmegen against determined German resistance highlighted the 80th AAA's increased combat efficiency due to reorganization and Normandy combat experience.

Despite the lessons learned from Operations *Neptune*, circumstances conspired to prevent the 80th from delivering the overwhelming anti-tank firepower it desired into its next fight. Once the high command decided to try to end the war dramatically and concurred with newly promoted Field Marshal Montgomery's plan to dash to the Rhine, the First Airborne Army turned to determining how to get all the men and equipment necessary into Holland as quickly as possible.

From the start, aircraft availability limited how many troops could drop or ride into the fight on any given day. The goal was to swarm an objective using speed and surprise to provide a tactical advantage. Given the overall number of bridges to be seized (nine in all), over 60–plus miles of road, and the need to deliver nearly simultaneously the 1st British Airborne Division, along with the 82nd and 101st Airborne Divisions, the IX Troop Carrier Command and the Royal Air Force ran out of airplanes and gliders well before the ground troops ran out of men and equipment to be transported. The solution was to move sections of each division in lifts over a period of days, reinforcing each airhead with additional combat power as aircraft became available. Experienced officers recognized the danger inherent in this plan. General Stanislaw Sosabowski, commanding the Polish 1st Independent Parachute Brigade, spoke for the airborne community when he criticized the plan, stating that "an airborne operation is not a purchase by installment."[11] Thus, an ambitious plan and a lack of resources set the stage for a repeat of Operation *Husky*, but on a larger scale.

The 80th AAA's primary lesson from Normandy was that men and guns needed to be delivered to the battle as quickly as possible. However, Normandy proved to be the pinnacle of the rapid insertion of the battalion. From the start, the plan to send the battalion across the channel into Holland allotted fewer gliders per lift to the 80th. In Normandy, Batteries A and B went into LZ "O" simultaneously (or at least attempted to in the confusion of combat). For *Market Garden*, only Battery A made the initial lift on 17 September, followed by Battery B on 18 September.

The battalion history records 72 hours of frenetic activity, noting on 14 September that "operation 'MARKET' seemed a certainty."[12] Between 14 and 16 September, all batteries completed the preparation of combat loads for arrival by glider, departed for their respective departure airfields, and participated in final intelligence updates and dissemination of information. Given the size of the air armada carrying the assault to Holland and the time phasing of the battalion's assets entering the battle, the unit spread across four different airfields on 15 September. Batteries A and B moved to Balderton, C and E moved to Cottesmore, and HQ Detachment and D and F Batteries moved to Fulbeck. The medical detachment, along with one anti-tank cannon and vehicle from C and E Batteries, moved to Langar. Lieutenant Colonel Singleton would accompany Battery A on the initial assault, so after final coordination with the headquarters at Fulbeck, he relocated to Balderton for final preparations, along with the battalion operations NCO, Sergeant Koch.[13]

Battery A departed Balderton Field in England on 17 September as part of serial 1-A, flown by the 439th Troop Carrier Group. Elements of the division headquarters, along with signal assets, the division recon platoon, and air support elements, completed the roster of troops assigned to the serial. The initial wave commenced takeoff at 1100 on 17 September 1944. By 1122, with all aircraft launched, the assault force was en route to their assigned drop zones. Battery A arrived on time, between 1336 and 1400, and the pilots of their gliders made good landings in their

A USAAF CG-4A Waco glider is prepared for Operation *Market Garden*. (Courtesy of Getty Images)

designated landing zones. Battery A reported no casualties from the initial landings, although Private Harold Clark died from enemy contact while conducting a reconnaissance patrol later that day.[i] Clark was killed near Beek, a suburb of Nijmegen, 3 miles north of Drop Zone "N." This indicates that members of Battery A were operating in support of 3rd Battalion, 508th PIR, which had responsibility for this sector of the division area of operations. Despite the loss of some men such as Clark, overall, especially compared to the opening hours of Operation *Neptune*, things proceeded like clockwork. The battalion history notes, somewhat ominously in retrospect, "It didn't seem like the same war."[14]

---

i   The 80th AAA Battalion History indicates Clarke died on 17 September 1944. Burns and Fary record Clarke died on the 18th, as does the 2006 version of the battalion roster.

Aircraft towing gliders for the air invasion of Holland. (Courtesy of Getty Images)

The initial assault landing went exceedingly well, and by 1343 in the afternoon, almost all gliders, including all carrying Battery A, reached their assigned landing areas. Units of the 82nd repeated this success throughout the area of operations, with General Gavin later writing that "early indications were that the drop was unusually successful. Unit after unit reported in on schedule, and with few exceptions, all were in their pre-planned locations."[15] Battery A immediately went into action upon landing. The gunners captured 21 enemy soldiers almost as soon as the glider men hit the ground. Despite this auspicious beginning, signs of trouble began appearing.[16]

The lack of combat power stands as the foremost of these indicators. Battery A had only eight guns and 80 crew members available to support the 504th, 505th, and 508th Parachute Infantry Regiments. General Gavin expressed concern during pre-mission planning about the many objectives assigned to the 82nd, spread across 20-plus square miles.

102 • NEVER A DULL MOMENT

OPERATION MARKET
80th AIRBORNE ANTIAIRCRAFT BATTALION

Battery "B"

Glider Serial No.	OK	DAM	DES	MISS	Glider Commander	No. Personnel				Equipment				Landed at
						NO	K	W	M	VEH	S	U		
379095		X			Cpl. Duncan, Norvil R.	4				T	X			LZ
273994 ?		X			1st Lt. Daley, Charles S.	9								LZ

Hdqs. Det.

277668	X				Major Keith, Warren C.	12								632537
256740		X			S/Sgt. Smith, Lonnie Y.	5				T	X			632537
277375		X			Capt. Neumann, Raymond A.	6				T	X			535634
256224	X				1st Lt. Cockrell, W. E. Jr.	2				J	X			629529
319732	X				1st Lt. Telford, W. S. Jr.	2				J	X			598529
277371	X				Capt. Coleman, Charles A.	2				J	X			634527

Med. Det.

| 42-77538 | X | | | | Capt. Galatzan, Joe S. | 2 | | | | J | X | | | 653525 |
| 43-13868 | | X | | | Capt. Block, Arnold S. | 6 | | | | T | X | | | 653525 |

Battery "C"

43-42025		X			Capt. Pratt, William W.	2				J	X			632533
42-56279		X			T/5 Mallamus, Paul Jr.	7				T	X			637533
43-27348	X				Cpl. Kemble, Aaron J.	7				T	X			637533
42-77710		X			1st Sgt. Someyock, Charles	11								635533
42-74029	X				Sgt. Baker, Truman L.	11								636538
42-73844	X				T/4 Trost, Robert F.	11								635533
43-41865		X			Cpl. Boteler, Roland	2				G	X			630520
42-73880	X				1st Lt. Stark, Marshall W.	2				J	X			629536
43-79457		X			S/Sgt. Grimes, Edward A.	2				G	X			645532
43-40549	X				S/Sgt. Keck, James H. K.	2				J	X			632542
42-62733	X				Cpl. Althaus, Edward H.	2				G	X			640525
43-19948		X			Sgt. Nawrocki, Walter A.	2				J	X			643557
42-56253		X			Cpl. Summan, Walter J.	2				G	X			630550
42-56519		X			S/Sgt. Hilgemyer, Norman	2				J	X			629534
43-39790	X				Sgt. Kane, Francis T.	2				G	X			640525
43-39804		X			1st Lt. Harrison, James M.	2				J	X			625540
43-40386		X			Cpl. Leuok, Paul L.	2				G	X			643657
43-40386		X			Sgt. McDonald, Harry L.	2				J	X			632542
42-73917	X				Cpl. Morgenstern, Charles	2				G	X			628538
43-36642	X				1st Lt. Lees, Avon Jr.	2				J	X			625541
42-73565		X			Cpl. Stuppy, Halvor	2				G	X			628538
43-40934	X				S/Sgt. Heath, William H.	2				J	X			632542

Glider manifest for Operation *Market*. (Photo courtesy of Thulai Van Maanen, and Joe and Micky Pratt)

Additionally, Allied intelligence indicated that German armor might be in force in a heavily wooded area southeast of the division's objective area known as the Reichswald—this combination of circumstances created a conundrum for Lieutenant Colonel Singleton and his anti-tank gunners.[17] On the one hand, the widely dispersed parachute infantry regiments could use all the support the men of Battery A could provide. Conversely, the threat of German tanks emanating from the Reichswald called for the anti-tank guns to concentrate on defending against this significant threat.

Throughout the afternoon of the 17th, elements of the division continued to consolidate from the initial assault landings and head out to their objectives. Lieutenant Colonel Singleton co-located the anti-tank command post (CP) near Drop Zone N with Gavin's division CP. The vehicles allocated to the division headquarters suffered damage upon landing. General Gavin found himself constrained to moving from position to position on foot. Therefore, Singleton provided the commanding general with one of Battery A's jeeps.[18] Gavin put this jeep to good use as night fell and moved from unit to unit to observe the situation firsthand.[19]

On 18 September, Battery B made its landing in the vicinity of Drop Zone N. Gavin's focus was taking the critical terrain and bridges between Mook and Nijmegen to ensure the rapid passage northward of Horrocks's armored XXX Corps; however, the dispersed formations of the division began to affect the 82nd's ability to conduct offensive operations.[ii] Gavin had insufficient troops to secure the landing area, which was soon under attack by German ground troops. Airborne infantrymen whose primary mission was securing and holding bridges changed focus to clear the enemy from the vicinity of the landing areas. Four enemy tanks, supposedly situated east of the landing zone near Horst, represented the most significant threat. Therefore, half of the available anti-tank firepower, four guns in all, went to the 505th PIR to bolster their defenses.[20] Battery A provided two additional guns to the

---

ii   Gavin also broke two vertebrae while landing during the jump into Holland. While he was unaware of the injury's severity during the battle, his mobility suffered accordingly. John C. McManus, *September Hope: The American Side of a Bridge Too Far.* (Caliber, 2013), 106.

104 • NEVER A DULL MOMENT

508th PIR moving toward its objective of the large bridge at Nijmegen. Fortunately, many of the German troops were not front-line infantry, but anti-aircraft gunners reassigned to the role of riflemen. As Gavin said, they proved to be no match for his aggressive, veteran paratroopers, who soon secured the landing zone for the scheduled glider landings.[21]

Battery B planned to bring nine more jeeps and eight anti-tank cannons into the battle. Upon landing, the battery could not account for one of its eight jeeps, and it soon discovered that the missing jeep was not its most significant issue. The larger problem was that the battery commander, the wide-ranging Arthur Kroos, was missing in action. Kroos served as General Ridgway's aide throughout Normandy. Once promoted to corps commander, Ridgway brought his previous aide, Major Don Faith, along to the new assignment. Faith had served Ridgway faithfully in Sicily and Italy, and the two men worked well together. Kroos elected to return to the 80th AAA and received command of Battery B in August 1944.[22] Reports later indicated that others witnessed Kroos, along with Staff Sergeant John F. Bonk and Private First Class William V. Smurr, go down near the coast when the C-47 towing their glider sustained damage and went down. Smurr, having joined the battalion as a replacement in August, was on his first combat assignment and had been with the battery for less than two months.[23]

B Battery went into the fight immediately upon landing and secured four prisoners by day's end. Meanwhile, having driven the enemy off the landing zone, the 505th Parachute Infantry Regiment went into the attack against the German-held village of Mook. Battery A supported this attack with anti-tank gunnery, killing an estimated 15 enemy soldiers.[24] Battery B's eight 57mm guns doubled the capability available to the 82nd, and Singleton put six of them into action as soon as the crews unloaded their gliders. The remaining two cannons allowed the battalion commander a reserve he could commit if the enemy threatened any sector too heavily.

Meanwhile, in England, the 80th AAA Headquarters detachment, Battery D, and Battery F received briefings on their scheduled glider movement on the following day, Tuesday 19 September. Weather delays ultimately postponed the movement of these elements to Holland. In contrast to their comrades already in contact, the men stuck at their departure airfields passed the time watching movies and enjoying Red Cross coffee and doughnuts.[25] The rain and fog that prevented the arrival of the rest of the battalion also affected other elements of the Allied attack. The weather delayed the 325th Glider Infantry Regiment and weakened the 82nd Airborne Division.[26] All across the 82nd's front, the parachute infantry fought combined arms teams of German armor and infantry. Battery A sighted enemy tanks near Nijmegen on the morning of the 19th, but British armor from XXX Corps arrived later that day to reinforce the lightly armed paratroopers. Fighting raged throughout the division area, with the men of the 80th engaged alongside their infantry brothers, with Battery A heavily engaged at Mook southwest of DZ "N" and north at Beek, where Clark had died earlier. Four German *Kampfgruppen* struck at various points in the division areas, including Mook, Beek, the town of Wyler, and Groesbeek.[27] A Kampfgruppe was a combined arms unit consisting of infantry, armor and artillery, normally consisting of 1,000 soldiers.

A summary of Battery A's actions at Mook reveals the ferocity of the action. Lieutenant Jake Wertich led his platoon of gunners in three days of street fighting. Corporal John Barton participated in 1st Battalion, 505th PIR's assault that netted 75 German prisoners, while Staff Sergeant Steve Banish captured six enemy soldiers on his own. The battalion roster published in 2006 reflects that Banish received a Bronze Star, but whether it was for this specific action is unclear. Banish's actions certainly deserved recognition. Private First Class Gordon S. Smital did receive a Bronze Star for his heroism at Mook, during which he repeatedly moved his 57mm under fire to positions of the greatest advantage. Smital would be killed in action three months later, on 21 December 1944, fighting in Belgium. Wertich and his men so impressed the 505th PIR that the operations officer of its 1st Battalion, Captain William Harris, specifically noted the performance of the glider men of the 80th AAA. Further north at Beek, outposts noted the arrival of additional German armor, and the 80th committed one gun apiece from Batteries A and B under the command of Lieutenant John Bullis.[28]

The men of the 80th continued to fight all along the 82nd's perimeter on 20 September 1944. Over the previous 72 hours, the three airborne divisions comprising Operation *Market* seized multiple objectives along the 60-mile route up to the Rhine and the German frontier. To the south, the 101st Airborne Division successfully took multiple bridges between the 18th and 19th, despite delays and fierce resistance, allowing XXX Corps, the *Garden* element, to drive northward to the 82nd and Nijmegen.[29] By mid-morning on the 19th the lead element of Horrocks's corps linked up with paratroopers from the 504th PIR at the town of Grave. Gavin welcomed the firepower of the British armor column but could not yet pass the XXX Corps through his lines over the Waal River to reach the men of the British 1st Airborne Division at Arnhem. The 82nd had not yet seized the critical bridge at Nijmegen, connecting that city to Arnhem.[30]

Gavin had his hands full securing the route between Grave and Nijmegen to ensure the arrival of the British armor and defending the division perimeter from increasingly ferocious German assaults. He gave priority to seizing the high ground at Groesbeek Heights to secure the route into Nijmegen rather than dispatching a heavy force to seize bridges over the Waal immediately on the 17th.[31] By the 19th, the bridges remained in German hands. Additionally, the bad weather kept the 325th Glider Infantry and supporting arms grounded in England, denying Gavin additional combat power that he could use to hold both his positions and launch powerful attacks on the bridges over the Waal. With the arrival of XXX Corps, Gavin had the means at hand to launch a combined-arms assault on the bridges. However, the Germans had reinforcements of their own, in the form of the units from the 10th SS Panzer Division. At the end of the day on the 19th, the Germans still retained control of the bridges.[32] The morning of 20 September dawned as a make-or-break day for Gavin and his men. They had to seize the bridges to get the XXX Corps over the Waal and on to Arnhem. The paras of the 1st Airborne Division depended on it.

Despite the high level of combat throughout the division's area of operations, the main effort focused on capturing the Nijmegen bridges. These objectives consisted of both a railroad and a highway bridge over the Waal. 3rd Battalion, 504th Parachute Infantry, commanded by Major Julian Cook, received the mission of crossing the Waal under fire in boats to take the northern end of the bridges, while 2nd Battalion, 505th Parachute

Infantry, attacked the southern approaches. Battery B detailed two guns to support Cook's amphibious assault (an action for which Cook would receive the Distinguished Service Cross); while Battery A sent a cannon to assist the 505th PIR's paratroopers. The Battery A 57mm found itself involved in an anti-tank gun duel with German 88mm guns that wreaked havoc on British armor attacking the bridgehead from the south.[33] Lieutenant James Cliff, whose combat performance at Sainte-Mère-Église earned him a Silver Star during the Normandy campaign, distinguished himself while fighting in Nijmegen. A Battery's gun could not find a clear field of fire to engage the German gun position, so Cliff moved out under fire to clear away a barbed-wire entanglement. This action created a clear field of fire for the cannon and netted Cliff a Bronze Star, marking him as among the most highly decorated officers in the battalion.[34] Cook's paratroopers, supported by the valiant combat engineers of the 307th Airborne Engineer Battalion and followed by the equally brave men of the 1st Battalion, 504th PIR, succeeded in establishing their bridgehead on the north bank of the Waal, as the 505th Parachute Infantry took the southern ends of the bridges. Interestingly, historian Guy LoFaro recounts that Cook's action and that of Ben Vandervoort's 2nd Battalion, 505th PIR, occurred independently and were not part of one coordinated attack. In the event, the assaults produced an overwhelming effect, and, despite fierce and confused fighting on both the railway and highway bridges, the paratroopers, supported by elements of XXX Corps, succeeded in taking the bridges by the evening of the 20th.[35]

The British 1st Airborne Division had endured a grueling battle over the previous 96 hours. On 17 September, the 1st Parachute Brigade and 1st Airlanding Brigade executed their drop. However, they used drop zones located some distance from their objectives over the Lower Rhine due to a concern that German anti-aircraft emplacements would unduly jeopardize the transport aircraft if they jumped closer to the center of the town.[36]

Unexpectedly strong resistance from the defending Germans, including the 9th and 10th Panzer Divisions, hampered the British troopers from gaining more than one side of the main bridge across the river, a position they continued to hold tenaciously. However, despite reinforcements from the 4th Parachute Brigade on 18 September and the Poles on

XXX Corps troops cross Nijmegen Bridge over the Waal River during Operation *Market Garden*. (Photo courtesy of Getty Images)

19 September, the Germans continued to impede the British paras' attempts to seize the entire bridge.

The delay of the XXX Corps at Nijmegen on the 20th contributed to an ever-worsening situation, and by the morning of the 21st, the British defense of the Arnhem bridgehead collapsed. The men of the 1st Airborne Division, bravely supported by their comrades in the Polish Parachute Brigade, fought valiantly. Still, the unexpected enemy strength, prolonged wait for the arrival of XXX Corps, and weather-induced delays preventing timely reinforcements doomed their efforts.[37]

While the bridges occupied much Allied attention and effort, fighting continued unabated all day on the 20th and into the 21st throughout the 82nd's area of responsibility. Oddly, the 80th AAA Battalion History notes that "activities this day were exceptionally quiet in Holland." Things were nowhere near as quiet in Holland as that statement leads a reader to believe.[38] The fighting at Wyler grew especially fierce, as the village was located on German rather than Dutch soil.

An intelligence report endorsed by the 80th AAA Battalion's intelligence officer, Captain Ray Newman, vividly conveys the nature of the combat in Wyler. The report notes the presence of enemy armor in unknown strength and describes the actions of Technician Fifth Class Charles Hineman of B Battery on 20 September 1944. Hineman, while exposed to heavy enemy fire crawled to a jeep and, while still on the ground, reached inside the vehicle and started it. Hineman then operated the jeep with only his hands, allowing the jeep to drag his body while also protecting him from German fire and pulling the battery's anti-tank cannons to safer positions. The report notes Hineman evacuated three guns in this manner and that the NCO received a recommendation for the Silver Star for his bravery.[39]

German troops proved especially tenacious in defending their native soil, and by 1945 on the night of 20 September, nine members of B Battery found themselves trapped. They remained so through the morning of 21 September. One of its anti-tank guns destroyed a German personnel carrier, killing 23 of the 25 enemy passengers. The battery also recorded capturing an additional six prisoners.[40] Mook continued to occupy the attention of 1st Battalion, 505th PIR, with the town continually changing hands between the paratroopers and German troops. Lieutenant Wertich continued to lead from the front, and his A Battery glider men succeeded in capturing an additional 15 prisoners. Similarly, further North at Beek, the battle seesawed back and forth, with both sides taking and then losing the same positions, only to retake them once again.[41]

By 22 September, as the 504th guarded the Nijmegen bridges, Batteries A and B consolidated their platoons, sending A Battery to support the 505th PIR and B Battery to support the 508th PIR. In a testament to the heavy fighting that continued, the 80th recorded the death of A Battery's Private First Class Charles O'Leary and the wounding of B Battery's Lieutenant McFadden, as well as two of his soldiers, by a bursting shell.[42] Poor weather continued to delay the reinforcements scheduled to arrive from England.

On 23 September, the 80th AAA Battalion experienced "a cold, clear morning" indicative of the fact that the rest of the battalion, along with the other badly needed elements of the 82nd Airborne Division, would arrive.[43] The remaining glider-borne elements of the battalion departed England at 1300 and landed at Landing Zone "O" northeast of Grave, in the 505th PIR's sector sometime after 1700. The flights were unopposed except for some flak as they crossed into Holland. Despite the delays imposed by weather, Operation *Market* marked the most significant airborne operation conducted by the 80th AAA during the war: 525 officers and men, along with 52 jeeps, 25 trailers, 32 anti-tank guns, and 24 .50-caliber machine guns, arrived to the battlefield via 124 Waco gliders without sustaining significant landing casualties. The battalion was airborne in fact as well as in name.[44]

Sergeant James C. Fellers of C Battery recalls the glider flight from England to Holland. Fellers crouched on the trails of his 57mm anti-tank gun, reading a mystery novel, as his friend Corporal Paul Leuck occupied the copilot's seat in the nose of the Waco. Of course, Leuck did not know how to fly, but every available space was used to get gun squads into the fight. Fellers was making his second combat glider assault, having first gone into Normandy on the night of 6 June. Fellers was on the same glider with Lieutenant Stark when the officer was injured during a hard landing under fire during Operation *Neptune*.

Compared to Normandy, this flight was initially uneventful. However, the mission grew hotter as they passed over the coast and encountered German anti-aircraft batteries. Fellers could see black clouds of flak blossoming, and the glider rocked violently due to its proximity to the bursting shells. Fellers recalled an escorting fighter approaching the glider at this time, and the pilot pointing downward. The P-51 Mustang then peeled away, only to return shortly. The pilot shot the glider riders an upturned thumb and flew off. At this moment Fellers realized the hostile anti-aircraft fire had ceased, most likely due to the good efforts of that pilot. The landing at Drop Zone "N" was uneventful, but Fellers saw that the enemy fire had shredded the glider's tail.[45]

The arrival of reinforcements precipitated a shift of regiments throughout the division area on the 24th. The fresh 325th Glider Infantry assumed responsibilities of the area to the south of Groesbeek from the 505th Parachute Infantry, which withdrew for rest and refitting. A Battery withdrew along with the paratroopers. Meanwhile the

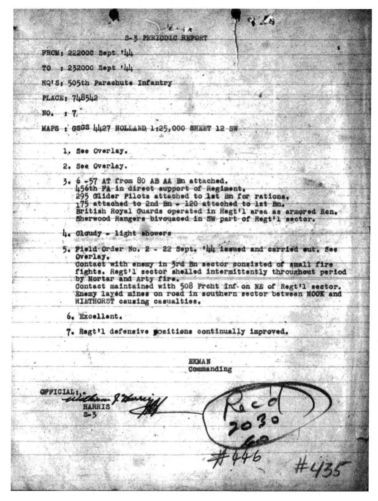

505th PIR daily report during *Market Garden*, 23 September 1944. Note the attachment of 57mm AT guns from the 80th AAA Battalion. (Photo Courtesy of Thulai Van Mannen)

325th GIR prepared to defend against suspected German elements still sheltering in the nearby Reichswald forest. The 505th PIR moved into Nijmegen to cover the newly captured bridges while also reorganizing and consolidating its subunits. Batteries D and F of the 80th provided protection for A Battery as it occupied its new gun positions.

Meanwhile, the 504th PIR assumed responsibility for the sector previously covered by the 508th Parachute Infantry along the

112 • NEVER A DULL MOMENT

Nijmegen–Beek–Wyler line in the eastern part of the division area. Batteries C and E supported the 504th Parachute Infantry in this new role. Battery E, in its new anti-tank role, initially provided a division reserve but soon found itself committed to assist the 325th GIR around Grave.[46] Combat continued apace, with Corporal Glenn Kaufman of B Battery engaging an enemy strongpoint with two high-explosive rounds, destroying four machine guns. Kaufman would lose his life during the heavy fighting to come in Belgium on Christmas Eve, 1944.[47]

With all four anti-tank batteries on the ground in Holland, Lieutenant Colonel Singleton moved his command post (CP) from its original position near Grave north to Nijmegen to collocate with Gavin's CP. This move ensured the battalion commander could properly act as the division's anti-tank officer, staying aware of the situation facing the unit and of the command general's priorities to task the batteries to move where they were most needed, and to coordinate maintenance and resupply as necessary.[48] This was an improvement from previous campaigns, where a lack of situational awareness resulted in the battalion dissipating the batteries throughout the divisional footprint, to be retained by each regimental commander regardless of the situation in their area of operations.

The Germans held Arnhem, and there would be no rapid outflanking of the Siegfried Line by the Allies. General Horrocks pressed north out of Nijmegen and moved within 5 miles of Arnhem between 21 and 25 September. However, although the 82nd Airborne and elements of XXX Corps held some ground beyond the Nijmegen Bridge, the enemy controlled most of the terrain between the Waal and Lower Rhine. After a week of fierce combat with no relief, the 1st Airborne Division had ceased to be an effective fighting unit. Of the over 10,000 men who went into Arnhem, over 10 percent were casualties, and another 30 percent were captured or hiding out from the enemy. No force existed north of the Waal to protect Horrocks's flanks during a further advance. Thus, on 25 September, the commanding general XXX Corps decided he would not continue to reinforce positions north of the Waal. The British and Polish troops around Arnhem who had thus far eluded capture would need to evade the Germans while the Allies organized an evacuation.[49]

Although this book is a campaign history of the 80th AAA Battalion, no discussion of Operation *Market Garden* is complete without considering whether the 82nd Airborne Division's failure to seize the bridges over the Waal River before the arrival of XXX Corps contributed to the failure of the plan. Opinions differ on whether Gavin—as the commanding officer of the 82nd and thus responsible for everything his division did or failed to do—should have pressed the 508th Parachute Infantry Regiment into Nijmegen to immediately take the bridges, which at that time were lightly defended.

Rather than drive straight for the Nijmegen bridges, Gavin directed the 508th Parachute Infantry Regiment to secure the Groesbeek Heights once the division completed its jump near Nijmegen. The mission to secure this terrain feature was just one of many assigned to Colonel Roy Lindquist's regiment, another being securing the ground identified as landing zones for follow-on glider reinforcements. Both missions contributed to the overall ground tactical plan and were necessary to ensure the security and successful buildup of the division area of operations. The Nijmegen bridges were vital to the operation but useless if the 82nd did not secure the southern approaches to Nijmegen.

Upon learning from Dutch underground agents that the Germans had not heavily fortified the bridges in Nijmegen, Gavin directed that the 508th PIR send a battalion to take the bridges. By the time the battalion moved into the town, they ran into the newly arrived 9th SS Reconnaissance Battalion, which had deployed south from Arnhem.[50]

Had Gavin identified the Nijmegen bridges as a primary objective and assigned a regiment to seize it immediately upon landing, would the outcome of *Market Garden* have been different? Would XXX Corps have been able to proceed to Arnhem in time to relieve the beleaguered 1st Airborne Division? While speculative history is rarely productive, one can examine the possibility by considering what occurred.

If the 508th Parachute Infantry had succeeded in taking the Nijmegen bridges on 17 September, the regiment would then have had the further responsibility of holding it. Meanwhile, further to the south, the 101st Airborne would still have been left to deal with its tactical challenges. These challenges include the Germans destroying the Son Bridge over the Wilhelmina Canal at Eindhoven. Installing

114 • NEVER A DULL MOMENT

temporary crossings and engineering repairs took time, and it was not until the 19th that the Irish Guards, the lead element of XXX Corps, crossed over and proceeded to Nijmegen. The operation was behind schedule before XXX Corps even reached Nijmegen. At this point, the 1st Airborne Division faced severe resistance from the 9th and 10th Panzer Divisions at Arnhem.

Had XXX Corps been able to cross the Waal on 19 September, there is nothing in the historical record to indicate the ground troops would have driven immediately for Arnhem. In reality, when the first troops crossed on the evening of 20 September, they stopped and consolidated their position. They did so for the tactically sound reason that, after driving up the road from the Belgian–Dutch border, XXX Corps' subordinate units needed to organize for the final move to Arnhem. The British troops would likely have behaved identically had they crossed on 19 September. Thus, 20 September would probably be the first day XXX Corps would attempt to move toward Arnhem, and even still, Horrocks would be faced with the fact that the 1st Airborne Division lacked the combat power to protect the flanks of the road leading to Arnhem.

Just as the commanding general XXX Corps determined on 25 September that he proceed no further, in this alternate reality, the same circumstances would confront Horrocks a day earlier, on 24 September. The failure of *Market Garden* was not due to the delay in seizing the bridges over the Waal but more due to the Germans' unexpectedly overwhelming combat power in Holland in the days before 17 September. The American and British airborne divisions faced a far more powerful enemy than anticipated: an enemy capable of upsetting the critical timing the operation demanded.

Between 25 and 27 September, all elements of the 82nd Airborne Division continued to face combined enemy attacks by infantry and armor, indirect fire, and strafing aircraft. For the 80th, this meant integrating their anti-tank weapons with British gunners from the 73rd Anti-Tank Regiment, who came forward with XXX Corps as part of Operation *Garden*.[51]

Additionally, the final sections of the battalion, service, and support troops, such as mechanics and cooks, arrived under the command of

Captain Edward Dittmar and Lieutenant Edward MacLean.[52] These troops landed by sea and came up the highway behind XXX Corps. The seemingly routine appearance of the remainder of the battalion illustrates a significant point that can be easily overlooked in the dramatic story of the fight for the bridges and the XXX Corps drive to try to reach Arnhem. Once the Allies took the bridges and XXX Corps advanced, the airborne troopers had to continue to fight to keep the roads open. If they lost their hold and the Germans succeeded in cutting them off, there was no way to receive reinforcements, resupply, or rearmament. The advantage of the broad-front strategy lay in the fact that, as the Allies advanced, they could rely on secure flanks that the enemy could not exploit in a counterattack. The rapier thrust advocated by Montgomery posed the risk of the rapier being broken off at the hilt by an enemy counterthrust. As the last days of September passed, the men of *Market Garden* continued to fight off the German ripostes.

The battalion command post noted significant enemy air activity over the division area of responsibility on 26 September. Messerschmitt fighters, Junkers fighter-bombers, and newly deployed German jet aircraft tangled with British fighters, while on the ground, the glider men and paratroopers endured increasing enemy artillery fire. The men of the 80th AAA interpreted these signs as precursors of a German counterattack. The following day, reports of significant German armor reached the battalion. An initial report from a Dutch civilian stated that he witnessed dozens of tanks moving about; however, by around 1400, Allied aircraft reported only five German tanks observed from the air. This smaller number still represented a serious threat. The anti-tank command post ordered B Battery to relocate six anti-tank guns northeast of Groesbeek, collocated with the 508th PIR. Meanwhile, German artillery fire continued to strike. In Pratt's C Battery, indirect fire killed Staff Sergeant Edward Grimes and Private First Class Alvin Copeland.[53]

That evening, at 1900, two British officers, identified as Lieutenants Brooks and Day, reported to Lieutenant Colonel Singleton at the anti-tank command post. The men commanded eleven 17-pounder anti-tank guns. These cannons fired shells 3 inches or 76.2mm in diameter and had an effective range of almost a mile. Their maximum range was over 6 miles. These powerful additions significantly bolstered the division's

116 • NEVER A DULL MOMENT

anti-tank defenses. Captain William Pratt, commander of C Battery, also participated in the discussions about where best to emplace these weapons. The officers determined to deploy the guns in support of the 325th GIR at Grave and with Pratt's C Battery working with the 504th PIR east of Nijmegen.[54]

It's getting light. The sun isn't up, but the deep dark of night is giving way to a grayish murkiness. The 19-year-old gunner is up and alert, on guard against any German infiltrators probing the lines. He's on his feet, not behind cover, taking advantage of the darkness to move about a little and shake off the morning cold. The battery lost a couple of guys yesterday to Kraut artillery, but it's been quiet for a while. And then it's not.

The all-too-familiar tearing sound rends the air, and he dives for the nearest foxhole. A German 88 is hitting their position. He makes it to the hole without getting hit and hunkers down, hoping the shelling won't last. He hopes in vain. The barrage grows in intensity, with what sounds like the CHUNNK of mortars adding to the cacophony. He stays in the hole for he doesn't know how long, maybe 30 minutes? Maybe more.

The morning light continues to dawn, and he looks up out of the foxhole. He's startled to see someone crouched down by the pile of dirt forming the berm but immediately relieved that he can make out from the apparition's helmet that it's an American paratrooper. One of the guys from 2nd of the "oh-four" (2nd Battalion, 504th PIR) that his battery is supporting. The paratrooper is shouting and gesticulating, but the gunner cannot make out what he's saying over the exploding mortar rounds. Finally, one word gets through: "TANK!"

The gunner pulls himself up and out of the hole and looks in the direction the trooper is pointing. It's a German tank emerging from the woods to the right of his gun section's position. Immediately the gunner is running toward his buddies' foxholes, looking for Boteler and Atkinson. The two men are already moving, and he joins them as they rush to their 57mm gun, a couple of dozen yards behind the foxholes. He notices the indirect fire is lifting, a sign that a ground attack is on the way. The Kraut tank is going to have infantry support, and maybe some other tanks along with it.

The men reach their cannon and frantically tear away the net used to camouflage the position and get the gun into action. The German tank, which looks like a Mark IV, is a bit more than a football field away and it's moving quickly. The gunner can't hear his section's other anti-tank cannon firing, but the tank is firing its machine gun at a target to its front. The American anti-tank crew shifts the cannon to try to line up a shot. The gunner grabs an armor-piercing projectile and slams it into the cannon's breech, then he and Atkinson leap onto the trails of the gun, out of Boteler's way. Boteler sights down the barrel, bore-sighting his shot as the tank is now less than 70 yards away. Boteler fires and the cannon rocks. The shell hits home, a great shot that hits the tank right in the drive sprocket! The motor's roaring but the tank can't move. Mobility kill.

There's still German infantry in sight and Boteler yells, "C'mon," leading the other two forward to a shallow depression in the ground. The rest of the squad's there, Thacker, Concillio and Richgels, carbines pointed toward the enemy. But the Kraut infantry is falling back. It looks like they only had that one tank and are reluctant to press forward without it.[55]

The date 28 September marked a significant day of fighting for C Battery, 80th AAA. Private Fary's gun's engagement with the Mark IV was the opening round of a prolonged fight during which the Germans sought to push the 82nd Airborne back from its hard-won positions.

Lieutenant Marshall Stark, leader of 1st Platoon, C Battery, left a detailed account of the fight in which Ray Fary's gun destroyed the German Mark IV. C Battery destroyed two additional tanks beside the one accounted for by Fary's crew. Almost a kilometer east of Fary's position, a gun team under Corporal Walter Sluman engaged another German tank and destroyed the vehicle with one round. Stark himself destroyed a third tank.[56]

Stark reported that he observed the shot made by Corporal Roland Boteler, whose crew consisted of Privates First Class Robert Atkinson and Ray Fary. Stark noted, as did Fary, that the number two gun in the section remained silent while Boteler engaged the Mark IV, so he took it upon himself to investigate. He found the weapon's crew still under cover due to the incoming artillery, so he manned the cannon alone, loading and firing twice at the tank disabled by Boteler's shot. Stark reported that the German tank crewmen attempted to escape, but American fire cut them down. Lieutenant James Baugh and Private First Class Ken Shenafelt of D Battery noted that their unit engaged dismounted Germans running from a damaged tank.

118 • NEVER A DULL MOMENT

After witnessing the wounding of the tank crew, Stark further engaged another tank approximately 700 yards from his position. He reported that he never saw a clear view of the enemy vehicle. However, he witnessed firing and smoke from the suspected enemy position and fired three armor-piercing rounds at that location, after which no more fire came from that spot. Stark further stated he observed dismounted Germans near the same position and fired one high-explosive round in their direction.[57]

Overall, Stark personally observed the destruction of one tank and had good evidence that he had hit a second. While surveying the platoon sector, looking for locations to emplace his guns for better fields of fire, he noted the third disabled German tank. He thought that perhaps the tank, unseen by him, sustained damage from one of the three rounds he fired earlier.

C Battery sustained one cannon damaged, although recoverable, and three men wounded throughout the fighting on the 28th. Because of these casualties and the intensity of the German attacks, A Battery relocated two guns to support Captain Pratt's troops on the northeastern section of the division perimeter. Further south, at Grave, Battery E faced similar challenges, fighting with their fellow glider men of the 325th GIR. The actions of Corporal Leslie Hansen illustrate the intensity of the fighting.

At 0710 that morning, Hansen and his gun crew engaged two German tanks, attacking in support of a regiment of German infantry. Hansen's crew successfully destroyed an enemy Mark III tank, but the second tank fired a round that killed Corporal Hansen, Private First Class George Schubert Junior, and Private Daniel Jacks. Corporal Hansen received a Silver Star for valor, while Private First Class Schubert and Private Jacks received Bronze Stars for their bravery under fire.[58]

British anti-tank units continued reinforcing the division's anti-tank defenses throughout the day. Lieutenant Day, of "G" Troop, 73rd Anti-Tank Regiment, arrived with four self-propelled (SP) tank destroyers. These SP guns, American M10s, formed a mobile reserve for the division.[59] The M10 featured a 3-inch gun mounted on the chassis of a Sherman tank, combining maneuver and firepower that the 80th lacked with its

57mm cannons.[60] The long day of the 28th ended with an enemy air raid and artillery duel between German and Allied batteries.[61]

German pressure abated on 29 September, although the battalion continued sustaining casualties. D Battery lost Private First Class Paul Lettieri and Private Samuel Johnson when artillery struck their machine-gun position. Despite the losses, the day passed with no action beyond "sporadic artillery fire." However, most troopers anticipated a renewed German attack at any time.[62]

Between 28 and 30 September, British and American anti-tank units continued to build an integrated defense of the 82nd's perimeter. The division operations officer, Lieutenant Colonel Weineke, and Lieutenant Colonel Singleton built an enlarged anti-tank plan, incorporating road-blocks and minefields, while British troops from the 340th Anti-Tank Battery arrived with 12 additional 17-pounder cannons. C Battery received four of these cannons to bolster their sector, while eight remained in reserve with Lieutenant Day's M10s.

These assets arrived just in time as the Germans launched a night attack around 2100 on the 30th. This night assault was a departure from previous German practice and marked a change of tactics that would continue into early October. The Germans got within small-arms range of the 80th AAA Battalion CP, and the men of the headquarters took to foxholes, prepared to repel the attack. However, the German assault withdrew almost as quickly as it appeared. The pattern of quiet days followed by German nighttime attacks continued on 1 October. The Germans struck Battery E in the vicinity of Groesbeek, and Private Samuel McNeill, along with Private First Class Raymond Mullenax, remained at his post under heavy fire, and drove back a German infantry attack and destroyed an enemy machine gun supporting the assault. For his actions Private McNeill received a Silver Star for gallantry. The Germans approached within 25 yards of McNeill's position, but he continued to man the 57mm cannon despite receiving multiple wounds and prevented the enemy from overrunning his position.[63] Despite repeated displays of skill and courage such as McNeill's, the battalion continued sustaining casualties, losing C Battery's Private Forest Abell and F Battery's Technician Fifth Class Joe Majoros (attached from the

120 • NEVER A DULL MOMENT

80th's Medical Detachment) and Private Andy Hudak. F Battery also lost five additional men to wounds.[64]

On 2 October, E and F Batteries found opportunities to participate in local attacks against the Germans. Battery F provided plunging fire for the 505th Parachute Infantry during the regiment's attack on positions southwest of Groesbeek, around the former Drop Zone "N" at the beginning of Operation *Market*. The enemy set up strongpoints using the remnants of abandoned gliders, and the 505th PIR decided to drive them off. F Battery's fire accounted for an estimated 10–20 enemy casualties. E Battery provided the 325th Glider Infantry with similar support with its anti-tank guns, with Corporal Anthony Jaeger receiving credit for destroying a German machine-gun position. E Battery fired a total of 25 high-explosive rounds during the engagement.[65]

After the initial days of Operation *Market Garden*, the troops settled into a long period of defending positions and aggressive patrolling. Doing the routine properly and consistently, such as weapons maintenance, observing and reporting on the enemy, and proper field hygiene, became of paramount importance to maintain combat effectiveness. Holland was the longest period of sustained combat faced by the 80th thus far in the war, for a total of 55 days before being pulled off the line in November 1944 and being relocated to a rest camp in France.

By this point in the campaign, the combat, in the words of Phil Nordyke, a respected scholar of the 82nd Airborne Division in World War II, evolved into "static warfare reminiscent of the First World War."[66] The drive to force the Lower Rhine had failed; however, the Germans could not eject the American and British forces from their positions around Nijmegen and further south. Day after day, the troops endured intermittent rain, intermittent cold, and intermittent enemy artillery attacks, punctuated by occasional opportunities to return fire. Casualties continued as shrapnel found its mark, with the battalion losing First Sergeant Keith Alredge and Technician Fifth Class Carl Miller of D Battery killed by artillery on 9 October, while Captain William Pratt, commanding officer of C Battery, was wounded. At this point, the good habits and professional routines established by the battalion assumed greater importance. The batteries remained in action despite the positional nature of the combat, and succumbing to boredom, inattentiveness, or the temptation to take shortcuts could cost lives. Private First Class Kenneth Shenafelt of D Battery recounts that after weeks of British field rations, he decided to dig for potatoes to add variety to his diet. He became so engrossed in his impromptu gardening that he did not realize he was under enemy observation until the Germans opened fire on him. According to Shenafelt, "it sounded like a bunch of bees were circling me. I realized I was being fired at so I jumped in my hole, potatoes flying, and landed on top of William Clouse who was at the gun. I came down right on top of his ankle and nearly broke it."[67]

The 82nd Airborne Division remained on the line until relieved on 10 November 1944 by Canadian troops. The division had spent over 50 days on the line. By 17 November, the 80th AAA had departed Holland and moved to Camp Suippes, France. The paratroopers and glider men expected to rest, reconstitute, and refit. None of the men could anticipate that their next fight was a month away.

Officers of the 80th AAA Battalion, Camp Suippes, France. (Photo courtesy of Micky and Joe Pratt)

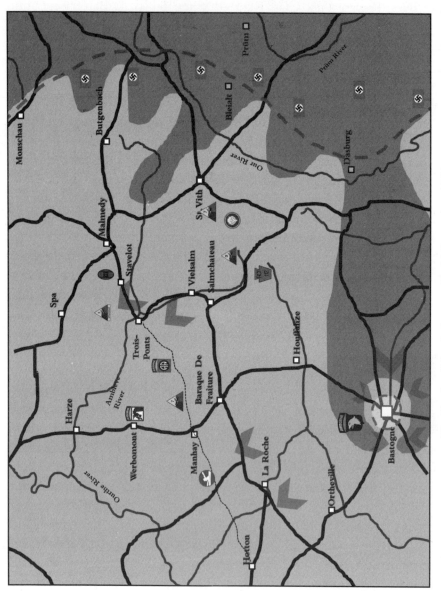

The Battle of the Ardennes, 17–26 December 1944.

CHAPTER 5

Rising to the Occasion—The Bulge

By the time of the Battle of the Bulge in December 1944–January 1945, specifically the defense of Trois-Ponts, Belgium, the 80th AAA was so capable they served as the foundations of a stalwart defense that stopped a German armored advance in its tracks. The strategic situation in December 1944 saw Allied movement eastward slowed, but German offensive action was not anticipated. The Germans launched a surprise attack westward through the Ardennes Forest in Belgium. American front-line units initially fell back in a disorganized manner in the face of the attack. The 82nd Airborne Division, along with the 101st, were alerted for movement from their rest camps into combat.

In the early winter of 1944, Nazi Germany faced the prospect of losing the war in Europe. The Soviet Union was advancing westward and had crossed the Vistula River the previous summer, driving ever closer to eastern Germany. The Allies in the West, despite the failure of Operation *Market Garden*, occupied positions along the German frontier. Hard fighting by First Canadian Army troops had opened the port of Antwerp the previous month, and Allied armies, after difficult battles in the Hürtgen Forest where the Germans waged successful defensive warfare, were taking an operational pause to resupply and replace losses from the fall fighting.[1]

German military leaders realized that fighting solely on the defensive ceded the initiative to the Allies and determined to strike westward in a bid to drive to Antwerp and retake the port facility, while also splitting the various Commonwealth and American armies threatening its western border. While the Germans could not hope to assemble enough combat power to retake all the territory lost since 6 June 1944, they planned to cause enough chaos and destruction to convince the Western Allies that suing for a separate peace made strategic sense. Having thus secured its western frontier, Germany would be free to concentrate its power in the East against the Soviet threat.[2]

Germany achieved strategic and tactical surprise when it launched its offensive on 16 December 1944. It had maintained an air of secrecy around its planning, and Allied intelligence declared the sector targeted by Germany for the assault, the Ardennes Forest, to be a quiet sector. Commanders considered the Ardennes a good place to break in infantry divisions newly arrived from the United States due to low expectations for significant fighting. Despite the official intelligence assessments that the Germans would remain on the defensive, some intelligence officers assigned to the individual Allied armies, such as Oscar Koch, G-2 (Intelligence) of General George Patton's Third Army, predicted from collating information from various services that the Germans were both capable of and preparing for offensive action sometime in December 1944.[3]

The speed and shock of the initial German attack resembled the blitzkrieg, or lightning war, tactics for which the German army received renown in the opening days of World War II.[i] On 16 December 1944, the Germans struck, initially moving to encircle a heavily forested region of the Belgian–German border called the Schnee Eifel. They largely succeeded by the night of 17 December, and in doing so largely cut off the American 106th Infantry Division from Allied lines. The 106th was new to the European Theater of Operations, having just replaced the 2nd Infantry Division on the front line less than a week earlier.[4] The German attack isolated over 8,000 American soldiers, including two of

---

i   The Germans themselves did not use the term "blitzkrieg" but referred to their preferred method of war as *Bewegungskrieg* or "War of Movement." The goal of this doctrine was swift and overwhelming action to achieve decisive results as quickly as possible. Robert Michael Citino, *The German Way of War* (University Press of Kansas, 2005), xiv.

the 106th Division's three infantry regiments, the 422nd and 423rd, and a variety of field artillery, engineer, tank destroyer, and cavalry units.[5]

The movement encircling the 106th Infantry Division started a series of blows against General Courtney Hodges's U.S. First Army. Hodges initially committed his own reserves against the German onslaught and called upon support from General William Simpson's U.S. Ninth Army. However, the surprise and tempo achieved by the enemy overwhelmed these efforts, and Hodges found he needed to request that his boss, General Omar Bradley, now commanding the 12th U.S. Army Group, ask Supreme Allied Headquarters to commit its strategic reserve to stem the tide. The reserve consisted entirely of XVIII Airborne Corps' 82nd and 101st Airborne Divisions.[6]

The 82nd spent the five weeks since its movement off the line in Holland at a rest camp in France. Rest is perhaps a misnomer because, despite amenities such as passes, movies, and stage shows, the men spent much of their time engaged in tasks, to include police calls (cleaning details), inspections, and repairing clothing and equipment. Despite what might be regarded as the drudgery of garrison soldiering, the 80th AAA Battalion headquarters issued two day passes for the men to visit Paris during this time.[7] For the men of the 80th, 17 December began much like the previous days of their times at the Suippes rest camp. Men attended religious services and a presentation of Ballet Russe; however, during the performance came an announcement for unit commanders to report to the commanding general at 2200 hours, soon followed by orders for officers and NCOs to begin returning to their units.[8]

General Gavin, in his role as the commanding general of the 82nd and also acting as the commanding general of XVIII Airborne Corps due to the absence of Ridgway in the United Kingdom, received the warning order to be prepared to move both divisions to Belgium to support First Army at 1900 on 17 December. By 2100 new orders specified to get both the 82nd and the 101st on the road as soon as possible.[9]

The men of the 80th AAA Battalion recalled receiving the news in a variety of ways. Battery A's Private First Class Malcolm Neel recounted that he was attending the Ballet Russe when the announcement for the officer call came down, leaving the enlisted men in the audience wondering what fate had in store for them. He further states he was asleep

126 • NEVER A DULL MOMENT

in barracks when an alert order came down. In short order Malcolm was heading to the battery supply NCO to draw cold weather boots and ammunition while his pal Jim Bell (Private First Class James Bell) headed to the range with a detail to retrieve sandbags.[10] Second Lieutenant William Fuller of D Battery noted in his diary, "December 18, 1944 0130 ALERTED FOR MISSION!" A Battery's Corporal Gordon Walberg noted he did not receive word until being awakened around four in the morning by his squad leader Sergeant Lawrence Fox. Walberg noted he had time to draw as many supplies as possible but still eat breakfast in the chow hall before departing for Belgium in a jeep with his gun crew, Technician Fifth Class Paul Schlupp and Private First Class Morris Karshenbaum.[11]

All members of the battalion hurriedly prepared their gear to move out on the morning of the 18th. The column departed Suippes between 0830 and 0950, initially headed for Bastogne.[12] Gavin departed France with an advanced party to confer with General Hodges, commanding First Army, whose troops bore the brunt of the German attack. Hodges had control of XVIII Airborne Corps now that SHAEF committed its reserve, and Gavin (later Ridgway as he made his way to the front) would fall under his orders. Gavin initially ordered the first elements of both the 101st and 82nd Airborne Divisions to head for Bastogne in Belgium to shore up the southern flank of the Allied positions; however, Hodges told Gavin the 82nd was needed in the north to support the troops in the vicinity of Werbomont, Belgium. Enemy armor, identified as a *Kampfgruppe* under German commander Joachim Peiper, was known to be driving westward, seeking to cross the Amblève and Salm rivers in the drive to Antwerp. As the meeting between Hodges and Gavin broke up, word came that enemy armor was spotted by First Army liaison aircraft proceeding north out the village of Trois-Ponts. This armor could either threaten the rear of First Army or, by turning west, disrupt the arrival of the 82nd Airborne Division. The U.S. Army 30th Infantry Division was currently operating in that area and received orders to defend against this threat. The 30th Division responded by splitting its 119th Infantry Regiment to both cover Werbomont and defend along the Amblève.[13]

The 82nd initially took up positions in the vicinity of Werbomont, with the mission to defend against the 1st SS Panzer Division, looking to reinforce Kampfgruppe Peiper, spearhead of the initial German attack on the Allied northern positions. The 80th initially adopted its standard anti-tank role, but eventually assigned Batteries D and F to anti-aircraft defense, while Batteries A, B, and C provided anti-tank support to the division's infantry, and Battery E maintained a division reserve of firepower.

Despite the surprise of receiving a new combat assignment while in a rear area, the officers and men of the 80th performed the task of preparing for departure within short order. Within 12 hours of division headquarters ordering them to be prepared to move, they had supplied and equipped themselves as well as possible and were on the road to Belgium. The men were "convinced that they had helped establish a record for speed with which a division sized element prepared and left for a combat mission."[14]

The 80th AAA Battalion elements arrived near Werbomont after dark on 18 December, most likely between 2000 and 2100. The batteries immediately prioritized anti-tank defense given the threat posed by Kampfgruppe Peiper. On an individual level, the troops prioritized finding somewhere to sleep out of the cold. Not all succeeded. While D Battery's Lieutenant Fuller located a barn in which to bed down, A Battery's Corporal Walberg and crew made do with curling up under sleeping bags in their jeep. Walberg recalls waking, the chill penetrating his body down to the bone. Despite the sleeping bags, the men experienced severe cold. As Walberg explained, "we didn't want to get inside the bedrolls because of the delay in getting out of them." The men of A Battery had learned that seconds count in combat.[15]

Throughout 19 December, the officers and men of the 80th AAA applied all of their training, experience, and skill to preparing for the defense of Werbomont. Lieutenant Colonel Singleton directed D and F Batteries to revert to their primary mission of anti-aircraft protection, as some concern existed that enemy fighters and fighter-bombers could strafe the division area of operations. By late afternoon, the battalion commander, along with the leaders of the division's infantry regiments, received the latest field order from Major General Gavin and set about executing their new assignments. Singelton dispatched A Battery to work with their compatriots from Sainte-Mère-Église, the 505th PIR. The 508th PIR welcomed B Battery and its complement of anti-tank guns, while C Battery rejoined with their comrades from Nijmegen, the 504th PIR. E Battery was to act as the division reserve, while D and F Batteries retained their mission of air defense.[16]

Pratt's C Battery moved north with the 504th PIR, whom Gavin directed to make contact with the 30th Infantry Division, who faced the 1st SS Panzer Division. Kampfgruppe Peiper found itself nearly cutoff while fighting near Stoumont that same day, with American elements to its east. The 1st SS Panzer Division was expected to try to cut Peiper's group out from the trap; thus, Gavin sent the 504th, under the command of Colonel Reuben Tucker, to support the 30th Infantry Division in dealing with this threat.[17] While separated from the remainder of the German force, Kampfgruppe Peiper remained formidable, with an estimated 4,000 troops and 200 armored vehicles. If the 504th Parachute Infantry could take the town of Cheneux, where Peiper maintained a bridgehead, it would go a long way to completing the encirclement of the German task force.[18]

Meanwhile, patrols from the 505th PIR moved east and made contact with C Company, 51st Engineers, and outposts of the 7th Armored Division further to the southeast. The engineers reported that the bridges in Trois-Ponts were not viable for the Germans to use.[19] The 505th Parachute Infantry's commander, Colonel William Ekman, immediately dispatched infantry armed with 2.36-inch rocket launchers to reinforce the engineers at Trois-Ponts, with his second battalion following as quickly as it was able. The battalion occupied Trois-Ponts by late afternoon on 20 December.[20]

While the parachute infantry regiments closed on their objectives, an officer from the 703rd Tank Destroyer Battalion, Lieutenant Louis Capelle, arrived at Lieutenant Colonel Singleton's Command Post. Cappelle commanded a company of 12 self-propelled guns, which Singleton promptly integrated into the division's anti-tank defensive scheme.[21] The M36 featured a 90mm cannon, front armor varying between 1½ and

RISING TO THE OCCASION • 129

2 inches thick, and could achieve speeds of 26 miles per hour on hard surfaces. The attached M36s provided the 82nd Airborne Division with firepower and defensive flexibility unlike anything they had seen up to this point in the war.[22]

Emphasis quickly shifted to limited offensive operations, with elements of the 504th Parachute Infantry Regiment moving to seize the town of Cheneux. Battery C provided the 504th PIR with direct support during the assault, taking casualties and performing their duties using captured German equipment. Meanwhile, the remainder of the battalion was occupying positions throughout the division area of operations.

The 504th PIR's 1st Battalion drew the mission to take Cheneux. B and C Companies of the 504th hit German defenses within half a mile of Cheneux. The Germans possessed significant firepower in the form of anti-aircraft batteries operating in a supporting role like batteries of the 80th AAA Battalion. The airborne infantry lacked the weapons to overpower the German guns, but they did have access to a captured German half-track equipped with a 77mm cannon. Privates First Class Harold Kelly and Harry Koprowski from C Battery, 80th AAA, volunteered to man the cannon, despite never having fired one. A member of the 504 PIR drove; a Private First Class Snow, and two additional paratroopers, Privates Holliday and Hoover of 1st Platoon, B Company, 504th PIR, joined them with Browning Automatic Rifles to keep away German infantry. The improvised tank destroyer attacked multiple German positions throughout the afternoon, destroyed at least one German half-track, and disrupted a German infantry counterattack. At some point, Kelly received wounds to his lower face but continued to fight until the crew ran out of ammunition. The men retreated outside of Cheneux. Kelly and Koprowski, along with Snow, Hoover, and Holliday, managed to relieve the enemy pressure on B Company, 504th PIR; all five men later received the Bronze Star.[23] However, the town remained in German hands.[24]

Despite the efforts of Kelly and Koprowski and the 504th crew, the Germans still defended Cheneux in strength. The battalion commander of the 1st Battalion, 504th, determined he had to take the town by

130 • NEVER A DULL MOMENT

storm and committed his B and C Companies to the attack. The assault went forward after a brief artillery preparation and sustained over 60 percent casualties. The paratroopers fought with their trademark aggression, going after German gun positions using only grenades and small arms. Eventually, tank destroyer support came forward and began to shell the buildings of the town. This fire forced German defenders outside, where the men of the 504th Parachute Infantry faced them on more equal terms.

While the 504th PIR assaulted Cheneux, the men of the 2nd Battalion, 505th, established their defensive positions around Trois-Ponts. The village comprised key terrain as it boasted three different bridges that the Germans could use to cross the water obstacles presented by the confluence of the Amblève and the Salm rivers, which would allow both Kampfgruppe Peiper and the 1st SS Panzer Division to continue to drive on Antwerp.

Trois-Ponts possessed similar significance to the more famous town of Bastogne, further south. The town provided three crossing points over the Amblève and Salm rivers, hence its name. Trois-Ponts was also a crossroads town at which several roads running through the Amblève and Salm valleys converged. An improved road ran west from Trois-Ponts, connecting Stavelot to the northeast, to Werbomont to the west. Should the Germans control the town, crossing points, and highway, they would possess a transportation hub accessible by wheeled and tracked vehicles, useful for launching combat and resupply operations.[25]

A Battery positioned two 6-pounders under Lieutenant Jake Wertich, who had fought so effectively at Mook the previous September, directly at the village with the bulk of Vandervoort's battalion. Meanwhile, 1st Battalion, 505th, supported by two guns commanded by Lieutenant Neil McNeill advanced to the town of Grand Halleux, and an additional two-gun section joined 3rd Battalion, 505th at Rochelinval, to overwatch additional bridges.

Vandervoort's battalion threw themselves into preparing to defend Trois-Ponts. E Company, 505thParachute Infantry, crossed the damaged bridge over the Salm River to establish a forward defensive position, while D Company remained on the west bank and dug in to cover a second bridge to the south of the village. Airborne engineers from the 307th along with their brethren from C Company, 51st Engineers, who had been holding the village since before Vandervoort's unit arrived, prepared the bridge for demolition in the event the Americans had to abandon Trois-Ponts to the enemy. One of Lieutenant Wertich's guns accompanied E Company as it occupied positions on high ground overlooking the village and the primary avenue approach to the town. If the A Battery's gun could dominate this route, called the Aisomont Road, it held the key to stopping approaching German armor. The 2nd Battalion, 505th, and its supporting guns arrived none too soon, as combined-arms teams from the 1st and 9th SS Panzer Regiments were even then in assembly areas near the town of Wanne, preparing to force a crossing of the Salm to relieve Peiper and his men. If they were successful, the Germans still had a chance to fulfill their goal of splitting the Allied armies and seizing Antwerp.[26]

Lieutenant Wertich along with Corporal Stokes Taylor positioned their anti-tank cannon within 30 yards of the E Company, 505th Parachute Infantry's command post. The paratroopers busily prepared an anti-armor defense, digging in and emplacing mines and rocket-launcher teams. Corporal Taylor emplaced an outpost using half of his six gunners, sending forward Corporal William Ballentine, and Privates First Class Harry Robison and Gordon Smital. The gun crew manning the cannon consisted of Technician Fifth Class Jay Graham, Sergeant Richard Scott, and Private Edward Delsignore. These eight glider riders comprised the heart of the defense of Trois-Ponts and would soon face down two SS Panzer regiments.

E Company and the anti-tank gunners did not have long to wait. A column of enemy grenadier half-tracks hit their position around 2000 on 20 December. The mines and bazooka teams destroyed two vehicles while the remainder withdrew; however, they would be back. On the morning of the 21st, a combined arms team of German *Panzergrenadiers* supported by armor struck E Company in strength, taking prisoners and overrunning some defensive positions. However, the men of A Battery succeeded in destroying a German reconnaissance car that provided the enemy with fire support from its 7.5cm cannon.[27]

132 • NEVER A DULL MOMENT

The Germans continued to maneuver to get around E Company's flanks, and Lieutenant Colonel Vandervoort committed F Company, his battalion reserve, to cross the Salm and shore up the beleaguered Company E. Meanwhile, the commander of A Battery, 80th AAA, Captain Norman Nelson, arrived and directed Corporal Walberg to move his gun forward to support Corporal Taylor and Lieutenant Wertich. Walberg requested that the commander accompany his gun team, and together they moved across the river and established a new firing position about half a football field behind Taylor's cannon. The terrain allowed Walberg to engage any armor that bypassed Taylor's gun team from the side rather than head-on. Throughout the morning and into early afternoon, German infantry advanced in dispersed formations, taking advantage of cover and concealment while their armor support moved closer to E Company's lines to prepare for an all-out strike. Around 1400, the hammer blow came.

Walberg and Taylor heard small-arms fire from south of their locations. No supporting infantry was available for the A Battery guns, so Corporal Walberg dispatched his two crewmen, Karshenbaum and Schlupp, to occupy an outpost and act as infantry support. Their role was to engage German infantry with their rifles, while Walberg operated his cannon solo if enemy armor approached. While not an optimal solution, it did offer some protection from German *Panzergrenadiers*. Soon enemy infantry approached in large numbers—too many for the small outpost—and Schlupp warned Walberg to withdraw to avoid being killed or captured. As Walberg attempted to evacuate his gun by jeep, however, four Germans approached and opened fire.[28] Walberg received wounds to his shoulder and chest, the impact of the enemy rounds knocking him to the ground. Gordon recovered enough to return fire before his rifle eventually jammed and then warned Schlupp that enemy infantry was all around. Schlupp managed to wound two Germans while withdrawing under pressure. Corporal Walberg then retreated to the battalion aid station in Trois-Ponts, a significant journey while wounded. Schlupp would eventually receive a Bronze Star for his role in the Trois-Ponts fight. Back at the E Company lines, the Germans continued to try to break the American position.[29]

The battle devolved into an infantry fight, and the A Battery gunners were forced to fight to defend their 6-pounder. Company E, 505th Parachute Infantry's 2nd Platoon, along with the bazooka teams, took heavy casualties as German *Panzergrenadiers* advanced through their positions.[30] Corporal Taylor's outpost also took heavy casualties. Privates First Class Robison and Smital were killed. Corporal Taylor advanced at this moment, carrying a Browning Automatic Rifle. Taylor took the advancing enemy under fire while Lieutenant Wertich continued to man the anti-tank gun single-handedly.[31]

With E Company under tremendous pressure, the report of the fight at Trois-Ponts made its way to the regimental commander, Colonel William Ekman, coordinating with the 508th PIR further to the south. When word of the danger to company reached Ekman, he consulted with the assistant division commander of the 82nd, General Swift, and determined to pull E Company back from its exposed position across the Salm.[32] Lieutenant Colonel Vandervoort directed that his command post send the withdrawal order to his companies via radio and then crossed the Salm himself in a jeep to personally oversee the evacuation of the east bank. Vandervoort witnessed the confused combat, and at least four tanks supporting the German assault. However, Stokes Taylor and Jake Wertich were still in the fight.

Corporal Taylor opened fire on the Germans trying to seize his anti-tank gun, forcing them to take cover. He additionally engaged the enemy maneuvering against the E Company soldiers still in their foxholes. Taylor kept up a continuous fire until he exhausted his ammunition and was killed in his position. His valor allowed time for some of his crew members to make their escape.[33]

Lieutenant Wertich likewise held his ground. While Corporal Taylor engaged enemy infantry, Lieutenant Wertich operated the anti-tank gun by himself. He accounted for two German tracks before dying at his gun, and slowed the armored advance. Had the German vehicles been able to overrun his gun and gain the Aisomont road, Trois-Ponts would have been rapidly invested with enemy armor.[34] Both Lieutenant Wertich and Corporal Taylor received the Distinguished Service Cross for their valor, posthumously.

Lieutenant Wertich's and Corporal Taylor's stand demonstrated the level of competence and professionalism achieved by the 80th AAA Battalion by this point in the war. From his time as a replacement platoon leader, Wertich had become an effective combat officer over a very short period, as evidenced by his performance during the fighting in Holland. Likewise, Corporal Stokes Taylor was at the critical place at the critical time to protect the withdrawal of both his crew and a large part of E Company, 505th PIR. These men had learned from their previous combat experiences and placed themselves and their weapon system where they and it could be most effective on the battlefield. As a result of their experience and skill they were prepared to rise to the occasion when the crisis came.

While fighting raged at Trois-Ponts, the division continued to receive additional reinforcements. C Company of the 563rd Anti-Aircraft Artillery (Automatic Weapons) Battalion, commanded by Captain Englebert, arrived. Lieutenant Colonel Singleton assigned Englebert the role of providing air defense to the division's 319th and 320th Glider Field Artillery Battalions. The 80th AAA command post noted during this period of combat that "reports were flowing in properly and the Battalion seemed to be functioning smoothly."[35] This entry is remarkable for its routine straightforwardness. The 80th AAA was in the middle of some of the most significant combat experienced by the 82nd Airborne Division, and the command post was coordinating not only its own batteries, but numerous anti-tank and air defense attachments.

The anti-armor command post concept was proving its worth as the headquarters managed a variety of unfamiliar assets with significantly heavier firepower than the 80th normally had at its disposal. For the command post to record it functioning properly illustrates how they had mastered the routine and were now able to function at a high level, even during critical periods of combat.

Only T/5 Schlupp, Corporal Ballentine, and Private Delsignore remained unwounded after the fight in front of Trois-Ponts. Eight A Battery officers and men were killed or wounded. The surviving gunners managed to withdraw along with the bulk of E Company down to the bank of the Amblève, with the German attackers following. 2nd Battalion,

505th, managed to stop the enemy assault at the river. For the time being, the 505th PIR continued to hold.

The Germans pressed the 82nd Airborne Division across its front throughout 21 December. In addition to the fighting at Cheneux and Trois-Ponts, paratroopers endured German attacks at Grand Halleux, along the Salm River south of Trois-Ponts. 1st Battalion, 505th (1–505th) PIR's G Company, commanded by Captain Jack Issacs, held positions there west of the Salm, with one platoon east of the river. The company endured assaults by the enemy on 21 December and expected renewed pressure from the Germans on the morning of 22 December. The 80th AAA Battalion took advantage of the additional flexibility provided by C Company, 563rd AAA (Automatic Weapons), and reassigned assets from D Battery to move south to support the 505th PIR. One platoon would support Issacs and his men, and a second would support 1–505th PIR. Alerted to move at 0130, Lieutenant Fuller led his platoon of D Battery to Grand Halleux and reported to Captain Issacs early in the morning of the 22nd.[36] The next assault occurred that night.

Two companies from the 9th SS Panzer Regiment struck several 505th PIR positions along the Salm. One company assaulted G Company at Grand Halleux with a direct attack. Fuller's D Battery .50-caliber machine guns, augmented by an M45 Quadmount (known colloquially as a "Quad .50" because it featured four M2 Browning .50-caliber machine guns mounted on a two-wheeled trailer[37]) joined in with the G Company troopers to create what one paratrooper called, "a concentrated wall of fire."[38]

A Company, 1–505th PIR, fended off a similar attack with support from 2nd Platoon, D Battery, under Lieutenant Henry Coustillac and anti-tank support from an A Battery, 80th AAA 6-pounder. Private First Class Malcolm Neel recalled that the German infantry approached "screaming, more like roaring as they came down the hill on the other side of the river [Salm]." Neel further stated this was the only time in the war he threw up, as he waited for the charging Germans to assault his position. The combined firepower of A Company, 505th PIR, and the 80th AAA gunners stopped the Germans cold. Private First Class Kenneth Shenafelt of D Battery later said, "we sowed them down like

136 • NEVER A DULL MOMENT

cabbage in a cabbage patch." By the end of 22 December, D Battery recorded expending 80,000 rounds of ammunition.[39]

At this point in the fighting, the 82nd Airborne Division's area of operations around Werbomont resembled a vast horseshoe, lying on its side. The open end of the horseshoe faced west with the northern, or top, prong consisting of the 504th PIR, holding positions from the vicinity of the towns of Rahier and Cheneux and then arching south to just north of Trois-Ponts. The 505th Parachute Infantry formed the curve of the horseshoe's "U," holding Trois-Ponts, Grand Halleux and Petit Halleux, and tying into the 508th Parachute Infantry Regiment north of Vielsalm. The 508th PIR completed the "U" and began the southern prong, curving along the Salm River until reaching Salmchâteau, and then turning west to link up with the 325th Glider Infantry Regiment East of Hébronval. The 325th held the remainder of the southern prong covering the division's southern flank, terminating at the town of Fraiture.[40]

By 23 December, the fighting in the vicinity of Grand Halleux had died down; however, enemy armor did threaten the 505th PIR's positions during the day. The mobile firepower of the 703rd Tank Destroyer Battalion provided support and soon destroyed the threat. Private First Class Neel's gun team sought shelter from the cold in a nearby house when the Germans hit the area with indirect fire. Both Private First Class Peter Jensen and Corporal Ernest Seddon were wounded in the shelling. In the 508th PIR's sector, B Battery reported engaging and destroying a Mark III tank, while Battery F moved to the southern flank to provide support to the 325th GIR.[41]

With the 1st SS Panzer Division's attempts to force river crossings to relieve Kampfgruppe Peiper somewhat stabilized, Gavin turned his attention to the division's right flank. In the confusion of the early days of the German attack and the 82nd's occupation of its area of operations east of Werbomont, it was difficult for General Gavin to cover 80 square miles with only four regiments, which caused him to spread his troops thinly along the front, in the horseshoe fashion described above.

First Army Commanding General Hodges directed Gavin, then acting in command of XVIII Airborne Corps, to tie in with the 30th Infantry Division on his left flank and General Maurice Rose's 3rd Armored

Division on his right. The 30th had been in heavy fighting in the Malmedy–Stavelot area north of Trois-Ponts, and the 82nd had a decent idea of its positions and area of responsibility.[42]

The 3rd Armored Division was to occupy positions south of Gavin's 82nd Airborne; however, General Rose could not easily accomplish that task. American armored divisions in World War II were formidable fighting units. These divisions possessed significant firepower and mobility, which they tailored for missions under tactical headquarters called combat commands. The combat commands, labeled "CCA," "CCB," and "CCR" for "Reserve," had no standing units under them, but received troops as the tactical situation dictated. The 3rd Armored Division had six tank battalions and three armored infantry battalions, supported by artillery. While this would seem more than enough to go toe to toe with the attacking German Panzer divisions, both of Rose's combat commands already had missions when the 82nd Airborne Division occupied Werbomont. CCA was First Army's reserve, and CCB was deployed north supporting the 30th Infantry Division with blocking positions on the road network.[43]

To accomplish its mission of establishing a defense along the 82nd's southern flank, 3rd Armored Division could only initially deploy a small armored force composed of "little task forces." These forces were mobile and patrolled the void in that area but created no specific positions to defend or with which Gavin's men could make contact.[44] The commander of the 325th Glider Infantry Regiment, Colonel Charles Billingslea, summed up the situation from the 82nd's perspective in a later interview, stating, "The non-appearance of the 3rd Armored was a source of worry to everyone concerned."[45]

Beginning on 21 December, Gavin directed the 325th Glider Infantry to establish its positions along the division's right flank, while retaining two companies of 2nd Battalion, 325th GIR, as the division reserve. This remained the situation until 22 December, when the German 2nd SS Panzer Division drove straight for the void between the 82nd and 3rd Armored Divisions' "little task forces" to break through to the west.

3rd Armored Division's CCA and CCB redeployed to meet the new threat. At the same time, Gavin had to deal with a fluid situation wherein

138 • NEVER A DULL MOMENT

no cohesive defensive line could be maintained. Gavin directed the 80th AAA Battalion to commit E Battery, the division anti-tank reserve, in support of the 325th GIR. Three of the battery's guns participated in the defense of the village of Regne, where the 325th established an outpost; however, German armor soon pushed the glider men out of the town. The loss of Regne, as well as the crossroads at Baraque de Fraiture created a situation where German armor could now get in the rear of the 82nd, threatening it with encirclement. Private First Class John Leh participated in the attack to retake Regne, stating that E Battery posted two 6-pounders to the east and west of the town, for a total of four guns, in support of the counterattack.[46] Company B, 325th GIR, led the attack, supported by armor as well as the E Battery guns. During this fight, the glider troops captured the adjutant of a German Panzer regiment, who had several valuable pieces of intelligence regarding the 2nd Panzer Division's plans.[47]

While the 325th GIR retook Regne, other American forces continued to retreat eastward in the face of the 9th SS Panzer Division. These American units, retreating from the town of St. Vith about 12 miles east of the 82nd's lines, crossed bridges held by the 508th PIR at Vielsalm on 23 December. A Company engaged in intense combat against the lead elements of the 9th SS, who surged to the east banks of the Salm to capture bridges across the river. American engineers struggled to destroy bridges but could not detonate the charges on the final intact bridge. 508th troopers ultimately destroyed it by firing a 2.36-inch rocket into a box of plastic explosives placed on the span. For the time being, the 82nd held the 1st, 9th, and 2nd SS Panzer Divisions at bay, but the airborne force was in jeopardy of being encircled.[48]

By this point in the battle, British Field Marshal Montgomery received temporary command of the entire northern section of the Allied line from General Eisenhower to restore a level of unity to a confused command situation. XVIII Airborne Corps fell under Montgomery's command because of this change. Montgomery met with General Ridgway, now in the field at Werbomont where the corps had its command post, on Christmas Eve 1944 and directed the airborne general to order the 82nd to contract its lines to better defend against the relentless German pressure. A shorter line would allow for better flank protection between regiments, as there would be less overall ground to cover.[49] Although surrendering ground won was not part of the airborne ethos, General Gavin agreed with the tactical soundness of the directive, and the division carried out the maneuver on the night of 24 December.[50] Ridgway's XVIII Airborne Corps previously ordered the 82nd not to withdraw to ensure the forces retreating from St. Vith could use the crossing points of the Salm. With this action complete, the danger of Allied units being cut off east of the river was no longer a consideration.[51]

The 82nd's readjustment of its lines was not without incident for the 80th AAA Battalion. The beleaguered Private First Class Neel's squad at Grand Halleux suffered another casualty while working to displace a 6-pounder. Private Richard Kibbe was working to free the gun, which was frozen to the ground, using hot water, while another soldier tried to pull the gun free with the squad's jeep. One wheel of the gun carriage broke free, but the other remained stuck, causing the cannon to pivot, and its barrel collided with Kibbe's knee. Kibbe's injury was sufficiently bad that he could not walk, and his squad was forced to use their cannon as an improvised litter, securing the injured private to the towing trails of the cannon for the retrograde movement to the town of Basse-Bodeux.[52] Kibbe's trials were not yet over.

During the road march away from Grand Halleux, the jeep towing Kibbe slid off the roadway down a long embankment. The other passengers included Lieutenant McNeill, Sergeant Jim Kish, and Privates Jim Bell and William Chadwick. Chadwick suffered a broken leg; Kibbe suffered no further injury, but the fall did not help his condition. Both men were moved by ambulance later that night. Bell suffered severe injuries and had to wait to be medically evacuated the following morning. McNeill and Kish were unharmed.[53]

The withdrawal reduced the amount of territory that the 82nd Airborne Division defended by almost half, with the three parachute infantry regiments defending a line from Trois-Ponts running southwest to near the village of Manhay.[54] The 325th GIR maintained the division reserve. The 30th Infantry Division remained positioned on the 82nd's left flank, and the 7th Armored Division, recently withdrawn from St. Vith, was on the airborne's right flank.[55]

The 3rd Armored Division departed from the area south of the 82nd's positions, no longer attached to XVIII Airborne Corps. Combat Command A, 7th Armored Division, recently withdrawn from Saint Vith, was moving into position, but unaware of 3rd Armored Division's departure. On the night of 24 December, elements of the 2nd SS Panzer Division took advantage of the confusion caused by the flurry of American activity and advanced northward to seize the town of Manhay, destroying five tanks of 7th Armored Division's CCA while losing two panzers.[56]

As a result of this confusion, a gap existed between 7th Armored Division and the 82nd Airborne Division's right flank. On Christmas morning General Gavin committed Colonel Billingslea's 1st Battalion, 325th GIR, to occupy the village of Tri-le-Cheslaing, which was actually in 7th Armored Division's area of responsibility; however, Gavin needed to do something to protect his division's flank. 1-325th GIR took the village without a fight. No Germans were found, despite the village being just over a mile east of Manhay. Although the 7th Armored and 82nd Airborne Divisions had yet to tie their flanks together, Gavin was in contact with CCA, 7th Armored Division, via radio and knew that formation to be positioned further north along the highway connecting Werbomont and the Belgian city of Liège.[57] Germans shelled Tri-le-Cheslaing once the glider men took up their positions in the village; however, no ground attack occurred until the morning of 26 December. 1st Battalion, 325th GIR, succeeded in defending the position, as well as the right flank of the division. That night the 7th Armored Division deployed an armored infantry battalion to assume control of Tri-le-Cheslaing, with 1st Battalion, 325th GIR, shifting to the east, ensuring the 7th Armored and 82nd Airborne Divisions remained tied-in on their left and right flanks, respectively. However, further to the east, along the 82nd's line, the last battle of this phase of the campaign was being played out.

By 24 December, the German attacks were blunted enough that the 82nd could conduct a withdrawal to consolidate and reorganize its positions, while the division remained on the defensive as momentum shifted. By 28 December, German combat power was sufficiently blunted that the initiative began to pass to the Allied forces.

When the 82nd Airborne Division conducted its withdrawal to "tidy up the line" in the words of Field Marshal Montgomery,[58] their movement created a void that the German attackers moved quickly to fill. The 9th SS Panzer Division and the 62nd Volksgrenadier Division both conducted aggressive reconnaissance of the center of the 82nd's lines, held by the 508th PIR. The village of Erria, held by the 3rd Battalion, 508th PIR, came under heavy artillery attack the night of 27–28 December, followed by a ground attack by the 19th Panzergrenadiers, 9th SS Panzer Division. The 19th Panzergrenadiers struck G Company, 508th PIR, head on, and then tried to maneuver around the paratroopers. This maneuver was met by devastating fire from F Company, 2nd Battalion, 508th PIR, stalling the attack. The commander of the 508th PIR, Colonel Roy Lindquist, committed his regimental reserve and drove the Germans from the village. Among the 82nd's casualties in this fight was Private First Class John McCormick from B Battery, 80th AAA Battalion. By this point in the campaign, after a week and a half of going up against the 82nd, the German divisions facing them could no longer mount an effective attack. The 82nd was prepared to transition to the attack.[59]

During this period, in addition to Private First Class McCormick, the 80th AAA lost four men to German fire: Corporal Glenn Kaufman, B Battery; Private First Class Jesse Dillon and Private Andrew Matsko, F Battery; and Private First Class C. W. Smith, B Battery. Despite the casualties, the battalion experienced a relatively quiet period, with time dedicated to training new personnel on combat radio use, providing instruction to the men of 325th Glider Infantry on the proper use of the ground mount for the .50-caliber machine gun, and preparing maps for the upcoming offensive "push."[60]

The 80th AAA Battalion History for the period 25–31 December 1944 records that the battalion command post relocated several times as the division prepared to transition to the offensive. Revealing more information about the types of chores required to make a command post run, the entry for the 27th states that the battalion radio jeep conducted a reconnaissance of prospective locations to establish the battalion command post at Neuville, Belgium. Having accomplished its mission, the vehicle then became mired in a muddy road on its return to the battalion, and the driver radioed to request assistance to recover the radio team. The last entry for this incident notes laconically that the incident delayed the planned displacement of the command post until the following day.

Along the front the Allies resumed the offensive. To the south of Field Marshal Montgomery's 21st Army Group, American General George Patton's Third Army resumed its attacks on 30 December 1944. Montgomery's attack would kick off on 3 January 1945, with General J. Lawton Collins's VII Corps as the main effort, attacking east with a total of four divisions. To the north, XVIII Airborne Corps would protect the VII Corps left flank, with the 82nd Airborne driving southeast to recapture the territory it withdrew from previously. The 82nd received reinforcements in the form of the 517th PIR, from the newly arrived 17th Airborne Division, along with a tank destroyer battalion and a tank battalion.[61] On New Year's Day, the 628th Tank Destroyer Battalion reported to Singleton's anti-tank command post, providing the division with 36 M36 tank destroyers.

The attack kicked off on 3 January 1945 with the 80th AAA's anti-tank command post hosting numerous liaison officers coordinating support across the front. Heavy weather made the prospect of the attack a dubious affair, but the regiments proceeded to move out as scheduled. In the first 48 hours of combat, A and D Batteries captured 11 prisoners between them. By 5 January, the 505th PIR had seized the village of Abrefontaine, and the 80th CP relocated to that area as the division continued its advance.[62]

On 7 January, D Battery accompanied 2nd Battalion, 505th PIR, as it attacked Goronne, going up against a company of *Panzergrenadiers* supported by two German tanks. Lieutenant Henry Coustillac felt that his platoon's .50-caliber machine guns would do little against armor, and received the assistance of one section of 6-pounders from Battery A. D Company, 505th PIR, led the attack supported by American M4 Sherman tanks; however, the German armor soon disabled the Shermans, which had the added result of blocking the paratroopers' advance into Goronne.

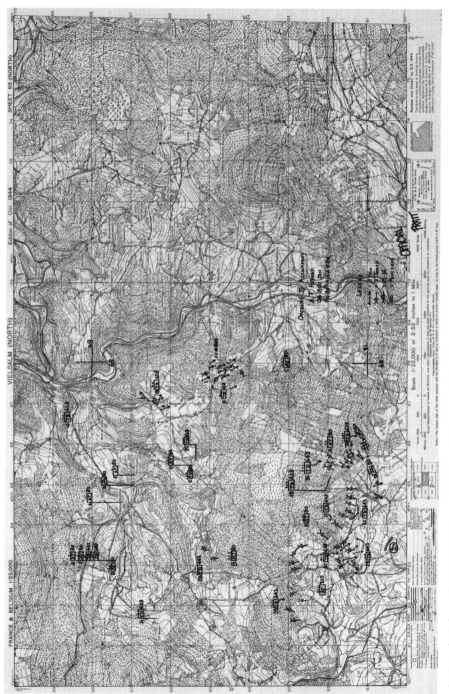

Anti-tank defense for 82nd Airborne Division, 6 January 1945. (Photo Courtesy of Thulai Van Maanen, and Micky and Joe Pratt)

144 • NEVER A DULL MOMENT

The battalion commander, the irrepressible Ben Vandervoort of Normandy and Holland fame, dispatched Coustillac to D Company's aid. The lieutenant conferred with the D Company commander, and the two officers determined that if D Company could seize a good firing position for the anti-tank cannon under Coustillac's command, the gunners would try to position the cannon to take the German tanks under fire. Soon after, Coustillac was killed by enemy mortar fire, which also wounded Lieutenant Colonel Vandervoort; however, the A Battery gunners eventually emplaced their weapon where they could open fire on the enemy tanks. The battalion history indicates that this 6-pounder may have been accompanied by an M36 from the 628th Tank Destroyer Battalion, but it does not state this explicitly. The 82nd Airborne Division anti-tank overlay for 6 January 1945 illustrates that a platoon from the 628th was in action with D Battery the previous day, so this is a valid assumption. In any event, the gunners succeeded in destroying the German armor, and D Company, 505th PIR, resumed its attack. E and F Companies of the 2nd Battalion followed in their wake and the paratroopers soon took their objective.[63]

The 80th AAA log recorded that "in general" the division experienced "much success in the attack." F Battery and the 628th Tank Destroyer Battalion reported destroying one enemy Mark IV tank, one half-track, and one anti-tank gun, while C Battery reported capturing 12 prisoners. E Battery lost a 57mm gun to enemy fire. In the days following, the battalion received its baggage, left behind in the rush of departing Camp Suippes the previous month. Rather than a cause for celebration, the rumor circulated among the troops that this meant they would not be pulled off the line anytime soon, but would remain in contact, thus necessitating the additional gear. Fortunately, like many soldiers' rumors, this proved unfounded. By 10 January, the log records the battalion would be relieved and moved to a rest area at Creppe, Belgium.[64] In the midst of the move, the battalion received a letter from Captain Arthur Kroos of all people, who wrote to inform his comrades that he was alive and well, but a prisoner of war at Stalag Luft I.

Gavin's performance during the opening stages of the Ardennes campaign is open to criticism, specifically charges that he elected to defend over too broad an area initially, thus making his lines vulnerable to penetration by German infiltrators, and that he failed to properly anchor his southern flank on either the 3rd Armored Division, or subsequently the 7th Armored Division. This failure provided the 2nd SS Panzer Division with an opportunity to cut off the 82nd Airborne Division, thus threatening the unit with isolation, if not destruction, and opening the way for the German invasion to drive on to Liège and then to Antwerp. On the contrary, Gavin's decisions, both in his choice of defensive tactics and how he defended the southern prong of his defensive "horseshoe," were the best he could make given the tactical situation from 17 to 25 December 1944.

During the Battle of the Bulge, the 82nd Airborne Division rushed from rest camps in France to the vicinity of Werbomont, Belgium, to establish a hasty defense against the surprise German attack that had launched the campaign. It faced three SS Panzer divisions and one *Volksgrenadier* division, consisting of the best SS armored formations and tasked with driving west, hard for the Belgian port of Antwerp. Other American units, reeling from the initial onslaught, were still retreating westward and relied on the XVIII Airborne, temporarily under Gavin's command, and the 82nd, to hold the crossings over the Salm River until they could safely cross.

Given the necessity of defending both Werbomont and the Salm River crossings, Gavin had to hold an incredibly broad front. The 82nd's defense was of necessity spread out and lacked depth. He had to rely on the tenacity of his paratroopers and glider men, and the aggressiveness of his subordinate commanders to stem the German advance. Gavin's faith in his troops was rewarded during the defense of the Salm River bridges, where his men held for days, denying the enemy the crossing points over the River Meuse. German elements repeatedly penetrated the American lines; however, the division held its positions and repeatedly sealed off these penetrations until ordered to withdraw.

Regarding his southern flank, Gavin could not properly tie in with the 3rd Armored Division because the tank division lacked the strength to establish defensive positions. The bulk of the 3rd Armored Division's combat power was committed to other tasks, and the small mobile task

146 • NEVER A DULL MOMENT

forces operating along Gavin's right were insufficient to create a proper, coordinated boundary between the two divisions. Likewise, when 7th Armored Division assumed responsibility from 3rd Armored Division for the sector southwest of the 82nd, they faced a fluid situation and could not conduct a proper relief. Gavin compensated for these issues by committing his division reserve to the southern flank when faced with German attacks along that line.

Gavin was faced with establishing a defense in support of an Allied offensive drive that had been shattered by an unexpected enemy counterattack across a broad front. He had no choice but to defend the line assigned to him. The defensive line was necessarily thin to cover the breadth of Gavin's assigned sector. Similarly, with no support along his southern flank, he took what steps he could to secure that line against German attacks. The task of covering a broad front impacted Gavin's ability to maintain a robust reserve, but preserved what amount of combat power he could to commit in moments of crisis. From 17 to 25 December 1944, Gavin played a bad hand as well as possible.

Once off the line, the officers and men of the 80th AAA set about refitting and refurbishing for their next mission, but they also took the opportunity to increase their knowledge about anti-tank warfare. Captain Al Neumann began examining captured German anti-tank weapons called "Panzerfausts."[65] The *Panzerfaust* was a more effective anti-tank weapon than the 2.36-inch rocket, or bazooka, primarily because its warhead consisted of a shaped charge, which proved far more effective against armor.[66] The shaped charge's effectiveness came from the fact that it produced a high-velocity jet capable of penetrating metal or concrete.[67] Neumann's initial experiments were carried out against a captured enemy tank, and he recorded the warhead was capable of penetrating armor 7 inches thick.[68] Neumann gave several classes on the weapon from 13 to 15 January, when he injured himself during a firing demonstration. He remained hospitalized until 29 January; however, the batteries all continued to train with the new weapon. General Gavin attended one demonstration on 14 January, before Neumann's injury.

Over the last two years, the 80th AAA Battalion had undergone a metamorphosis. From its beginnings at Camp Claiborne in September 1942, the unit had become an elite formation. Its officers understood its capabilities as well as those of the enemy, and could employ it under a variety of conditions to overcome enemy armor and air attacks to enable the infantry regiments to achieve their objectives. The men had displayed competence, valor, and endurance in battles from Italy, through France and Holland, and on to Belgium. Had the 80th AAA not learned from its formative experiences, made the necessary changes and adaptations, reinforced good combat habits, and developed high esprit de corps as a result, the unit would not have been ready for the crucible of the Battle of the Bulge.

The battalion stood poised to join the division's final drive into Germany.

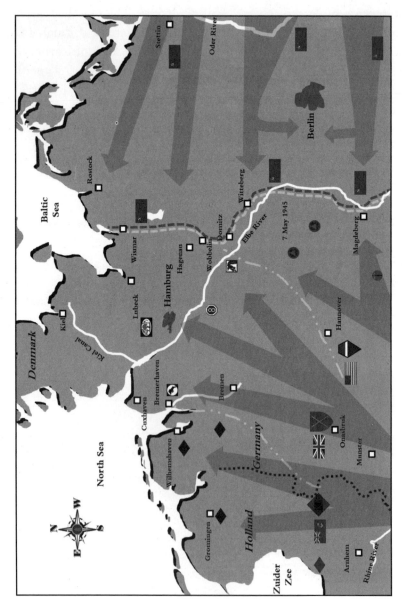

Entering Germany, 28 January–7 May 1945.

CHAPTER 6

Maintaining the Standard—Germany and VE Day

The entry in the battalion history entry for 13 January 1945 states, "B Battery alerted for possible move," but makes no further mention of any impending operation until over a week later. B Battery departed Creppe along with the 508th and 517th Parachute Infantry Regiments, en route to join an attachment of the 7th Armored Division. The B Battery gunners would support their former comrades from the fighting along the Salm to retake the Belgian town of St. Vith.[1] The 7th Armored had previously evacuated St. Vith in the face of the German offensive, and this operation provided the division an opportunity to avenge itself.

B Battery moved to an assembly area at Deidenburg, prepared to support the 508th PIR in the pending assault. The 7th Armored Division kicked off its drive westward that same day, taking the town of Born on 22 January and seizing St. Vith on the 23rd. Lieutenant Claire Jones and Private First Class Darrel P. Willoughby reported to the 508th PIR command post on 23 January to discuss emplacement of the battery's guns. The Germans mortared the position during this meeting. Willoughby recalled taking cover under a nearby truck. The enemy fire killed Lieutenant Jones and wounded two other Battery B men, Sergeant Louis Burnansky and Sergeant Estell Morris.[2] B Battery returned to Creppe after the St. Vith operation to join the rest of the battalion and prepare for the division's next big operation.[3]

150 • NEVER A DULL MOMENT

Over the previous month, the Allies had pushed back the Germans and repaired their lines. While the Germans had never fully "broken through" and made it into the Allied armies' rear areas, their attack had pushed deep into the Allied territory. This push resulted in the eponymous nickname for the Ardennes campaign, "the Battle of the Bulge." The disposition of German forces when marked on situation maps created a massive westward bulge in the Allied forward line of troops drawn on the charts. Once the German attack culminated and the the Allied armies began moving eastwards once more, the bulge gradually shrunk, until the American VII and VIII Corps made a junction at the town of Houffalize on 16 January, an action which fully restored the integrity of the Allied front.[4] With this action accomplished, the First Army troops temporarily under Field Marshal Montgomery reverted to General Omar Bradley's 12th Army Group, and Bradley began planning for a renewed campaign to enter Germany. Likewise, Montgomery had ideas about what move the Allies should next make.

Meanwhile Lieutenant General Brereton was eager to get XVIII Airborne Corps, along with the 82nd and 101st Airborne Divisions, off the line and back under his command. The First Allied Army remained largely dormant in the aftermath of *Market Garden*. No large-scale airborne drops occurred during the Ardennes fighting,[i] and Brereton sought to get his army a more active role. He proposed to Eisenhower and Supreme Headquarters Allied Expeditionary Force that if the airborne divisions could be pulled off the line to reconstitute then the First Allied Airborne Army would be able to plan a series of airborne operations, at the rate of one every 60 days that would restore strategic flexibility to the campaign in Western Europe.[5] General Ridgway disagreed with Brereton's proposal, stating that winter weather would preclude the successful execution of airborne operations, and that the time necessary for planning such operations was too lengthy to support the advance into Germany. Author Guy LoFaro notes that *Market Garden* illustrated the speed at which an airborne operation could be devised, prepared, and executed, and that cold conditions did not preclude the use of airborne

---

i   Although IX Troop Carrier Command did perform aerial resupply when the weather allowed.

forces. LoFaro points to General Gavin's assessment of Ridgway's personal motivations for an alternate explanation for Ridgway's objections. Gavin believed that Ridgway wanted to continue to lead XVIII Airborne Corps on the drive into Germany. Pulling the airborne units out of combat to refit for future operations would cost Ridgway that opportunity. There was no guarantee that Ridgway would command any future airborne mission devised by First Allied Airborne Army. Frederick Browning had commanded *Market Garden*, and Ridgway had had no combat role the previous September. Ridgway was determined to not allow that to occur again. His corps was in the field now, under First Army, and Ridgway would not have things any other way.[6]

Senior American commanders had their own reasons to be reluctant to release the airborne troops. Both the 82nd and 101st Airborne Divisions had established excellent records, and their troops continued to display valor, skill, and professionalism. Even though the divisions had fewer men, less firepower, and less tactical mobility than the standard U.S. Army infantry division,[ii] they successfully carried out any mission assigned. Neither Bradley, Hodges, nor any other commander was willing to surrender such fine divisions on the eve of a new campaign.[7]

In the event, Brereton did not get his way, and XVIII Airborne Corps and its subordinate airborne divisions remained in Belgium, allotted to Hodges's First Army for an offensive schedule to begin 28 January 1945. The next major airborne operation in the European Theater of Operations would not occur until March 1945, when First Allied Airborne Army conducted Operation *Varsity*, inserting airborne forces over the Rhine River. Interestingly, XVIII Airborne Corps and Ridgway exercised tactical command over the U.S. 17th Airborne and British 6th Airborne Divisions, which comprised the attacking force for that mission. Neither the 82nd nor 101st participated. But that lay in the future.[8] At the end of January 1945, the 82nd found itself deploying by truck rather than airplane for its next battle. The division occupied assembly areas near freshly liberated St Vith on 26 and 27 January, in anticipation of kicking off their attack on 28 January.

---

ii Although Ridgway proposed changes in the organization and equipment of airborne units to provide them with more organic firepower after Normandy. LoFaro, 501.

152 • NEVER A DULL MOMENT

The 80th AAA Battalion faced a new challenge as it deployed for the campaign—complacency. Having forced back the German offensive in the Ardennes, the men of the 80th experienced a growing feeling that the end of the war was approaching. While not like the heady days of August and September 1944, when the collapse of enemy resistance seemed imminent, it was still apparent to the troops that the German army was on the ropes. While it was doubtful that Germany would be able to resume a strategic offensive in the West after the Battle of the Bulge, the enemy was still capable of conducting a skillful retreat eastward, making the Allies pay for every yard of ground gained. This was especially true as the Allies entered Germany, where the enemy troops had the added motivation of defending homes and families. The 82nd troopers only needed to recall the stubbornness with which the Germans fought to defend Wyler during Operation *Market Garden* to get an idea of how tenacious the enemy defense could be. With the end of the war potentially in sight, the men of the 80th AAA had to continue to perform competently and courageously. If they lowered their guard, they put their lives and the lives of their friends in jeopardy.

General Hodges's First Army kicked off the 28 January attack as the main effort of Bradley's 12th Army Group. Hodges directed the V Corps and XVIII Airborne Corps to lead his advance, attacking abreast with the V Corps to the north and Ridgway's XVIII Airborne to the south. Ridgway entrusted the 82nd Airborne Division, along with the veteran 1st Infantry Division,[iii] to lead his Corps' advance. Given Ridgway's longtime association with and regard for the 82nd, this was no surprise to any member of the division.[9]

---

iii The 1st Infantry Division, known as "The Big Red One" due to the distinctive insignia worn by its soldiers, had an enviable reputation from World War I, much like the 82nd. The division's first World War II combat occurred during Operation *Torch* in French Morocco, through the end of the North African campaign. The 1st Infantry Division subsequently fought with distinction in Sicily, Normandy (spearheading the landing at Omaha Beach), and the Ardennes. "1st Infantry Division—Order of Battle of the United States Army—WWII—ETO." U.S. Army Center of Military History. history.army.mil, n.d., https://history.army.mil/documents/ETO-OB/1ID-eto-ob.htm.

Gavin's paratroopers attacked after first light on 28 January, moving quickly. The 325th GIR and the 504th PIR led the way, followed closely by the 505th PIR and the 508th PIR. German forces were initially surprised; however, both the 325th GIR and 504th PIR gained little ground that first day due to severe winter weather. Deep snow, frigid temperatures, and intermittent precipitation sapped the strength of the advancing troops, regardless of whether they engaged in any fighting. Simply advancing was a struggle, especially as the heavy snow cover could conceal German minefields and other obstacles. The hard going over rough terrain also created situations where the men would perspire while advancing, only for their perspiration to freeze during inevitable halts.[10] Climate and geography proved to be enemies as much as the Germans. Progress remained slow throughout the remainder of January. With the Germans now alerted that the Americans were on the move, their defense grew more robust and the weather remained a factor. By 1 February, General Eisenhower, dissatisfied with the lack of progress, cancelled the offensive and focused his attention on Field Marshal Montgomery's 21st Army Group's attacks to the north of 12th Army Group. Montgomery was now SHAEF's main effort for entering Germany.[11]

Despite Eisenhower's formal termination of the 12th Army offensive, the men in the field were in the middle of a battle, and a decision made at headquarters did not have an immediate effect on the fighting along the 82nd Airborne Division's and 1st Infantry Division's front. Both divisions remained in contact with the enemy and continued to advance as the situation allowed. By 1 February the weather improved, but the increased temperatures brought an increase in combat activity. B Battery reported firing 25 high-explosive rounds, resulting in the destruction of six enemy vehicles.[12] By the morning of 2 February, the division was poised to breach the Siegfried Line, with the 325th Glider Infantry in the van of the attack.[13]

1-325th GIR and 2-401st GIR (the regiment's 3rd Battalion from March 1944, as a result of a reorganization of airborne forces preparing for Operation *Neptune*)[14] attacked the villages of Neuhof and Udenbreth. Batteries E and F supported the 325th GIR's attack. 80th AAA Battalion historian Bob Burns recounts that Lieutenant Bill Fuller of D Battery noted in his diary that "325th caught hell in Neuberg."[15] The glider men fought house to house and pillbox to pillbox while under heavy German fire,

154 • NEVER A DULL MOMENT

with support from the 307th Airborne Engineer Battalion and the gunners of the 80th AAA. Captain Wayne Pierce, the acting executive officer of 1-325th GIR, wrote that "there were plenty of tracers flying through the air that morning so no doubt the 80th contributed much to that attack."[16]

Lieutenant Joseph A. P. Hart led the F Battery effort to support the 1-325th GIR and 2-401st GIR. He established firing positions in a nearby wood line and opened fire when the attack kicked off. His battery's fire drew the attention of the defending Germans, while also suppressing many of the enemy positions. This fire support relieved the pressure on the infantry sufficiently to allow them to maneuver against the German pillboxes. F Battery reported expending 4,000 rounds of ammunition during the fight, and capturing seven prisoners, while E Battery accounted for an additional three prisoners.[17]

The 504th PIR and 505th PIR both experienced similar success against their objectives. All three regiments held their ground against German counterattacks the following day. The doorway to Germany was now open, and the men of the 82nd Airborne made their way inside. Over the course of 4–6 February, the 99th Infantry Division arrived to relieve the 82nd Airborne. Its services were required elsewhere.[18]

The end of 12th Army Group's offensive and the focus on 21st Army Group resulted in Hodges's First Army reverting to a supporting role. However, supporting did not mean inactive. The U.S. Ninth Army, commanded by Lieutenant General William Simpson and operating under 21st Army Group, faced a challenge of crossing the low ground of the Roer River as part of his army's advance. The German army retained control of the Roer River dams, which they could destroy to flood the Roer and impede Simpson's movement eastward. Hodges had the assignment to assault the Hürtgen Forest to seize the dams and prevent their destruction. A similar operation in the fall of 1944 caused no end of heartache and thousands of American casualties, while the Roer dams remained in German hands.[19]

General Gavin received orders for the temporary assignment of his 82nd Airborne Division to the U.S. V Corps, under General Clarence Huebner, for the attack on the Hürtgen Forest. However, in the interest of speed, Huebner elected to commence his attack on the Hürtgen and the Roer dams on 5 February, before the arrival of Gavin's men. The attack did not succeed, and the Germans succeeded in destroying the floodgates of the dams, resulting in flooding that would delay Simpson's attack for weeks.[20] Despite this setback, V Corps' attacks had to continue in order to drive the German defenders eastward to set the conditions for 21st Army Group's and Ninth Army's eventual advance. The 82nd Airborne commenced its attacks into the Hürtgen Forest on 8 February and continued its attacks until relieved on 18 February.[21]

A and D Batteries, 80th AAA, supported the 505th Parachute Infantry throughout this period of combat, while one platoon of B Battery under Lieutenant William Cockrell went to the 508th PIR. The remnants of fierce fighting from the previous fall, which included the bodies of dead troops and wrecked, mangled equipment peeking through the snow cover, reminded Gavin of Dante's *Inferno*.[22] Corporal Carson Shirley of D Battery was more pragmatic, recalling that "The Hürtgen Forest was a mess."[23] Neither battery recorded any successful engagements with enemy armor or vehicles, capturing any prisoners, or large expenditures of ammunition. The terrain of the Hürtgen Forest did not lend itself to either the use of armor or the rapid maneuver of support weapons; thus, the batteries found themselves in regimental reserve. Lieutenant Colonel Singleton did, however, take the precaution of establishing the anti-tank command post near the Hürtgen to ensure proper coordination of the division's assets.[24] By 12 February, the battalion was out of the line and, along with the rest of the division over the next 10 days, moving back to rest camps in France.[25]

The 80th AAA Battalion's return to France was a welcome respite after the bitter cold of fighting along the Siegfried Line and in the Hürtgen Forest. With the exception of the brief respite at Creppe after the worst of the fighting in the Ardennes, the battalion had been in combat for two months since departing France the previous December. The men used the time to relax and unwind, while the inevitable round of refitting, training, and refurbishing equipment occupied their duty hours. On 7 March Lieutenant Colonel Singleton, accompanied by the division ordnance officer, observed the firing demonstration of a 57mm self-propelled anti-tank gun. The division artillery commander, Brigadier General Francis March, also attended the firing. The gunners firing the new weapon obtained "excellent" results, to the satisfaction of those officers in attendance.[26]

80th AAA glider men pose with a captured German AT gun in Belgium. (Photo courtesy of Bob Burns)

This new SP gun mounted the cannon directly on a jeep, eliminating the need to tow a cannon mounted on a separate gun carriage. The benefits to airborne operations were immediately obvious, as the weapon system would occupy less space on gliders for a combat assault, and gun crews would not have to go through the machinations of hitching and unhitching the gun carriage to the jeep when going into action or displacing to another position.[27] The new system was not without disadvantages, however. The weapon could not be maneuvered by a dismounted crew over rugged terrain in support of infantry, and if the jeep were damaged or suffered mechanical failure, the cannon could not simply be hitched to another available vehicle.

The battalion continued its regimen of classes, drill, and inspections interspersed with 48-hour passes and recreational activities until 30 March 1945. On that day, the battalion log notes all leaves and passes were cancelled, much to the chagrin of troops who were scheduled to depart for furloughs in England the following day, and the officers and

80th AAA Battalion troopers at work. (Photo courtesy of Bob Burns)

men prepared to move east. The 82nd Airborne Division was on tap to join the final push into Germany.[28]

Much had occurred over the past month while the 80th AAA and other elements of the 82nd rested and refit. The First Allied Airborne Army and Ridgway's XVIII Airborne Corps had conducted Operation *Varsity*, an airborne operation to seize a bridgehead over the Rhine, primarily executed by the U.S. 17th Airborne and the British 6th Airborne Divisions, and the Canadian 1st Parachute Battalion. *Varsity* was an element of the larger Operation *Plunder*, Field Marshal Montgomery's drive into northern Germany. *Varsity* went off on 24 March 1945, and its success paved the way for ground troops to cross the Rhine and continue 21st Army Group's eastward attack.[29]

Further south, U.S. III Corps, commanded by Major General John Miliken, under Hodges's First Army and Bradley's 12th Army Group,

158 • NEVER A DULL MOMENT

had seized the Ludendorff Bridge over the Rhine at the town of Remagen. From 7 to 25 March, Milikin pushed six divisions across the Rhine, spearheaded by the 9th Armored Division. Although the partially damaged Ludendorff Bridge collapsed on 17 March, by that point engineers had installed additional temporary bridges over the river and troops continued to cross.[30] With troops across the Rhine both in 21st Army Group's and 12th Army Group's areas of responsibility, SHAEF had an opportunity to execute a double envelopment of the enemy forces defending western Germany and trap as many troops as they could. As the Allies moved to exploit this opportunity, SHAEF ordered the 82nd and 101st Airborne Divisions to move to the west bank of the Rhine to act as an on-call, strategic reserve.[31]

The afternoon of 1 April, at 1500, the battalion's advance party under Lieutenant Worthington S. Telford departed for Mödrath, Germany, with the remainder of the battalion moving by truck and train to assemble at Lövenich, Germany, by the evening of 3 April.[32] The value that the 80th AAA Battalion command post placed on communication is inferred from the fact that Lieutenant Telford commanded the advanced party. Telford held the position of battalion communications officer, responsible for ensuring satisfactory radio and wire connectivity between the anti-tank command post, the division command post, and the batteries supporting the various regiments of the division. Selecting a site for the 80th AAA Battalion's headquarters that facilitated clear communications was a high priority. Lieutenant Telford and his men, especially at this point in the war, had the experience, skill, and technical assets to select a satisfactory location.[iv]

April 1945 was the critical time for the 80th AAA as they were involved in supporting the final the push into Germany, but at the

---

iv Lieutenant Telford's assignment as the battalion communications officer is listed in the unpublished history of the battalion provided to the author by Robert Burns, son of Edward Burns, D Battery, 80th AAA Battalion. The summary of Telford's responsibilities regarding the advanced party and the battalion command post are based on the author's experience as a U.S. Army signal officer, including two years as the communications officer of an airborne infantry battalion, one year as the communications officer for an armor battalion, and a year as the commander of a tactical signal company.

same time there was prevailing sense that the war was almost won. The 80th's discipline and experience were critical to maintaining superior performance while preserving the lives of the troops to the greatest extent possible.

SHAEF did not intend to commit either the 82nd or the 101st to the Rhine crossing but directed that they remain on the west bank of the river unless the operational situation demanded a rapid commitment of reinforcements. SHAEF's intent was to guard against a German riposte like the attacks in Belgium in December 1944. While such a surprise was highly unlikely, the Allies had very little manpower available to deal rapidly with such a contingency, so the 82nd and 101st moved westward from France.[33] The War Department anticipated relocating the two veteran airborne divisions to the Pacific in preparation for the invasion of Japan; thus, SHAEF did not want them to incur unnecessary casualties.[34] Despite the caution of the higher headquarters, Gavin encouraged aggressive reconnaissance and patrolling across the Rhine. He noted in his diary on 9 April that his division had responsibility for securing 35 miles of riverfront and 60 square miles of German territory. Gavin specifically described the tenacity of the German defenders on the opposite bank, recording that one patrol from the 504th PIR sustained 30–35 percent casualties patrolling across the Rhine on 6 April.[35]

The firing batteries of the 80th AAA occupied their positions along the Rhine two days earlier, on 4 April. Batteries A and F supported the 505th PIR, while C and D backed up the 504th. The 325th GIR received Battery E. By implication, B Battery remained in reserve, as the log makes no mention of it being assigned a mission with one of the infantry regiments. C Battery supported the 504th PIR on its 6 April foray across the Rhine, destroying an enemy armored anti-aircraft vehicle in the process. The log refers to this piece of equipment "as a flak wagon," implying that it was most like a self-propelled anti-aircraft gun, or SPAAG. The formal name for the SPAAG was the *Flakpanzer*.[36] Several variants of the weapon were produced; however, this late in the war it is likely this gun was a Flakpanzer IV variant, mounted on a Mark IV tank chassis and equipped with a 3.7cm cannon.[37]

From 5 to 12 April 1945, the battalion engaged in a type of warfare that was very different from the way the men were used to fighting.

160 • NEVER A DULL MOMENT

Rather than maneuvering on-line with the infantry and repelling attacks from enemy armor and low-flying fighters and fighter-bombers, the batteries engaged in a "defensive harassing mission" that provided the time and space for the batteries to dig in and establish fixed, battery-level command posts.[38] The fire missions between 6 and 11 April paint a picture of this manner of combat. In addition to the flak wagon accounted for by Battery C, the batteries recorded the following engagements:

- **6 April**—Battery F destroyed mortar positions across the RHINE with .50-cal. Fire
- **7 April**—Battery A with the 505th CT (combat team) fired seven rounds at a church steeple. They scored seven hits.
- **8 April**—A Battery reported that about six rounds of rifle fire was received by men who were guarding train cars on Cologne siding.
- **9 April**—Lieutenant Hart reported firing approximately 400 rounds of .50-caliber into Langel at a factory chimney.
- C Battery fired 40 rounds of APC and 24 rounds of HE at suspected CPs across the RHINE.
- E Battery fired three rounds of HE and one round of APC at a portable MG (machine-gun) nest across the Rhine.
- **10 April**—Battery A fired four rounds of APC and three rounds of SABOT at a suspected pillbox on the east bank of the Rhine. They also fired three rounds of HE harassing fire into the area. Three rounds of HE and eight rounds of APC plus 1,250 rounds of .30-caliber were fired at other targets across the Rhine. One petrol dump was set on fire, an enemy OP (outpost) destroyed, and a dugout received two direct hits with APC.
- **11 April**—D Battery fired .50-caliber at two MG positions on the east bank of the Rhine River.[39]

While the tone of the entries remains professional, there is an undertone of routine, if not boredom, over this week as the gunners engage targets across the Rhine. While this activity was not random destruction, it lacked the frenetic purpose of fighting tanks in the hedgerows of Normandy, seizing bridges in Holland, and fighting off the attacking SS Panzer divisions in Belgium. However, the tempo of operations picked up on 12 April.

Lieutenant Neil McNeill, who had a long-standing affiliation with the 505th Parachute Infantry, crossed the Rhine with a Lieutenant Saunders from that regiment, to retrieve two wounded children. The pair crossed once more that day and captured seven Germans, whom they brought back over to the 82nd's lines. The following day the officers repeated the performance and brought in an additional six prisoners and a high-value captive, identified in the battalion log only as "a NAZI leader."[40] Two towns across the Rhine also surrendered on 13 April, Lülsdorf and Niederkassel. The news also came to the battalion that the President of the United States was dead. The unit held a ceremony in honor of the fallen commander in chief on 14 April 1945.[41] The Allied drive was advancing further east and there was less need for the 82nd to maintain its aggressive patrolling along the Rhine. Soon, the 82nd Airborne Division began to assume the functions of an occupying force, responsible for law and order and civil administration as the American military took control of German territory.[42] The division notified the 80th AAA Battalion that all batteries except for one were to stand down from the defensive/harassing mission along the Rhine and "prepare for a police mission."[43] The battalion selected C Battery to maintain its combat support mission while the remainder prepared for their new roles; however, by 16 April all batteries had transitioned to occupation duty.

Thus began a strange period of transition for the 80th. The United States of America and Nazi Germany remained at war; however, the fighting had moved eastward, but the 80th AAA did not follow the sound of the guns. The gunners now found themselves inspecting passes, processing displaced persons, and rounding up German soldiers fleeing west to ensure they were not captured by the advancing Russians. Additionally, a very real concern emerged about the existence of Nazi guerrilla forces in the areas where the 82nd Airborne Division performed its occupation duties. Called "Werewolves," these units supposedly consisted of a nucleus of trained resistance fighters who would foment insurgency against the occupying Allies, like the cells created by the French and Dutch resistance against Nazi occupation earlier in the war.[44] The threat of these forces was more apparent than real, and the Werewolves

162 • NEVER A DULL MOMENT

constituted more of a propaganda threat that preyed upon the minds of the Allies than a significant resistance organization.[45]

The battalion assigned each battery a town in which to conduct patrol and security duties on 16 April. Almost immediately, the troops ran across refugees from a variety of European countries, displaced Germans who had lost their homes, and German soldiers either trying to avoid capture or actively surrendering. The troops had their hands full inspecting documents, processing enemy soldiers as prisoners of war, and escorting refugees and the homeless to shelter in what were termed "displaced persons camps." They also handled a variety of law enforcement tasks, such as arresting Germans who were found abroad after curfew or in possession of American military rations. The latter offense was evidence of potential black marketing.[46] Given the food scarcity many displaced persons experienced this might seem unnecessarily harsh, as people must eat to survive. However, unregulated commerce could wreak havoc with the economy, encourage fraternization, which commanders forbid as a state of war still existed between the United States and Germany, and potentially cause an increase in violent crime among the civilian population.

On 20 April, the commanding officer of the 505th Parachute Infantry Regiment, Colonel William Ekman, along with his operations officer, visited the 80th AAA command post to discuss a pending combat operation. However, the actual operation was to assist the 505th PIR in conducting house-to-house searches for illegal weapons or other contraband.[47] The battalion continued to execute patrolling and security functions until it received orders to relocate to the town of Rheinbach on 22 April. Orders for a subsequent combat mission came early on 25 April, after a visit from the 82nd's assistant division commander, Brigadier General Ira Swift. After an early battery commanders' meeting, an advanced party under Captain William Pratt departed for Oitzendorf, Germany. The batteries underwent preparations for the move, spent time on the anti-tank range between 26 and 27 April, and departed for Oitzendorf on the 28th.

The impetus for this move was concern from SHAEF headquarters about the rapidly advancing Russian army. Concern existed that the

MAINTAINING THE STANDARD • 163

Russians could occupy Denmark, and General Eisenhower wanted to ensure that their path would be blocked by units of the Allied Expeditionary Force. Field Marshal Montgomery's 21st Army Group had operational responsibility for this mission, but to ensure rapid execution SHAEF assigned Ridgway's XVIII Airborne Corps for the role. The 82nd Airborne, along with the British 6th Airborne Division, and U.S. 7th Armored and 8th Infantry Divisions, fell under XVIII Airborne Corps for the mission. By 29 April, the 80th AAA Battalion staged at Oitzendorf and on the 30th supported the crossing of the Elbe River, with the 505th PIR in the lead. The 82nd would then head east to make contact with the Russians before they could turn north for a drive to Denmark.[48]

C Battery crossed the Elbe with the 504th Parachute Infantry on 30 April. Private First Class Ray Fary recalls making the crossing and having to deal with booby traps left by the retreating German troops. The bridgehead across the river was heavily congested with advancing Americans, and the improvised mechanical ambushes found several victims. Fary stated that once over on the eastern side of the Elbe a loud explosion occurred further up the column, bringing forward movement to a halt. Once the troops moved out, they passed a destroyed American vehicle, struck by a dynamite charge left by the enemy. The explosion killed eight soldiers of the 8th Infantry Division. Reports circulated that another vehicle suffered a similar fate, killing two more soldiers. The young C Battery gunner saw grim reminders of the incidents along the roadside as C Battery continued its advance.[49]

General Gavin noted in his memoirs that the charges planted by the defending Germans were actually magnetic sea mines. Gavin recalled that "the mines were planted along the roads, preset to detonate when a specific number of vehicles passed." Gavin witnessed the first detonation, when a jeep that had just crossed the river detonated a mine, the resulting explosion hurling the vehicle high enough to turn in the air several times. Gavin stated he had never seen anything like that explosion previously in the war.[50]

While the 82nd Airborne and 8th Infantry Divisions moved eastward, the British 6th Airborne Division secured the frontiers of Denmark

164 • NEVER A DULL MOMENT

through a rapid advance to the Baltic by 2 May. The British troops ensured the Russians would be unable to occupy the tiny country by mere hours.[51] Days before, Hitler had committed suicide as the Russian army brought the city of Berlin down around his head, and Grossadmiral Karl Dönitz assumed leadership of the German Reich.

By 1 May, the entire 80th AAA Battalion was over the Elbe and establishing the anti-tank command post and battery command posts in towns throughout the region. Over the course of 2 and 3 May, the 80th continued to advance, having "eaten three meals in three different cities the day before," as noted in the battalion log.[52] The 82nd Airborne Division advanced at a terrific rate as organized resistance collapsed. D and B Batteries reported clearing the town of Göhlen and assisting in processing over 500 enemy prisoners, primarily German and Hungarian, who were set on surrendering to anyone but the Russians.[53] This processing of prisoners continued as the division approached the town of Ludwigslust, where General Kurt von Tippelskirch, commanding general of the German 21st Army Group, met with Gavin to discuss the formal surrender of German forces. In practical terms, the surrender had already begun, as the 82nd troopers were actively rounding up German troops who, in Gavin's words, "wanted to surrender." At this point, the 82nd had advanced 36 miles from its crossing points along the Elbe and captured approximately 100,000 prisoners.[54]

On 3 May, reconnaissance elements from the 82nd Airborne reported making contact with Russian forces in the town of Grabow, and by 5 May the batteries of the 80th AAA stood down for their support assignments with the regimental combat teams, and established bivouacs near the battalion command post at Göhlen. The troops transitioned once again to the policing, security, and patrolling functions they had performed earlier along the Rhine.[55]

During this period, the 505th PIR Infantry made a horrifying discovery. Near the village of Wöbbelin, they uncovered a concentration camp. The camp was for political prisoners, evacuated from camps in the east as the Russians overran their locations. While not specifically an extermination camp equipped with the apparatus for industrial murder, Wöbbelin remained a horrifying place. General Gavin described it thus: "One could smell the Wobelein [sic] Concentration Camp before seeing it … Living skeletons were scattered about, the dead distinguishable from the living only by the blue-black color of their skin compared to the somewhat greenish skin, taut over the bony frames of the living. There were hundreds of dead about the grounds."[56]

Captain Philip Hannan, a Catholic chaplain in the 505th PIR, did what he could to organize assistance for the prisoners, an effort which eventually blossomed into the division arranging for billeting for the living in an airfield hangar and the administration of intravenous feeding once it became apparent that the inmates could not yet stomach solid food. The local Nazi mayor had, according to Gavin, decided not to distribute scarce foodstuffs to the political prisoners of Wöbbelin.[57] Gavin ensured the townspeople of Ludwigslust were made to properly bury the dead, and held a funeral service for the deceased victims, requiring all townspeople to participate. Colonel Singleton ordered the men of the 80th to view the camp on 6 May, in response to a directive from General Gavin that as many men of the division as possible make the visit. The battalion history described the scene as an "almost unbelievable atrocity."[58] Sergeant James Fellers of C Battery could not comprehend the horror when he witnessed "bodies stacked like cordwood this way and that" or learned that some prisoners were made to lie on beds of barbed wire.[59] The following day, the 80th AAA Battalion and the rest of the division learned that the German armed forces had officially surrendered.

The 80th AAA Battalion greeted an unanticipated but welcome visitor to the command post on 7 May 1945, Captain Arthur Kroos, freshly released from captivity.[60] He and his men endured much after the Germans shot down their aircraft on 18 September 1944, or more specifically shot down the C-47 towing their aircraft.[61] Kroos and his men departed England from Beverton airfield en route to Landing Zone "N," south of Groesbeek, with the mission of making their way to Grave upon landing. Kroos was accompanied by Sergeant John F. Bonk and Private First Class William V. Smurr.[v] Bonk's role in Battery B was that

---

v   Kroos recalls Bonk as a staff sergeant and Smurr as a corporal; however, the roster of the 80th AAA Battalion records their ranks as sergeant and private first class, respectively. Kroos's memoir and 80th Airborne AA Unit Roster, 16 September 2006.

Taken at around the time the 80th visited, this photo shows townspeople burying the deceased victims of Wöbbelin concentration camp. (Photo courtesy of Getty Images)

of reconnaissance sergeant, while Smurr acted as Kroos's driver and radio operator. Their glider, piloted by Second Lieutenant George Hall, made up part of serial 50, of which Kroos acted as serial commander.

The C-47 towing Hall's glider received damage to its left wing from enemy anti-aircraft fire as it approached the coast of Holland, and Hall made the decision to cut free from the tow rope, as the tug plane veered off course. This decision ensured the glider would not make Landing Zone "N" but rather land on one of fortified islands just off Holland's coast. Kroos credits Hall with making as good as possible a landing. The German occupiers covered any terrain suitable for a glider landing with a variety of obstacles, including 10-foot-tall poles with barbed wire suspended between them.[vi] Hall managed to not hit any poles on the

---

vi Kroos describes the obstacle with the colloquial nickname "Rommel's Asparagus" for similar obstacles emplaced by the Germans along the French coast prior to the June 1944 D-Day invasion.

descent; however, he could not avoid the wires. The glider sustained significant damage, but the men remained unharmed. The German defenders immediately took the glider under fire.

The four men onboard got away from the aircraft immediately, seeking the protection of a handy ditch. Kroos recalls that he could locate the source of the enemy fire, but the small group could not remain where they were. He dispatched Smurr to return to the downed glider to retrieve weapons and anything else of use and then burn the aircraft, while Sergeant Bonk covered his movement. Kroos and Hall would scout about to gain any information they could on their whereabouts and enemy strength. The two men soon located a farm, and, leaving Hall to observe the buildings, Kroos returned to retrieve his soldiers. He found Bonk but could not locate Smurr until after exchanging fire with a German, whom Kroos believes he hit. Smurr eventually reported that he took additional fire on his return to the downed aircraft and was unable to complete his mission. Kroos then led the private first class back to Hall and Bonk.

By this point it was mid-afternoon on 18 September, and the small party captured a lone German soldier they found cycling between posts. With his help they navigated a minefield and passed within a quarter-mile of the crash site of the C-47 which had towed them to Holland. British aircraft were strafing the fuselage to destroy anything of value it may have contained. Kroos later learned the co-pilot was killed but the remainder of the crew were taken prisoner.

The small patrol continued moving and came across a German outpost consisting of an officers' mess and what appeared to be a headquarters building. The post was deserted, with the exception of what Kroos described as "a few German soldiers ... [who] disappeared without shooting when they saw us." Kroos surmised the post was for anti-aircraft troops manning the flak positions on the island. The air armada for Operation *Market* continued to pass overhead, and it seemed all available guns were opening fire on the passing planes. The Americans destroyed what they could and then talked over their next step.

Kroos elected to take cover in the minefield encircling the German position, deciding that nobody would think to look for them there. The troops remained there until dark when they resumed their odyssey, about

168 • NEVER A DULL MOMENT

2200 that night. They eventually made their way to another farmhouse, owned by a family called Quandt, where they hid in the barn's hayloft. Kroos made contact with the Quandt family the following day and learned that it would be difficult to escape to the mainland. The Germans had confiscated all boats, and a 600-man force occupied the island. The Quandts arranged for Captain Kroos to speak with a member of the Dutch underground, who promised to arrange a different hiding location for the Americans. They remained with the Quandts for another day, during which their German prisoner managed to escape. This placed both the Quandts and Kroos's party in danger, and he ordered his men to depart immediately.

Due to the difficult, flooded terrain of the island, the glider men did not get far, when they spotted a familiar vehicle. It was Kroos's jeep, obviously recovered from the crashed glider by the Germans. Kroos directed his men to take cover and waited for the jeep to approach their positions. They then opened fire on the Germans. The jeep ground to a halt, with one occupant returning fire. After a five-minute gun battle, the Americans gained the upper hand and broke contact. They moved for a quarter-mile when they made contact with a German squad. By this point, Kroos and his small band were on a small peninsula and surrounded on water on three sides. They had no choice but to fight. Kroos positioned his men around a nearby building and they opened fire when the Germans approached within 300 yards. After a 45-minute fight, during which the Germans brought up a machine gun to suppress the Americans, Kroos took stock of the situation. His men were out of ammunition and the Germans had fire superiority. Kroos elected to surrender. They threw their remaining gear into the water to keep it from the Germans and walked out of their defensive positions, hands in the air.

The Germans brought the Americans back to the outpost ransacked by Kroos and his men previously, searched them, and then locked them in an ammunition bunker overnight. The following afternoon they were fed a scant meal of cabbage soup and then escorted to the coast where they were placed in the hold of a ship and evacuated to the mainland. Kroos was distraught to learn that Mrs. Quandt and one her neighbors had been captured by the Germans as well. The farmer's wife was on the boat and Kroos tried to explain the situation to her as best he could. Eventually the Germans separated the Americans and evacuated them over a period of days to Germany. At Frankfurt, Kroos and his men were separated, and Kroos was interrogated and processed. He eventually found himself assigned to Stalag Luft I, a camp for downed American fliers. Kroos was one of only four infantry officers in the camp.

The most remarkable aspect of Kroos's captivity, as he relates in letters he sent to his wife Patricia, is how unremarkable it was. The tone of his letters home is upbeat, but the sense that time weighed heavily on the captive Americans permeates each one. He addressed the fact that rations could be scarce (he lost 60 pounds as a prisoner of war), but the shortage of food does not seem to be a result of a deliberate policy of starvation. Kroos himself noted that the prisoners were "certainly far from starving." Compared to the conditions under which prisoners of Imperial Japan suffered, the captives in Stalag Luft I were fortunate.[vii]

Kroos remained a prisoner from 9 October 1944 to 4 May 1945, when Russians liberated the prisoner-of-war camp. Kroos recounts that a Russian officer approached Stalag Luft I, riding a horse and, through an interpreter, instructed the prisoners to tear down the stockade around the camp as they were no longer German prisoners. The prisoners remained in the camp but were now at liberty to move about as they pleased.

Kroos soon had a tremendous stroke of luck. Members of the 82nd Airborne staff happened to be coordinating with the Russian officers responsible for the area that included Stalag Luft I. Upon learning that the 82nd Airborne Division was close by, Kroos immediately made

---

vii Western captives of the Japanese recorded significant weight loss and malnutrition during World War II. This weight loss came from a combination of labor conditions, general availability of food for all members of Japanese society during the war, cultural dietary differences, and Japanese attitudes toward prisoners. However, there does not seem to be a policy of deliberately denying food to prisoners by either Nazi Germany or Imperial Japan. Tackikawa Kyoichi, "The Treatment of Prisoners of War by the Imperial Japanese Army and Navy Focusing on the Pacific War," n.d., https://www.nids.mod.go.jp/english/publication/kiyo/pdf/2008/bulletin_e2008_5.pdf.

170 • NEVER A DULL MOMENT

his way to the camp headquarters and found the party from the 82nd, which included the division judge advocate general, a Colonel Moss, who exclaimed upon seeing the captain, "Kroos you S.O.B., I thought you were dead!" Moss arranged for Kroos to accompany the party back to American lines. Kroos had a true homecoming after visiting the 80th AAA, spending time with Generals Ridgway and Gavin, as well as comrades from his time as Ridgway's aide. He eventually made his way home to Wisconsin via Paris, New York, and Florida, before taking his discharge at Camp McCoy.

Kroos remained in touch with General Ridgway, who in a letter dated 1985, recalled the valor Kroos displayed in Normandy, over 40 years later.

Russell Weigley described the events of late April and early May 1945 in Germany as "the simple dissolution of resistance,"[62] as enemy formations melted away and the sight of a German soldier no longer meant impending combat to American troops.[63] German forces fighting in Italy surrendered on 29 April, and by 7 May Germany surrendered unconditionally on both its Western Front to the Supreme Allied Expeditionary Force and on its Eastern Front to the Russians, effective 2301 local time, 8 May 1945. The 80th AAA Battalion History declared on 9 May, "THIS IS IT—V E DAY." The war in Europe had ended.[64]

Sustaining a high level of professionalism remained important after the shooting stopped in May 1945 as the 80th AAA Battalion assisted in the occupation of Germany, resettlement of refugees and civilians, and the processing of prisoners of war. The men of the 80th AAA Battalion learned that a fine line existed between someone who was an enemy combatant and a refugee as they conducted checkpoints, patrols, and security operations.

The battalion continued to execute its security tasks throughout May and into June 1945. The batteries performed patrols, conducted inspections, and participated in athletic competitions. The troops also maintained their military skills, with the batteries sustaining their capabilities as glider troops through practice flights at the Ludwigslust airfield. The war was not over, a point driven home by a mandatory viewing for all troops of the War Department film entitled *Two Down, One to Go* on 9 May. Their routine was occasionally punctuated by the excitement of a small number of officers and men receiving the news that they had been selected to return to the United States. At times when manning roadblocks the gunners would come across former SS troops or concentration camp guards attempting to blend in with the crowds of refugees that continued to fill the roads. When the troopers identified such men, they were quickly detained, processed, and turned over to the Army Counter-Intelligence Corps. C Battery's Sergeant Fellers related that not all was military efficiency, though. He made the point that, despite orders to "stop all traffic and check everyone's papers," his inability to understand German limited his effectiveness. Fellers resorted to the expedient of waving through anyone he stopped who showed him papers of any kind.[65]

At 1200, 2 June 1945, British troops formally relieved the 80th AAA Battalion of its duties and the troops prepared to depart Germany for Camp Chicago in Laon, France. The battalion departed on 3 June via motor convoy and traveled via Belgium to France, arriving on the early morning of 5 June.[66]

The big question on everyone's mind was "what's next?" Germany had surrendered, but the United States was still fighting Imperial Japan in the Pacific. Would the 82nd Airborne refit for combat in the Far East? Would they remain in Europe as an army of occupation as had occurred at the end of World War I? Or, maybe, they'd be allowed to go home. But only if they had the points.[viii]

Points were on almost everyone's mind. An article appeared in *Stars and Stripes* newspaper on 11 May 1945, a periodical for servicemen by servicemen, explaining what the headline called the "G.I. Discharge Plan" and declaring the bulk of the troops would be out of Europe within a year. The article went on to explain that every soldier serving would be assigned an Adjusted Rating Score. The men would receive credit for the length of their military service, how much time they spent overseas, their combat service (calculated by whether they received a combat

---

viii Dr. Jeff Frost maintains a wonderful tribute blog to his 82nd Airborne Division ancestor William A. Clark, who served in every campaign with the division. His explanation of William Clark's personal experience with the point system is worth reading in full. Jeff Clark, "The Postwar Points Discharge Plan," Tribute to an 82nd Airborne Veteran, May 13, 2014, https://ww2tribute.blogspot.com/2014/05/.

172 • NEVER A DULL MOMENT

decoration as well as campaign participation credit), and whether they had dependent children. A cumulative total of 85 points became the gold standard. If a soldier had that many points or more, they were high priority for returning to the United States for discharge.[67]

Men received a point for every month spent in the Army, calculated from September 1940, and an additional point for every month spent overseas. A combat decoration or battle participation credit (determined from a list created by the War Department, not based on the number of individual fights in which a soldier may have participated) was worth five points apiece, and a dependent child under 18 was worth 12 points, with a limit of three children total. The 82nd Airborne Division participated in six official campaigns while abroad—Sicily, Naples–Foggia, Normandy, Rhineland, Ardennes, and Central Europe—and thus any trooper who had fought from Sicily to the Elbe qualified for 30 points toward their Adjusted Rating Score. Regardless of what came next for the division, it was clear that it would soon lose its most experienced men.[68]

General Gavin revealed what would become of the 82nd Airborne Division at a review on 9 June 1945. The 82nd would head to Berlin as an occupation force. Details would be forthcoming, but in the meantime the men would focus on continued training and inspections, with leaders granting the troops a liberal number of leaves and passes to tour the French capital of Paris. But if the division was to occupy Berlin, how was it to make up for the loss of its high-point troops?

This answer proved simple. The 17th Airborne Division would be departing the European Theater of Operations, and it contained a higher ratio of low-point men, having deployed overseas in late 1944, two years behind the 82nd Airborne Division, and having participated in fewer campaigns. The high-point men of the 82nd would transfer to the 17th Airborne Division for the return home, and the low-point men of the 17th would head to Berlin as new members of the 82nd.[69] For the men in the 80th AAA Battalion going home, this meant a transfer to the 155th AAA Battalion. Lieutenant Colonel Singleton would depart the 80th to assume command of the 155th, while Lieutenant Colonel John W. Paddock would take Singleton's place at the head of the 80th on 25 June.[70]

The rounds of training, inspections, and passes continued for the next seven weeks, with the added activity of preparing to move the battalion to Berlin. New types of classes appeared on the training schedule, with less time spent on the anti-tank range and more time dedicated to subjects such as riot duty, interior guard, and close-order drill. On 30 July, the advanced party of the 80th AAA departed for Berlin, closely followed by the main body on 11 August. The trip back to Germany was marred by the loss of Private First Class Edward Morrissey, listed in the battalion as having fallen from the train en route to Berlin. The battalion arrived in Berlin on 16 August 1945, prepared to assume its role as an occupation force. It immediately assumed a set of guard posts from the 325th Glider Infantry.[71]

The 82nd Airborne Division maintained its role as an occupation force until 18 November. The routine of peacetime soldiering, even in the occupied capital of a conquered enemy, comes through in the later entries of the 80th AAA Battalion History, with the standard entry "Battalion carried out regular garrison and guard duties" appearing repeatedly. The division performed its mission with the same dedication and attention to detail with which it performed its combat role, and formally turned its duties over to the 78th Infantry Division on 15 November 1945. Three days later, the 80th AAA departed for Camp Oklahoma City, near Rheims, France.[72]

C Battery, 80th AAA Battalion, Germany, 1945. Note the bloused jump boots. (Photo courtesy of the Stark Family)

174 • NEVER A DULL MOMENT

Back in France, the point system became of interest to the men of the 80th AAA Battalion once more. Japan had surrendered the previous September, after President Truman's decision to order the use of atomic weapons on the cities of Hiroshima and Nagasaki, to preclude invading the Japanese mainland. With the end of the War in the Pacific, the War Department accelerated demobilization, and the score a man needed to return home fell to 60 points. Men with fewer than 60 points would receive assignment to the 101st Airborne Division; however, the 101st received word that it would be placed on inactive status on 30 November 1945.[ix] Men with 60 or more points would be sent to other units for return to the United States. General Gavin appealed to his troops with more than the required number of points to remain with the division, revealing that the 82nd was returning to the United States as a unit, to be honored with a parade in New York City in early 1946. To Gavin's surprise, many 60-point men elected to leave the division to return home earlier. Men with fewer than 60 points from the 101st Airborne Division arrived at the 82nd's camp on 29 November to take the place of those who had departed.

The 80th Airborne Anti-Aircraft Artillery Battalion and the 82nd Airborne Division would return to the United States to march up New York City's 5th Avenue in January 1946. The final entry of the battalion history reads, "The unit moved through France to England where they were to board the QUEEN MARY home."[73]

---

ix   Originally the War Department had selected the 101st Airborne Division to remain on active status and the 82nd was to be deactivated in Europe. Gavin mobilized official support by asking General Ridgway to lobby the Chief of Staff of the Army on the 82nd's behalf and public support through his contacts with the press for the decision to be overturned.

82nd Airborne Division, New York City Victory Parade, January 1946. (Photo courtesy of Getty Images)

Afterword

Few of the men of the 80th Airborne Anti-Aircraft Battalion were professional soldiers. They came forward when their country called, did their duty as they saw it, and returned home as soon as they could after completing the job they set out accomplish. But in doing so, they displayed the hallmarks of true professionals. In training they dealt with every surprise the Army could throw at them, from their unexpected designation as glider troops with the attendant hazards of such duty, to the indifference if not actual hostility displayed by the paratroopers of their own division. They gained proficiency with the technical aspects of their weapons, developed tactics for deploying them in combat, and learned the intricacies of loading and lashing required to transport them by glider. When it left the United States for North Africa, the 80th AAA Battalion was a cohesive team.

In North Africa, Sicily, and Italy, the officers and men of the 80th realized that what they learned in training was not enough. Once overseas, they sought to learn from the practical experience of others so they would have a chance to defeat German armor once they were in battle. They took advantage of their relationship with veteran British units to obtain heavier firepower and created new battery organizations to employ it. More importantly, they learned from the experiences of Sicily and Italy that they needed to get their firepower to the battlefield as quickly as they could if they were to make any contribution to the fight.

They arrived earlier to the fight in Normandy, bringing their heavier firepower, and it had the desired effect on the enemy. However, they also learned that the battlefield evolved, and they needed to adapt with it. Thus, by the time they went to Holland they understood they faced a larger threat from enemy armor than enemy airplanes and adjusted accordingly, converting one battery from anti-aircraft to anti-tank. These adjustments paid off, and the men fought effectively, applying the hard-won knowledge, and turning it into a deadly combat routine.

By the time they reached Belgium, the men of the 80th were veterans and it showed. They had the skill and experience to meet the challenges of a surprise attack, terrible weather, and large concentrations of enemy armor, and prevail. Belgium is where the men of the 80th showed they were professional soldiers, even if they did not consider themselves such. They maintained this standard as they entered Germany in the final days of the war, shifting from a combat role to perform the duties of an occupation and security force with little if any loss of efficiency. From its formation in 1942 to its deactivation in 1946, the 80th Airborne Anti-Aircraft Artillery Battalion demonstrated how to train, fight, and win.

APPENDIX A

80th Airborne Anti-Aircraft Artillery Battalion Distinguished Service Cross Recipients[1]

The Distinguished Service Cross is awarded to a person who, while serving in any capacity with the Army, distinguished himself or herself by extraordinary heroism not justifying the award of a Medal of Honor; while engaged in an action against an enemy of the United States; while engaged in military operations involving conflict with an opposing or foreign force; or while serving with friendly foreign forces engaged in an armed conflict against an opposing armed force in which the United States is not a belligerent party. The act or acts of heroism must have been so notable and have involved risk of life so extraordinary as to set the individual apart from their comrades.[2]

First Lieutenant Jake L. Wertich

Headquarters, European Theater of Operations, United States Army
Award of the Distinguished Service Cross

First Lieutenant Jake L. Wertich, 0-01304472, Coast Artillery Corps, United States Army, for extraordinary heroism in connection with the

180 • NEVER A DULL MOMENT

military operations against an armed enemy on 21 December 1944 at Trois Ponts, Belgium.

When an enemy attack caused the forward troops to withdraw, Lt. Wertich refused to be driven from his gun. When all members of his crew were killed or wounded, he manned his gun himself, covering the withdrawal of the company from the hill. Even when the enemy over-ran his position, Lt. Wertich remained at his gun, thereby keeping the enemy tanks out of position and assuring success of the maneuver. His gallant action saved the lives of many members of his battalion and aided materially in repulsing a strong enemy attack [that] had the city of Liege, Belgium, as it objective.

Lt. Wertich is known to have knocked out two enemy tanks in the action which cost him his life. His personal bravery, invincible courage and self-sacrifice were an inspiration to those around him in keeping with the highest traditions of the United States Army.

First Sergeant Richard E. Rider

Headquarters, European Theater of Operations, United States Army
Award of the Distinguished Service Cross

By direction of the President, under the provisions of AR 600-45, 22 September 1943, as amended, the Distinguished-Service Cross is awarded to:

First Sergeant Richard E. Rider (then Staff Sergeant) (Army Serial No. 35500015), Coast Artillery Corps, United States Army, for extraordinary heroism in combat on 13 June 1944, near Baupte, Normandy, while accompanying a combat patrol of parachute infantry regiment. With utter disregard for his own personal safety, First Sergeant Rider exposed himself fearlessly to enemy machine-gun and cannon fire in order to direct accurately the fire of his antitank guns. When one gun was attacked by five enemy tanks, First Sergeant Rider personally took over from the gunner and directed fire against the approaching enemy. The first tank was destroyed immediately, as were the second and third in rapid succession. The other two tanks retreated to a position in less dangerous territory.

First Sergeant Rider followed, placing his gun in a location from which he could deliver destructive fire. From this position he destroyed both remaining tanks, and the German crew were destroyed by our infantry.

By his fearless attention to the mission, he was able to destroy completely a serious enemy tank threat, and his determination and enthusiasm supported him to pursue and destroy the retreating tanks. His courage and force before the entire patrol were of high standards and reflect the highest credit upon the armed forces of the United States. Entered military service from Ohio.

Corporal Stokes M. Taylor

Headquarters, European Theater of Operations, United States Army
Award of the Distinguished Service Cross

Corporal Stokes M. Taylor, 34192689, Coast Artillery Corps, United States Army, for extraordinary heroism in connection with the military operations against an armed enemy near Trois Ponts, Belgium on 21 December 1944.

Corporal Taylor's anti-tank squad was in position on a hill covering the road leading into Trois Ponts, Belgium. At approximately 1400 hours on 21 December 1944, the enemy launched a savage attack against the hill. Corporal Taylor's gun was put out of action by enemy fire during this enemy advance. Seizing a Browning Automatic Rifle and ammunition, Corporal Taylor ordered his men to fall back, while he took up a position on the road and covered their withdrawal by fire. With complete disregard for his personal safety, and with full knowledge of the overwhelming odds against him, Corporal Taylor raked the hillside with intense and accurate fire which prevented the enemy from gaining the edge of the woods to fire on his anti-tank squad as they effected their withdrawal. After his ammunition was exhausted, Corporal Taylor was seen to be hit by enemy rifle fire.

His unfailing courage and leadership were in keeping with the highest traditions of the United States Army and won the admiration and respect of all who witnessed his actions. Entered military service from Tennessee.

APPENDIX B

The Combat Infantryman's Badge

During World War II the Chief of Staff of the United States Army, George C. Marshall, himself an old infantryman, wanted a special distinction awarded to the soldiers of the infantry in recognition of the hardships they endured and the casualties they sustained when compared with other branches of the Army. Airmen who incurred great risks qualified for the Air Medal, and Marshall desired a similar award for the infantry. Eventually, in 1943, the War Department published WD Circular 269-1943 authorizing the Combat Infantryman Badge.[1]

The purpose of the badge was to recognize "exemplary conduct in action against the enemy." Further War Department instructions stated that only infantrymen serving in infantry units of regimental size or smaller were eligible for the award. According to the Board of Corrections of Military Records and the Awards Branch of the former Army Personnel Command (now Human Resources Command), the military occupational specialties (MOS) most regularly awarded the Combat Infantry Badge included the following:[2]

a. Light machine gunner (604)
b. Heavy machine gunner (605)
c. Platoon sergeant (651)
d. Squad leader (653)
e. Rifleman (745)

184 • NEVER A DULL MOMENT

f. Automatic rifleman (746)
g. Heavy weapons NCO (812)
h. Gun crewman (864)

The Combat Infantryman Badge did not bestow any points toward the total they needed for a return to the United States at the conclusion to the war; however it did provide its recipients with an additional stipend to their pay each month. But the importance of the award had nothing to do with money or points. The badge announced to the world that its wearer had done his duty under fire.

The men of the 80th Airborne Anti-Aircraft Artillery Battalion were ineligible to receive the Combat Infantryman Badge because the 80th was not designated an infantry unit. Because the coast artillery retained responsibility for anti-aircraft weapons in the United States Army at that time, the 80th was designated a coast artillery organization. This designation persisted even though the battalion had an anti-tank role (MOS 610 anti-tank gun crewman),[3] and routinely engaged the enemy with direct fire. The men who originally comprised the 80th AAA Battalion came from the 82nd's infantry regiments, particularly the 325th Infantry and 326th Infantry.[i] They thought of themselves as infantrymen, fighting alongside the men of the parachute and glider infantry. However, as the 80th AAA Association's newsletter, "The Outpost" stated, "Unfortunately, the 80th AA men were denied the Combat Infantry badge because they were 'Coast Artillery.'"[4]

---

i   Captain William Pratt's collection of military memorabilia contains a pair of crossed rifles, the insignia of the infantry, topped with the alphanumeric combination "80AAA."

Endnotes

Preface

1 George Marshall, "Biennial Reports of the Chief of Staff of the United States Army to the Secretary of War, 1 July 1939–30 June 1945" (US Army Center of Military History, 1996), https://history.army.mil/html/books/070/70-57/CMH_Pub_70-57.pdf, 3.
2 Ibid, 197.

Chapter 1

1 Jerry Autry, *General William C. Lee: Father of the American Airborne (Just Plain Bill)* (Airborne Press, 1995), 112–126.
2 Clay Blair, *Ridgway's Paratroopers* (Doubleday, 1985), 34.
3 Nikolaos Theotokis, *Airborne Landing to Air Assault* (Pen and Sword Military, 2020), 12.
4 William Mitchell, "Winged Defense," quoted in David Jablonsky, *Roots of Strategy, Book 4* (Stackpole Books, 1999), 427.
5 Autry, 74.
6 "The Knollwood Maneuver," arsof-history.org, accessed 8 March 2024, https://arsof-history.org/articles/v4n1_knollwood_page_1.html.
7 Theotokis, 30–31.
8 Autry, 122.
9 Ibid, 122.
10 Robert Burns, *History of the 80th AAA Battalion* (Unpublished).
11 Ibid.
12 Blair, 22–24.
13 Ibid, 38.
14 Ibid, 44.
15 Phil Nordyke, *The 82d Airborne Division: A Photographic History* (Historic Ventures, 2015), 75.

16 Discussion with Mark Vlahos, Colonel, USAF (Ret) and author of multiple books on WWII troop carrier operations, 31 January 2024, https://markcvlahos.com.
17 Nordyke, *The 82d Airborne Division: A Photographic History*, 73.
18 Ibid, 73.
19 Ibid, 73.
20 Ibid, 55–57.
21 James Baugh, *From Skies of Blue: My Experiences with the Eighty-Second Airborne during World War II* (iUniverse, 2003), 23.
22 Pratt letter dated 15 February 1943; Pratt diploma; Description of Officer's Advanced Orientation Course.
23 Army Air Force Manual 50–17, "Avialogs: Aviation Library – CG-4A Glider – Hadrian," www.avialogs.com, accessed 8 March 2024, https://www.avialogs.com/aircraft-w/waco/itemlist/category/1228-cg-4a-glider-hadrian.
24 Steven J. Zaloga, *US Anti-tank Artillery 1941–45* (Osprey Publishing, 2012), Kindle Edition, 6.
25 Ibid, 8.
26 Nordyke, *The 82d Airborne Division: A Photographic History*, 73.
27 Blair, 43.

Chapter 2

1 Burns, *History of the 80th AAA Battalion*.
2 Arthur Kroos, *One Soldier's Story: The WWII Memoirs of a Sheboygan County Man*, ed. Beth Dippel (Sheboygan County Historical Research Center, 2003), 22.
3 Robert Burns, "The Outpost – Newsletter of the 80th Airborne Anti-Aircraft Battalion" "505th Regimental Combat Team – 80th Airborne Anti-Aircraft," www.505rct.org, accessed 8 March 2024, http://www.505rct.org/80aa/80aa-outpost1.asp.
4 Kroos, 23.
5 Burns, *History of the 80th AAA Battalion*.
6 Ibid.
7 Zaloga, *U.S. Anti-tank Artillery*, 1941–45, 44.
8 Baugh, 61.
9 Ibid, 61.
10 Jonathan Woislaw, "The 1st Infantry Division in Sicily: A Case Study in Tactical Intelligence" (2021). Student Thesis. https://apps.dtic.mil/sti/trecms/pdf/AD1157541.pdf.
11 "Arthur Gorham – Recipient," valor.militarytimes.com, accessed 8 March 2024, https://valor.militarytimes.com/hero/23093.
12 Ibid.
13 Vlahos, 31 January 2024.
14 Kroos, 25.

ENDNOTES • 187

15 Baugh, 62.
16 Ibid, 62.
17 Dwight David Eisenhower, Joseph P. Hobbs, and George Catlett Marshall, *Dear General* (JHU Press, 1999), 118.
18 Gordon L. Rottman, *US Airborne Units in the Mediterranean Theater 1942–44* (Osprey Publishing, 2013), Kindle Edition, 163.
19 Ibid, 164.
20 "National Pathfinder Association History," NPA, accessed 8 March 2024, https://www.nationalpathfinderassociation.org/history.
21 "21st Independent Parachute Company: ParaData," www.paradata.org.uk, accessed 8 March 2024, https://www.paradata.org.uk/unit/21st-independent-parachute-company.
22 Blair, 128–155.
23 Burns, *History of the 80th AAA Battalion.*
24 Blair, 128–155.
25 Burns, "The Outpost."
26 Burns, *History of the 80th AAA Battalion.*
27 Ibid.
28 Burns, "The Outpost."
29 Burns, *History of the 80th AAA Battalion.*
30 Ibid.

Chapter 3

1 United States War Department. *FM 100-5: Operations* (United States Government Printing Office, 1941).
2 Russell F. Weigley, *Eisenhower's Lieutenants* (Indiana University Press, 1990), 37.
3 Dwight D. Eisenhower, *Crusade in Europe* (Doubleday, 1948), 230.
4 Carlo D'Este, *Decision in Normandy* (Konecky & Konecky, 1983), 35.
5 Ibid, 62.
6 Mitchell Yockelson, *The Paratrooper Generals* (Stackpole Books, 2020), 74.
7 Ibid, 77.
8 Blair, 184.
9 Phil Nordyke, *All American All the Way* (Zenith Press, 2005), 164.
10 Richard Hargreaves, *The Germans in Normandy* (Stackpole Books, 2006), 8–10.
11 Ibid, 16–17.
12 Williamson Murray, *Strategy for Defeat: The Luftwaffe, 1933–1945* (Tannenberg Publishing, 2015), 455.
13 Phil Nordyke, *Four Stars of Valor: The Combat History of the 505th Parachute Infantry Regiment in World War II* (Zenith Press, 2006), 180.
14 Steven Zaloga, *D-Day 1944 (2) Utah Beach and the U.S. Airborne Landings* (Osprey Publishing, 2002), 48.
15 Blair, 208.

16 82nd Airborne Division, *Normandy After Action Review* (n.d.), 2.
17 Ibid, 10.
18 Blair, 234.
19 Phil Nordyke, *Four Stars of Valor: The Combat History of the 505th Parachute Infantry Regiment in World War II* (Zenith Press, 2006), 153.
20 Baugh, 109.
21 Ibid, 112.
22 Ibid, 127–129.
23 Ibid, 133.
24 82nd Airborne Division, *Normandy After Action Review* (n.d.), 5–6.
25 Burns, "The Outpost."
26 Ibid.
27 Ed Ruggero, *The First Men In* (Harper Collins, 2006), 140–141.
28 Ibid, 153–156.
29 Burns, "The Outpost."
30 Ibid.
31 Ibid.
32 Ibid.
33 Ibid, and "Airborne at La Fière: Slugfest in Normandy," Warfare History Network, 15 October 2020, https://warfarehistorynetwork.com/article/airborne-at-la-fiere-slugfest-in-normandy/.
34 Mike Kelvington, "Battle of the Bridge: A Company, 1-505th at La Fiere Bridge," *The Havok Journal*, 9 July 2023, https://havokjournal.com/culture/military/battle-of-the-bridge-a-company-1-505th-at-la-fiere-bridge/.
35 Annex No. 5, Elmira Air Movement Order.
36 Ruggero, *First Men In*, 228.
37 Ibid, 229.
38 Burns, "The Outpost."
39 Ibid.
40 Ibid.
41 Ruggero, *First Men In*, 140.
42 Robert M. Murphy, *No Better Place to Die: Ste-Mère Eglise, June 1944: The Battle for La Fière Bridge* (Casemate Publishers, 2011), Kindle Edition, 151.
43 Ibid, 151.
44 "Weapons of Patton's Armies – PDF Free Download," epdf.pub, accessed 8 March 2024, https://epdf.pub/weapons-of-pattons-armies.html.
45 Murphy, *No Better Place to Die*, 151.
46 Burns, "The Outpost."
47 Ibid.
48 "The Battle of Sainte-Mere-Eglise 1944: D-Day and After," Maksym Chorny's personal blog on WWII, 30 October 2021, https://war-documentary.info/sainte-mere-eglise-1944/.
49 Burns, "The Outpost."
50 Ibid.

ENDNOTES • 189

51 Ben Powers, "The French Village of Cauquigny," Argunners.com, 8 June 2020, https://www.argunners.com/valor-french-village-cauquigny/.

52 Ibid.

53 "Charles N. Deglopper, World War II, U.S. Army, Medal of Honor Recipient," Congressional Medal of Honor Society, n.d., https://www.cmohs.org/recipients/charles-n-deglopper.

54 Ibid.

55 80th AAA Battalion History, 10 June 1944 Entry.

56 *Securing the Douve Line: Utah Beach to Cherbourg*, history.army.mil, accessed 8 March 2024, https://history.army.mil/books/wwii/utah/utah7.htm, 132.

57 Ibid, 132.

58 80th AAA Battalion History, 11 June 1944 Entry.

59 Burns, "The Outpost."

60 Ibid.

61 "First Sergeant Richard E Rider – DSC Recipient," WW2-Airborne.US, accessed 8 March 2024, https://ww2-airborne.us/units/80/rider_dsc.html.

62 Ray Fary, "Baupte Action Seen By 319th," *The Outpost*, 15 (Summer 2008), 3.

63 Joseph Covais, *Battery!* (Andy Red Enterprises, 2010), 230.

64 Ibid, 230.

65 Fary, "Baupte Action Seen By 319th," 3.

66 Burns, "The Outpost."

67 80th AAA Battalion History, 17 June 1944 Entry.

68 Blair, *Ridgway's Paratroopers*, 289.

69 80th AAA Battalion History, 19 June 1944 Entry.

70 *The Fall of Cherbourg: Utah Beach to Cherbourg*, history.army.mil, accessed 8 March 2024, https://history.army.mil/books/wwii/utah/utah11.htm.

71 Blair, *Ridgway's Paratroopers*, 293.

72 Burns, "The Outpost."

73 Ibid.

74 Blair, *Ridgway's Paratroopers*, 295.

75 "New Law Raises Pay for Glider Crews; President Signs Other Bills for Aid to Armed Services," *The New York Times*, 4 July 1944, sec. Archives, https://www.nytimes.com/1944/07/04/archives/new-law-raises-pay-for-glider-crews-president-signs-other-bills-for.html.

76 Nordyke, *Four Stars of Valor*, 153.

77 80th AAA Battalion History, 10 July 1944 Entry.

78 Blair, *Ridgway's Paratroopers*, 304.

79 "Combat Uniforms," 9th Infantry Division in WWII, 18 October 2012, https://9thinfantrydivision.net/combat-uniforms/.

80 "D-Day – Eyewitnesses – Singleton Raymond E," www.americandday.org, accessed 8 March 2024, http://www.americandday.org/Veterans/Singleton_Raymond_E.html.

81 Blair, *Ridgway's Paratroopers*, 304.

82 Sparky Sargent, "Targets Silent the Glider Gang behind the Lines," accessed 8 March 2024, https://www.flightjournal.com/wp-content/uploads/2016/10/4_Silent-Targets.pdf.

83 "NWWIIGPA-NORMANDY," www.ww2gp.org, accessed 8 March 2024, https://www.ww2gp.org/normandy/.

84 80th AAA Battalion History, 1–29 August 1944 Entries.

85 "The 80th Airborne Anti-Aircraft Battalion Unit History," www.ww2-airborne.us, accessed 8 March 2024, https://www.ww2-airborne.us/units/80/80.html.

86 Guy LoFaro, *The Sword of Saint Michael* (De Capo Press, 2011), 186.

87 "Command & Support Relationships Chart," chttps://alu.army.mil/alog/2016/julaug16/PDF/Command_and_Support_Relationships_Chart.pdf.

88 Burns, "The Outpost."

Chapter 4

1 80th AAA Battalion History, 17 July–1 August 1944 Entries.

2 R. G. Poulussen, *Lost at Nijmegen: A rethink on operation "Market Garden,"* Kindle Edition, 12.

3 80th AAA Battalion History, 31 August–5 September 1944 Entries.

4 *Logistics and the Broad-Front*, history.army.mil, n.d., https://history.army.mil/books/70-7_18.htm.

5 *Operation MARKET-GARDEN*, history.army.mil, n.d., https://history.army.mil/books/70-7_19.htm.

6 Major L. F. Ellis with Lieut-Colonel A. E. Warhurst, *Victory in the West Volume 2: The Defeat of Germany* (History of the Second World War United Kingdom Military Series), Internet Archive, 1968, https://archive.org/details/victory-west-vol-2/page/29/mode/2up, p. 29

7 Theotokis, 70.

8 Ellis, 29.

9 Theotokis, 25.

10 Ibid, 70.

11 "Major-General Stanislaw Sosabowski," www.pegasusarchive.org, n.d., https://www.pegasusarchive.org/arnhem/stanislaw_sosabowski.htm. Accessed 19 February 2024.

12 80th AAA Battalion History, 14 September 1944 Entry.

13 Ibid, 14–16 September 1944 Entries.

14 Ibid, 17 September 1944 Entry.

15 James Maurice Gavin, *On to Berlin* (Viking, 1979), 155.

16 Burns, "The Outpost."

17 Gavin, 147–148.

18 Burns, "The Outpost."

19 Gavin, 160.

ENDNOTES • 191

20 Burns, "The Outpost."
21 Gavin, 149.
22 Kroos, 39, 42.
23 80th AAA Battalion History, 18 September 1944 Entry; 80th Airborne AA Unit Roster, 16 September 2006.
24 80th AAA Battalion History, 18 September 1944 Entry.
25 Ibid, 18–19 September 1944 Entries.
26 Ibid.
27 Phil Nordyke, *The All Americans in World War II: A Photographic History of the 82nd Airborne Division at War* (Zenith Press, 2005), Kindle Edition, 122–123.
28 Burns, "The Outpost"; 80th Airborne AA Unit Roster, 16 September 2006.
29 Arthur Northwood Jr and Leonard Rapport, *Rendezvous With Destiny: A History of the 101st Airborne Division* (Konecky & Konecky, 1948), 315–322.
30 LoFaro, 344.
31 Ibid, 319.
32 "The Battle of Nijmegen," www.liberationroute.com, accessed 8 March 2024, https://www.liberationroute.com/pois/182/the-battle-of-nijmegen.
33 Burns, "The Outpost."
34 Ibid.
35 LoFaro, 367.
36 Ibid, 72.
37 Ibid, 76.
38 80th AAA Battalion History, 21 September 1944 Entry
39 80th AAA Battalion Intelligence Report, Captain Raymond Newman, courtesy of Thulai van Maanen.
40 Burns, "The Outpost"; 80th AAA Battalion History, 21 September 1944.
41 Ibid.
42 Burns, "The Outpost."
43 80th AAA Battalion History, 21 September 1944 and 23 September 1944 Entries.
44 Ibid.
45 Burns, "The Outpost."
46 Ibid.
47 Ibid.
48 80th AAA Battalion History, 21 September 1944 and 24 September 1944 Entries.
49 Evans, 56.
50 Nordyke, *The All Americans in World War Two*, 104.
51 80th AAA Battalion History, 27 September Entry.
52 Burns, "The Outpost."
53 Ibid.
54 80th AAA Battalion History, 26–27 September 1944 Entries.
55 Burns, "The Outpost."
56 80th AAA Battalion History, 28 September 1944 entry; Burns, "The Outpost."

192 • NEVER A DULL MOMENT

57 Ibid.
58 Ibid.
59 Ibid.
60 Weigley, 10.
61 80th AAA Battalion History, 28 September 1944 Entry.
62 Ibid.
63 Silver Star citation for Private Samuel McNeill.
64 80th AAA Battalion History, 30 September–1 October 1944 Entries; Burns, "The Outpost."
65 80th AAA Battalion History, 2 October 1944 Entry.
66 Nordyke, *The All Americans in World War Two*, 132.
67 Burns, "The Outpost."

Chapter 5

1 Weigley, 370.
2 David John Jordan, *Atlas of World War II* (Barnes & Noble Books, 2004), 169.
3 "Third Army G2 Predicts Battle of the Bulge, 9 December 1944," www.army.mil, n.d., https://www.army.mil/article/116038/third_army_g2_predicts_battle_of_the_bulge_9_december_1944. Accessed 25 February 2024.
4 "Chapter 7 – The Ardennes: Battle of the Bulge," www.history.army.mil, n.d., https://www.history.army.mil/books/wwii/7-8/7-8_7.htm, 140
5 Ibid, 165.
6 Ibid, 305.
7 80th AAA Battalion History, 18 November–16 December 1944 Entries.
8 Ibid, 17 December Entry.
9 Lewis Sorely, ed., *Gavin at War: The World War II Diary of Lieutenant General James M. Gavin* (Casemate Publishers, 2022), 142.
10 "The 80th Airborne Anit-Aircraft Battalion Unit History," www.ww2-airborne.us, accessed 8 March 2024, https://www.ww2-airborne.us/units/80/80.html.
11 Burns, "The Outpost."
12 Marshall Stark, "Operations of 1st Platoon of Battery 'C', 80th Airborne Antiaircraft Battalion in the Battle of the Bulge," 1947, https://mcoecbamcoepwprd01.blob.core.usgovcloudapi.net/library/DonovanPapers/wwii/STUP2/S-Z/StarkMarshall%20W.%20CPT.pdf.
13 "Chapter 7 – The Ardennes: Battle of the Bulge," www.history.army.mil, n.d., https://www.history.army.mil/books/wwii/7-8/7-8_7.htm, 336.
14 80th AAA Battalion History, 18 December 1944 Entry.
15 Burns, "The Outpost."
16 Ibid.
17 Ibid, and MacDonald, *A Time for Trumpets – The Untold Story of the Battle of the Bulge* (Perennial, 2002), 433.
18 Burns, "The Outpost."

ENDNOTES • 193

19 "Chapter 7 – The Ardennes: Battle of the Bulge," www.history.army.mil, n.d., https://www.history.army.mil/books/wwii/7-8/7-8_7.htm, 351.
20 Ibid, 352.
21 80th AAA Battalion History, 20 December 1944 Entry.
22 "Tankograd – Technical Manual 6036 – U.S. WWII & Korea M36, M36B1 & M36B2 90mm Gun Motor Carriage Tank Destroyers | PDF," Scribd, accessed 8 March 2024, https://www.scribd.com/document/683957824/Tankograd-Technical-Manual-6036-U-S-WWII-Korea-M36-M36B1-M36B2-90mm-Gun-Motor-Carriage-Tank-Destroyers.
23 Frank van Lunteren, *Blocking Kampfgruppe Peiper: The 504th Parachute Infantry Regiment in the Battle of the Bulge* (Casemate Publishers, 2015), Kindle Edition, 58–59.
24 Burns, "The Outpost."
25 "Chapter 11 – The Ardennes: Battle of the Bulge," www.history.army.mil, n.d., https://history.army.mil/books/wwii/7-8/7-8_11.htm.
26 Burns, "The Outpost."
27 Ibid.
28 Nordyke, *All American All the Way: From Market Garden to Berlin*, 209.
29 Ibid.
30 Nordyke, *All American All the Way: From Market Garden to Berlin*, 209.
31 Burns, "The Outpost."
32 Nordyke, *All American All the Way: From Market Garden to Berlin*, 209.
33 Burns, "The Outpost."
34 Nordyke, *All American All the Way: From Market Garden to Berlin*, 209.
35 80th AAA Battalion History, 21 December 1944 Entry.
36 Ibid, 22 December Entry; Burns, "The Outpost."
37 "Quad 50 Caliber M2," Estrella Warbird Museum (ewarbirds.org), accessed 28 February 2024, https://www.ewarbirds.org/armament/quad50m2.shtml.
38 Nordyke, *Market Garden to Berlin*, 215.
39 80th AAA Battalion History, 22 December Entry; Burns, "The Outpost."
40 Nordyke, *The All Americans in World War II*, 144.
41 80th AAA Battalion History, 23 December Entry; Burns, "The Outpost."
42 Nordyke, *The All Americans in World War II*, 185.
43 Blair, *Ridgway's Paratroopers*, 373–374.
44 Ibid, 374.
45 Lofaro, 457
46 Burns, "The Outpost."
47 Nordyke, *The All Americans in World War II*, 146.
48 Ibid, 146.
49 Weigley, 529.
50 Ibid, 529.
51 Lofaro, 471.
52 Burns, "The Outpost."

194 • NEVER A DULL MOMENT

53 Ibid.
54 Lofaro, 445.
55 Ibid, 478.
56 "Chapter 23 – The Ardennes: Battle of the Bulge," history.army.mil, accessed 8 March 2024, https://history.army.mil/books/wwii/7-8/7-8_23.htm.
57 Ibid.
58 Nordyke, *The All Americans in World War II*, 146.
59 Lofaro, 480–481.
60 80th AAA Battalion History, 29–30 December 1944 Entries.
61 LoFaro, 483.
62 80th AAA Battalion History, 2–6 January 1945 Entries.
63 80th AAA Battalion History, 7 January 1945 Entry; Burns, "The Outpost."
64 80th AAA Battalion History, 8 January–10 January 1945 Entries.
65 80th AAA Battalion History, 10 January 1945 Entry.
66 "Panzerfaust," panzerworld.com, accessed 10 March 2024, https://panzerworld.com/panzerfaust.
67 William Waters, "A Brief History of Shaped Charges," 2008, https://apps.dtic.mil/sti/tr/pdf/ADA497450.pdf.
68 80th AAA Battalion Histoey, 10 January 1945 Entry.

Chapter 6

1   80th AAA Battalion History, 13 January and 21 January 1945 Entries.
2   Burns, "The Outpost."
3   Blair, 423–424.
4   Ibid, 422.
5   LoFaro, 499.
6   Ibid, 499.
7   Ibid, 499.
8   James Fenelon, *Four Hours of Fury* (Scribner, 2020), 73–77.
9   Nordyke, *The All Americans in World War Two*, 165; LoFaro, 498–502.
10 Blair, 428.
11 Ibid, 429–430.
12 80th AAA Battalion History, 1 February 1945 Entry.
13 Nordyke, *The All Americans in World War Two*, 174.
14 "Airborne in Normandy," www.airborneinnormandy.com, accessed 10 March 2024, https://www.airborneinnormandy.com/2nd_bn_401st.htm.
15 Email exchange between Robert Burns and Wayne Pierce, 15 March 2004, copy provided to author.
16 Ibid; Nordyke, *The All Americans in World War Two*, 174.
17 80th AAA Battalion History, 2 February 1945 Entry; Burns, "The Outpost."
18 Ibid.
19 Blair, 431–432.

ENDNOTES • 195

20 Ibid, 433.
21 Nordyke, *The All Americans in World War Two*, 174.
22 Blair, 432.
23 Burns, "The Outpost."
24 80th AAA Battalion History, 7, 10, 11, and 14 February 1945 Entries.
25 Burns, "The Outpost."
26 80th AAA Battalion History, 7 March 1945 Entry.
27 80th Airborne AA Unit Roster, 16 September 2006.
28 80th AAA Battalion History, 30 March 1945 Entry.
29 Fenelon, *Four Hours of Fury*, 339.
30 Ken Hechler, *The Bridge at Remagen* (Novato, CA: Presidio, 2005), 159.
31 Blair, 478.
32 80th AAA Battalion History, 1–3 April 1945 entries; Burns, "The Outpost."
33 Weigley, 662.
34 Blair, 479.
35 Sorely, ed., 155–156.
36 80th AAA Battalion History, 4–6 April 1945 Entries.
37 MarkoPantelic, "Flakpanzer IV (2 Cm Flakvierling 38) 'Wirbelwind,'" *Tank Encyclopedia*, February 21, 2019, https://tanks-encyclopedia.com/ww2-germany-flakpanzer-iv-wirblewind/.
38 80th AAA Battalion History, 5 April 1945 Entry.
39 Ibid, 6–11 April Entries.
40 Ibid, 13 April 1945 Entry.
41 Ibid, 13–14 April 1945 Entries.
42 Nordyke, *All American All the Way: From Market Garden to Berlin*, 336.
43 80th AAA Battalion History, 13–14 April 1945 Entries.
44 Nordyke, *All American All the Way: From Market Garden to Berlin*, 336.
45 Lorraine Boissoneault, "The Nazi Werewolves Who Terrorized Allied Soldiers at the End of WWII History," Smithsonian Magazine, October 30, 2018, https://www.smithsonianmag.com/history/nazi-werewolves-who-terrorized-allied-soldiers-end-wwii-180970522/.
46 80th AAA Battalion History, 17–19 April 1945 Entries.
47 Nordyke, *All American All the Way: From Market Garden to Berlin*, 337.
48 Ibid, 337–339.
49 Burns, "The Outpost."
50 Gavin, 285.
51 Weigley, 723.
52 80th AAA Battalion History, 3 May 1945 Entry.
53 Ibid, 2 May 1945 Entry.
54 Gavin, 286–288.
55 80th AAA Battalion History, 3–5 May 1945 Entries.
56 Gavin, 288
57 Nordyke, *All American All the Way: From Market Garden to Berlin*, 346; Gavin, 289.
58 80th AAA Battalion History, 6 May 1945 Entry.

196 • NEVER A DULL MOMENT

59 Burns, "The Outpost."
60 80th AAA Battalion History, 7 May 1945 Entry.
61 All details of the actions of Captain Kroos and his soldiers, from landing in Holland until their capture, as well as the details of Kroos's captivity, are taken from his memoir, *One Soldier's Story*.
62 Weigely, 726.
63 Gavin, 286.
64 Weigley, 726; 80th AAA Battalion History, 9 May 1945 Entry.
65 Burns, "The Outpost."
66 80th AAA Battalion History, 9 May–2 June 1945 Entries.
67 John Sparrow, "History of Demobilization of Personnel in the United States Army," 1952, https://history.army.mil/html/books/104/104-8/CMH_Pub_104-8.pdf.
68 Jeff Clark, "The Postwar Points Discharge Plan," Tribute to an 82nd Airborne Veteran, May 13, 2014, https://ww2tribute.blogspot.com/2014/05/.
69 80th AAA Battalion History, 20 June 1945 Entry.
70 Ibid, 21–25 June 1945 Entries.
71 Ibid, 10–16 August 1945 Entries.
72 80th AAA Battalion, September–18 November 1945 Entries.
73 80th AAA Battalion History, 25 November, 29 November, and 30 November through December 1945 Entries.

Appendix A

1 "The 80th Airborne Anti-Aircraft Battalion Unit Citations." The 82nd Airborne. https://www.ww2-airborne.us/units/80/80_citations.html.
2 Army Regulation 600–8–22. Military Awards. https://history.army.mil/html/forcestruc/docs/r600_8_22.pdf.

Appendix B

1 Department of Defense. Electronic Reading Room for the Military Departments' Boards for Corrections of Military/Naval Records (BCM/NR). Af.mil, 2024. Accessed 8 March 2024. boards.law.af.mil/ARMY/BCMR/CY2012/20120007734. txt.
2 Ibid.
3 Richard Morgan, "Antitank Gun Crewman (610)," militaryyearbookproject. org, accessed 8 March 2024, https://militaryyearbookproject.org/references/old-mos-codes/wwii-era/army-wwii-codes/gunnery-and-gunnery-control/antitank-gun-crewman-610.
4 Burns, "The Outpost."

Bibliography

Books

Autry, Jerry. *General William C. Lee: Father of the American Airborne (Just Plain Bill)*. Airborne Press, 1995.

Bassford, Ronald A. *Let's Go!: The History of the 325th Airborne Infantry Regiment, 1917–1995*. First ed., 82nd Airborne Division Historical Society, 1995.

Battle Map of Normandy June–August 1944. Reprint of the 1947 map ed., Michelin Travel Partner, 2018.

Baugh, James. *From Skies of Blue: My Experiences with the Eighty-Second Airborne during World War II*. iUniverse, 2003.

Blair, Clay. *Ridgway's Paratroopers*. Doubleday, 1985.

Booth, T. Michael and Duncan Spencer. *Paratrooper: The Life of General James M. Gavin*. Casemate Publishers, 2013.

Breuer, William B. *Drop Zone, Sicily: Allied Airborne Strike, July 1943*. Presidio, 1997.

Calhoun, Mark. *General Lesley J. McNair: Unsung Architect of the U.S. Army*. University Press of Kansas. Kindle Edition, 2015.

Citino, Robert Michael. *The German Way of War*. University Press of Kansas, 2005.

Crookenden, Napier. *Dropzone Normandy*. Charles Scribner's Sons, 1976.

D'este, Carlo. *Decision in Normandy*. Barnes & Noble, 1994.

Eisenhower, Dwight D. *Crusade in Europe*. The Easton Press, 2001.

Eisenhower, Dwight D., et al. *Dear General*. JHU Press, 1999.

Fenelon, James. *Four Hours of Fury: The Untold Story of World War II's Largest Airborne Operation and the Final Push into Nazi Germany*. Scribner, 2020.

Gavin, James Maurice. *On to Berlin*. Viking, 1979.

Harclerode, Peter. *Wings of War: Airborne Warfare 1918–1945*. Weidenfeld & Nicolson Ltd., 2005.

Hargreaves, Richard. *The Germans in Normandy*. Stackpole Books, 2006.

Haskew, Michael E. *The Airborne in World War II*. Macmillan, 2017.

Hechler, Ken. *The Bridge at Remagen*. Presidio, 2005.

Jablonsky, David. *Roots of Strategy, Book 4: The Influence of Sea Power upon History, 1660–1783, Some Principles of Maritime Strategy, Command of the Air, Winged Defense*. Stackpole Books, 1999.

Jordan, David John. *Atlas of World War II*. Barnes & Noble Books, 2004.

Kroos, Arthur. *One Soldier's Story: The WWII Memoirs of a Sheboygan County Man.* Edited by Beth Dippel, Sheboygan County Historical Research Center, 2003.

LoFaro, Guy. *The Sword of St. Michael.* Hachette Books. Kindle Edition, 2011.

Macdonald, Charles B. *A Time for Trumpets: The Untold Story of the Battle of the Bulge.* Perennial, 2002.

Masters, Charles J. *Glidermen of Neptune.* SIU Press, 1995.

McManus, John C. *September Hope: The American Side of a Bridge Too Far.* Caliber, 2013.

Morgan, K. A. Martin. *Down to Earth: The 507th Parachute Infantry Regiment in Normandy.* Schiffer Publishing, 2004.

Mrazek, James E. *The Glider War.* Robert Hale and Co., 1975.

Murphy, Robert M. *No Better Place to Die: Ste-Mère Eglise, June 1944: The Battle for La Fière Bridge.* Casemate Publishers (Ignition). Kindle Edition, 2020.

Murray, Williamson. *Strategy for Defeat: The Luftwaffe, 1933–1945* [Illustrated Edition]. Pickle Partners Publishing, 2015.

Nordyke, Phil. *The 82d Airborne Division: A Photographic History.* Historic Ventures, 2015.

Nordyke, Phil. *All American, All the Way: The Combat History of the 82nd Airborne Division in World War II.* Zenith Press, 2005.

Nordyke, Phil. *The All Americans in World War II: A Photographic History of the 82nd Airborne Division at War.* Quarto Publishing Group U.S.A. Kindle Edition, 2022.

Nordyke, Phil. *Four Stars of Valor: The Combat History of the 505th Parachute Infantry Regiment in World War II.* Zenith Press, 2006.

Northwood, Arthur Jr and Rapport, Leonard. *Rendezvous. With Destiny: A History of the 101st Airborne Division.* Konecky & Konecky, 1948.

Otway, T. B. H. *Airborne Forces: The Second World War 1939–1945.* Naval & Military Press Ltd., 2019.

Poulussen, R. G. *Lost at Nijmegen: A rethink on operation "Market Garden."* Kindle Edition, 2011.

Roberts, Charles. *The U.S. 37-mm Gun in World War II.* Casemate Publishers, 2023.

Rottman, Gordon L. *U.S. Airborne Units in the Mediterranean Theater 1942–44 (Battle Orders 22).* Osprey Publishing. Kindle Edition, 2013.

Rottman, Gordon L. *U.S. World War II Parachute Infantry Regiments (Elite 198).* Osprey Publishing. Kindle Edition, 2014.

Ruggero, Ed. *Combat Jump: The Young Men Who Led the Assault into Fortress Europe, July 1943.* Harper, 2003.

Ruggero, Ed. *The First Men In: U.S. Paratroopers and the Fight to Save D-Day.* Harper, 2006.

Smith, Claude. *History of the Glider Pilot Regiment.* Pen and Sword Aviation. Kindle Edition, 2014.

Smith, Stephen and Simon Forty. *82nd Airborne: Normandy 1944 (Past & Present).* Casemate Publishers (Ignition). Kindle Edition, 2017.

BIBLIOGRAPHY • 199

Sorley, Lewis (ed.), *Gavin at War: The World War II Diary of Lieutenant General James M. Gavin*. Casemate Publishers, 2022.

Theotokis, Nikolaos. *Airborne Landing to Air Assault*. Pen and Sword Military, 2020.

Tucker-Jones, Anthony. *The Devil's Bridge*. Bloomsbury Publishing, 2020.

United States War Department. *FM 100-5: Operations*. United States Government Printing Office, 1941.

van Lunteren, Frank. *Blocking Kampfgruppe Peiper: The 504th Parachute Infantry Regiment in the Battle of the Bulge*. Casemate Publishers (Ignition). Kindle Edition, 2020.

Weigley, Russell F. *Eisenhower's Lieutenants*. Indiana University Press, 1990.

Yockelson, Mitchell. *The Paratrooper Generals: Matthew Ridgway, Maxwell Taylor, and the American Airborne from D-Day through Normandy*. Rowman & Littlefield. Kindle Edition, 2023.

Zaloga, Steven J. *D-Day 1944 (2): Utah Beah and U.S. Airborne Landings (Campaign)*. Osprey Publishing. Kindle Edition, 2013.

Zaloga, Steven J. *U.S. Airborne Divisions in the ETO 1944–45 (Battle Orders 25)*. Osprey Publishing. Kindle Edition, 2012.

Zaloga, Steven J. *U.S. Anti-tank Artillery 1941–45 (New Vanguard 107)*. Osprey Publishing. Kindle Edition, 2012.

Internet Sources

"1st Infantry Division – Order of Battle of the United States Army – WWII – ETO." U.S. Army Center of Military History. Accessed 14 May 2024. history.army.mil/documents/eto-ob/1id-eto-ob.htm.

"21st Independent Parachute Company." ParaData. Accessed 8 March 2024. www.paradata.org.uk/unit/21st-independent-parachute-company.

"505th Regimental Combat Team – 80th Airborne Anti-Aircraft." 505th Regimental Combat Team Website. Accessed 8 March 2024. www.505rct.org/80aa/80aa-outpost1.asp.

"Airborne at La Fière: Slugfest in Normandy." Warfare History Network. 15 October 2020. Accessed 8 March 2024. warfarehistorynetwork.com/article/airborne-at-la-fiere-slugfest-in-normandy.

"Arthur Gorham – Recipient." The Hall of Valor Project. Accessed 8 March 2024. valor.militarytimes.com/hero/23093.

Boissoneault, Lorraine. "The Nazi Werewolves Who Terrorized Allied Soldiers at the End of WWII." Smithsonian.com, 30 October 2018. Accessed 14 May 2024. https://www.smithsonianmag.com/history/nazi-werewolves-who-terrorized-allied-soldiers-end-wwii-180970522/.

Burns, Robert. "The Outpost – Newsletter of the 80th Airborne Anti-Aircraft Battalion." 505th Regimental Combat Team Website. Accessed 14 May 2024. www.505rct.org/80aa/80aa-outpost1.asp.

"CG-4A Glider – Hadrian." Avialogs: Aviation Library. Accessed 8 March 2024. www.avialogs.com/aircraft-w/waco/itemlist/category/1228-cg-4a-glider-hadrian.

"Chapter 7 – Breakthrough at the Schnee Eifel." *The Ardennes: Battle of the Bulge.* U.S. Army Center of Military History. Accessed 8 March 2024. www.history.army.mil/books/wwii/7-8/7-8_7.htm.

"Chapter 11 – The 1st SS Panzer Division's Dash Westward, and Operation Greif." *The Ardennes: Battle of the Bulge.* U.S. Army Center of Military History. Accessed 8 March 2024. history.army.mil/books/wwii/7-8/7-8_11.htm.

"Chapter 23 – The Battle Between the Salm and the Ourthe 24 December-2 January." *The Ardennes: Battle of the Bulge.* U.S. Army Center of Military History. Accessed 8 March 2024. history.army.mil/books/wwii/7-8/7-8_23.htm.

"Charles N Deglopper, World War II, U.S. Army, Medal of Honor Recipient." Congressional Medal of Honor Society. Accessed 14 May 2024. www.cmohs.org/recipients/charles-n-deglopper.

Clark, Jeff. "The Postwar Points Discharge Plan." Tribute to an 82nd Airborne Veteran. 13 May 2014. Accessed 8 March 2024. ww2tribute.blogspot.com/2014/05/.

"Combat Uniforms." 9th Infantry Division in WWII. 18 October 2012. Accessed 15 May 2024. 9thinfantrydivision.net/combat-uniforms/.

"D-Day – Eyewitnesses – Singleton Raymond E." American D-Day. Accessed 8 Mar. 2024. www.americandday.org/Veterans/Singleton_Raymond_E.html.

Den Brok, Hans. "NORMANDY: Operation Overlord 6-7 June 1944." National WWII Glider Pilots Association. Accessed 8 March 2024. www.ww2gp.org/normandy/.

Department of Defense. Electronic Reading Room for the Military Departments' Boards for Corrections of Military/Naval Records (BCM/NR). Af.mil, 2024. Accessed 8 March 2024. boards.law.af.mil/ARMY/BCMR/CY2012/20120007734.txt.

Ellis, Major L. F. with Lieut-Colonel A. E. Warhurst. "Victory in the West Volume 2: The Defeat of Germany" (History of the Second World War United Kingdom Military Series). Internet Archive, 1968, Accessed 8 March 2024. archive.org/details/victory-west-vol-2/page/29/mode/2up.

"First Sergeant Richard E Rider – DSC Recipient." Accessed 8 March 2024. ww2-airborne.us/units/80/rider_dsc.html.

"Glider Badge." U.S. Army Quartermaster Museum. Accessed 8 March 2024. qmmuseum.army.mil/research/airborne-special-operations/glider-badge.html.

Green, Michael and Gladys Green. "Weapons of Patton's Armies." Accessed 8 March 2024. epdf.pub/weapons-of-pattons-armies.html.

Kelvington, Mike. "Battle of the Bridge: A Company, 1-505th at La Fiere Bridge." The Havok Journal. 9 July 2023. Accessed 8 March 2024. havokjournal.com/culture/military/battle-of-the-bridge-a-company-1-505th-at-la-fiere-bridge/.

Kyoichi, Tachikawa. "The Treatment of Prisoners of War by the Imperial Japanese Army and Navy Focusing on the Pacific War." Accessed 14 May 2024. www.nids.mod.go.jp/english/publication/kiyo/pdf/2008/bulletin_e2008_5.pdf.

BIBLIOGRAPHY • 201

MacDonald, Charles B. "Chapter 19: The Decision To Launch Operation MARKET-GARDEN." U.S. Army Center of Military History. Accessed 14 May 2024. history.army.mil/books/70-7_19.htm.

"Major-General Stanislaw Sosabowski." Brigade HQ, 1st Polish Independent Parachute Brigade Group. Accessed 14 May 2024. www.pegasusarchive.org/arnhem/stanislaw_sosabowski.htm.

MarkoPantelic. "Flakpanzer IV (2 Cm Flakvierling 38) 'Wirbelwind.'" Tank Encyclopedia, 21 February 2019. Accessed 8 March 2024. tanks-encyclopedia.com/ww2-germany-flakpanzer-iv-wirblewind/.

Marshall, George. "Biennial Reports of The Chief of Staff of The United States Army to The Secretary of War, 1 July 1939–30 June 1945." U.S. Army Center of Military History. 1996. Accessed 14 May 2024. history.army.mil/html/books/070/70-57/CMH_Pub_70-57.pdf.

"Medal of Honor Citation: Emory Pike." Home of Heroes. Accessed 8 March 2024. www.homeofheroes.com/moh/citations_1918_wwi/pike.html.

Morgan, Richard. "Antitank Gun Crewman (610)." Accessed 8 March 2024. militaryyearbookproject.org/references/old-mos-codes/wwii-era/army-wwii-codes/gunnery-and-gunnery-control/antitank-gun-crewman-610.

National Pathfinder Association: History. Accessed 8 March 2024. www.nationalpathfinderassociation.org/history.

"New Law Raises Pay for Glider Crews; President Signs Other Bills for Aid to Armed Services." *The New York Times*, 4 July 1944. Accessed 8 March 2024. www.nytimes.com/1944/07/04/archives/new-law-raises-pay-for-glider-crews-president-signs-other-bills-for.html.

"Panzerfaust." Panzerworld.com. Accessed 10 March 2024. https://panzerworld.com/panzerfaust.

Piasecki, Eugene G. "The Knollwood Maneuver." General Arsof History. Accessed 8 March 2024. arsof-history.org/articles/v4n1_knollwood_page_1.html.

Powers, Ben. "The French Village of Cauquigny." *Argunners Magazine*. 8 June 2020. Accessed 8 March 2024. www.argunners.com/valor-french-village-cauquigny/.

"Quad 50 Caliber M2." Estrella Warbird Museum. Accessed 14 May 2024. www.ewarbirds.org/armament/quad50m2.shtml.

Quinn, Ruth. "Third Army G2 Predicts Battle of the Bulge, 9 December 1944." U.S. Army. 27 November 2013. Accessed 14 May 2024. www.army.mil/article/116038/third_army_g2_predicts_battle_of_the_bulge_9_december_1944.

Ruppenthal, Roland G. "Logistics and the Broad-Front Strategy." Accessed 14 May 2024. history.army.mil/books/70-7_18.htm.

Sargent, Sparky. "Silent Targets, the Glider Gang behind the Lines." Accessed 14 May 2024. https://www.flightjournal.com/wp-content/uploads/2016/10/4_Silent-Targets.pdf.

"Securing the Douve Line: Utah Beach to Cherbourg." U.S. Army Center of Military History. Accessed 8 March 2024. history.army.mil/books/wwii/utah/utah7.htm.

Sparrow, John. *History of Demobilization of Personnel in the United States Army.* Department of the Army. 1952. Accessed 14 May2024. https://history.army.mil/html/books/104/104-8/CMH_Pub_104-8.pdf.

Tankograd – Technical Manual 6036 – U.S. WWII & Korea M36, M36B1 & M36B2 90mm Gun Motor Carriage Tank Destroyers, Tankograd Publishing, Verlag Jochen Vollert, Militärfahrzeug. Accessed 8 March 2024. https://www.scribd.com/document/683957824/Tankograd-Technical-Manual-6036-U-S-WWII-Korea-M36-M36B1-M36B2-90mm-Gun-Motor-Carriage-Tank-Destroyers.

"The 80th Airborne Anit-Aircraft Battalion: Unit History." The 82nd Airborne—World War II. Accessed 8 March 2024. www.ww2-airborne.us/units/80/80.html.

"The 82nd Airborne Division, Action in Normandy France June–July 1944." Accessed 14 May 2024. www.eisenhowerlibrary.gov/sites/default/files/research/online-documents/d-day/1944-06-06-to-08-82nd-airborne.pdf.

"The Battle of Nijmegen." Liberation Route Europe. Accessed 8 March 2024. www.liberationroute.com/pois/182/the-battle-of-nijmegen.

"The Battle of Sainte-Mere-Eglise 1944: D-Day and After." Maxim Chornyi's Personal Blog on WWII. War Documentary. 30 October 2021. Accessed 8 March 2024. war-documentary.info/sainte-mere-eglise-1944/.

"The Fall of Cherbourg: Utah Beach to Cherbourg." U.S. Army Center of Military History. Accessed 8 March 2024. history.army.mil/books/wwii/utah/utah11.htm.

Waters, William. "A Brief History of Shaped Charges." Army Research Laboratory. 2008. Accessed 14 May 2024. https://apps.dtic.mil/sti/tr/pdf/ADA497450.pdf.

Unpublished Sources

Unpublished documents, including an unpublished history of the 80th Airborne Anti-Aircraft Battalion, U.S. military reports, histories, logs, and personal correspondence were provided from the collections of Mr. Robert Burns and Ms. Thulai Van Maanen.

Index

80th AAA. *See* 80th Airborne Anti-Aircraft Battalion
80th Airborne Anti-Aircraft Battalion
  325th Infantry Regiment and, 13
  326th Infantry Regiment and, 13
  activation, 13, 15
  as anti-tank battalion, 4, 5
  basic training, 17
  batteries, organization of, 15, 35
  command relationships and, 61–62, 90
  Distinguished Unit Citation and, 50
  dual role of, (anti-tank and anti-aircraft protection), 23
  first soldier killed in action, 48
  footwear, 87–88
  glider badge, 86–87
  hazardous duty pay, 18, 21, 27, 86, 87
  homecoming parade, 174
  informal anti-tank training with British – North Africa, 34, 35
  Involuntary status of glider men, 4, 21, 26
  Jack, Whitfield and command of, 16, 17, 31
  occupation of Germany, 161–162, 170–171, 173
  original title, 15
  Paddock, John W., command of, 172
  points system, 171–172, 174

  restructuring and, 93
  Singleton, Raymond, command of, 31, 60, 172
  training, 16, 19, 23–27, 60–61, 90
  Victory in Europe (VE) Day, 170
80th Airborne Anti-tank Anti-aircraft Battalion. *See* 80th Airborne Anti-Aircraft Battalion: original title
82th Airborne Division
  British 1st Airborne Corps and, 96
  325th Glider Regiment and, 30, 37, 48, 49, 77, 78, 105
  504th Parachute Infantry Regiment and, 37, 38, 40, 45, 48
  505th Parachute Infantry Regiment and, 37, 38, 43, 45, 48, 49, 58, 61, 65, 66
  507th Parachute Infantry Regiment and, 58, 65
  508th Parachute Infantry Regiment and, 58, 65
  as inheritor of 82nd Infantry Division, 3, 7, 8
  First Allied Airborne Army and, 93
  first deployment, 1943, 29
  "G.I. Discharge Plan." *See* Points System
  occupation force, Berlin, 172–173
  homecoming parade, 174
  points system, 171–172, 174
  training in North Africa, 33

204 • NEVER A DULL MOMENT

XVIII Airborne Corps and, 94, 125
82nd Infantry Division
as predecessor to 101st Airborne
Division, 7
as predecessor to 82nd Airborne
Division, 3, 7
conversion to airborne division, 7,
8, 18
Emory Pike and, 1–3
leadership of, 8
Sergeant York and, 8
World War II basic training, 1942, 7
90th Infantry Division, "Tough
'Ombres", 78–79
101st Airborne Division, 7, 8, 9, 80
British 1st Airborne Corps and, 96
invasion of Germany and, 158, 159
Lee, William and command of, 9
XVIII Airborne Corps and, 94
points system and, 174

Abell, Forest, 119
Albin, Ben, 73
Algeria, places
Camp Marina, 30
Oran, 50
Allegretti, Victor, 66
Alredge, Keith, 120
Ames, Charles, 72
Apicella, Anthony, 81
Armaments
.50-caliber M2 Browning machine
gun, 15, 47, 48, 80, 110, 135,
141, 142
2.36-inch rocket launchers,
"bazookas", 43, 49, 69, 74, 80,
128, 138, 146
6-pounder cannon, 4, 29, 34, 35–36,
41, 63, 130, 133, 135, 139, 142,
144
17-pounder anti-tank guns (76.2mm
shells), 115, 119

37mm anti-tank cannon, 4, 14, 15,
19, 25, 26, 29, 35–36
57mm cannon, 4, 29, 35–36, 46, 49,
60, 63, 65, 66, 67, 69, 73, 74, 75,
79, 80, 81, 85, 90, 104, 105, 107,
110, 116, 119, 144
57mm self-propelled anti-tank gun,
155
75mm cannon, 26
90mm cannon (mounted on M36),
128
Browning Automatic Rifle, 78, 129,
133
M45 Quadmount, 135
Number 82 Gammon grenade, 75,
80
Quad .50. See M45 Quadmount
Tank Destroyer, 118, 119, 128, 142,
144
German armaments
3.7cm cannon, 159
7.5cm cannon, 131
77mm cannon (German half-
track), 129
88mm gun, 82, 107
Flakpanzer. See Self-propelled
anti-aircraft gun (SPAAG)
Panzerfaust, 146
Self-propelled anti-aircraft gun
(SPAAG), 159
Atchley, John, 76
Atkinson, Robert, 116–117
Awards
Combat Infantryman's Badge, denial
of, 16
Distinguished Service Cross, 39, 69,
76, 80–81, 107, 133
Silver Star, 75, 76, 107, 109, 118,
119
Bronze Star, 47, 75, 80, 83, 105, 107,
118, 129, 132

INDEX • 205

Ballentine, William, 131, 134
Banish, Steve, 105
Barni, John, 77
Barre, George, 79
Barton, John, 105
Battle of the Bulge, 5, 123, 145, 147,
   150, 152
   Allied Units
      80th Airborne Anti-Aircraft
         Battalion and, 5, 125, 127, 129,
         134, 135, 138, 139, 141, 142,
         144, 146–147, 150
      17th Airborne Division and, 142
      82nd Airborne Division and, 123,
         125, 126, 127, 129, 134, 135,
         136, 137, 138, 139, 140, 141,
         142, 144, 145–146, 150, 151,
         153
      101st Airborne Division and, 123,
         125, 126, 150, 151
      307th Airborne Engineer
         Battalion, 131
      563rd Anti-Aircraft Artillery
         (Automatic Weapons) Battalion
         and, 134, 135
      3rd Armored Division, 136, 137,
         140, 145–146
      7th Armored Division and, 128,
         140, 145–146, 149
      21st Army Group, 153
      2-401st Glider Infantry Regiment
         and, 153
      51st Engineers and, 128, 131
      319th Glider Field Artillery
         Battalion and, 134
      320th Glider Field Artillery
         Battalion and, 134
      325th Glider Infantry Regiment
         and, 136, 137, 138, 139, 140,
         141, 153
      1st Infantry Division and, 152,
         153

      2nd Infantry Division and, 124
      106th Infantry Division and, 124,
         125
      119th Infantry Regiment and, 126
      422nd Infantry Regiment and,
         125
      423rd Infantry Regiment and, 125
      504th Parachute Infantry
         Regiment and, 128, 129, 130,
         136, 153
      505th Parachute Infantry
         Regiment and, 128, 130, 131,
         133, 134, 135, 136, 142, 144,
         153
      508th Parachute Infantry
         Regiment and, 128, 133, 136,
         138, 141, 149, 153
      517th Parachute Infantry
         Regiment and, 142, 149
      628th Tank Destroyer Battalion
         and, 142, 144
      703rd Tank Destroyer Battalion
         and, 128, 136
      First Canadian Army and, 123
      U.S. Army 30th Infantry Division
         and, 126, 128, 136–137, 139
      U.S. First Army and, 125, 126,
         136, 137, 151, 152
      U.S. Third Army and, 124, 142
      U.S. Ninth Army and, 125
      V Corps and, 152
      VII Corps and, 142, 150
      XVIII Airborne Corps and, 125,
         126, 136, 138, 139, 140, 142,
         145, 150, 151, 152
   Ardennes campaign, 144, 150
   German Units
      1st SS Panzer Division (German)
         and, 127, 128, 130, 131, 136,
         138
      2nd SS Panzer Division (German)
         and, 137, 138, 140, 145

206 • NEVER A DULL MOMENT

9th SS Panzer Division (German) and, 138, 141
9th SS Panzer Regiment and, 131, 135,
19th Panzergrenadiers and, 141
62nd Volksgrenadier Division and, 141
Kampfgruppe Peiper and, 126, 127, 128, 130, 136
Panzergrenadiers and, 131, 132, 133, 142
Peiper, Joachim, 126, 131
Baugh, James E., 17, 38–39, 61, 64, 82, 90, 118
Belgium, places
Abrefontaine, 142
Aisomont Road, 131, 133
Amblève River, 126, 130
Antwerp, 96, 123, 126, 131, 134, 145
Ardennes Forest, 123, 124
Baraque de Fraiture, 138
Basse-Bodeux, 139
Bastogne, 126, 130
Cheneux, 128, 129, 130, 135, 136
Creppe, 144, 149, 155
Deidenburg, 149
Erria, 141
Goronne, 142
Grand Halleux, 130, 135, 136, 139
Hébronval, 136
Houffalize, 150
Hürtgen Forest, 123, 154, 155
Liege, 140, 145
Malmedy-Stavelot, 137
Manhay, 140
Neuville, 142
Petit Halleux, 136
Rahier, 136
Regne, 138
River Meuse, 145
Rochelinval, 130

Salm River, 126, 130–131, 132, 133, 135, 136, 138, 139, 145, 149
Schnee Eifel, 124
St. Vith, 138, 139, 140, 149, 151
Stavelot, 130
Stoumont, 128
Tri-le-Cheslaing, 140
Trois-Ponts, 5, 123, 126, 128, 130, 131, 132, 133, 134, 135, 136, 137, 139
Vielsalm, 136, 138
Wanne, 131
Werbomont, 126, 127, 130, 136, 137, 138, 140, 145
Bell, James, 126, 139
Billingslea, Charles, 137, 140
Bonk, John F., 104, 165–167
Booth, Jasper, 73, 77
Boteler, Roland, 116–117
Bradley, Omar, 151
12th Army Group and, 94, 125, 150, 152, 157
28th Infantry Division, command of, 17–18
82nd Infantry Division, command of, 8, 17
Operations *Overlord* and *Neptune* planning and, 56, 57, 59
Brereton, Lewis, 95, 150, 151
British Forces
1st Airborne Corps, 96
1st Airborne Division, 96, 97, 98, 106
6th Airborne Division, 56
6th Battalion Grenadier Guards, 34
21st Army Group, 94, 142, 153
21st Independent Parachute Company, 44
52nd (Lowland) Division, 96
73rd Anti-Tank Regiment, 114, 118
201st Guards Brigade, 35
340th Anti-Tank Battery, 119

INDEX • 207

British 1st Parachute Brigade, 44
British Glider Regiment, 40
British Eighth Army, 34, 44
1st Air Landing Brigade, 37, 40, 107
Brooke, Alan, 55
Browning, Frederick "Boy", 96, 151
Buel, Paul, 74
Bullis, John, 105
Burnansky, Louis, 149
Burns, Edward, 90–91, 158n

Capelle, Louis, 128
Carter, Dent, 73
Churchill, Winston, 36, 55
Clark, Harold, 100
Chadwick, William, 139
Clark, Mark, 13, 86
Cliff, John, 76
Cliff, James, 107
Clouse, William, 121
Coburn, Donald, 66
Cockrell, William, 155
Coleman, Charles A., 17, 82
Collins, Lawton, 142
Concillio, Anthony, 117
Cook, Julian, 106
Copeland, Alvin, 115
COSSAC (Chief of Staff to the Supreme
    Allied Commander), 53–54, 55
Coustillac, Henry, 135, 142, 144
Crause, Earl, 73
Creek, Roy, 71, 72

Darby, William O., 46
DeGlopper, Charles N., 78
Delsignore, Edward, 131, 134
Dembovitz, Isadore, 73
Dillon, Jesse, 141
Dittmar, Edward, 115
Dittmar, Edward B., 17, 31
Dixon, Floyd, 47
Dolan, John "Red", 68–69, 71, 74, 75

Donitz, Grossadmiral Karl, 164
Doughty, Wilbur, 81
Downs, Floyd, 83
Duncan, Norvill, 83

Eisenhower, Dwight, 41, 54–55, 94, 95,
    96, 97, 138, 150, 153, 163
Ekman, William, 128, 133, 162
England, places
    Balderton airfield, 95, 99
    Beverton airfield, 165
    Camp Oadby, 95
    Cottesmore airfield, 99
    Fulbeck airfield, 95, 99
    Langar airfield, 95, 99
    Leicester, 86, 93
    Royal Airforce Field Ramsbury, 62,
        63
    Southampton, 86
Englebert, Captain, 134
Evers, William J., 85

Faith, Don, 104
Fary, Ray, 66, 69, 73, 75, 81, 116–117,
    163
Fellers, James, 110, 165, 170
Fields, James, 66
First Allied Airborne Army, 93, 94, 95,
    98, 150, 151, 157
Fisher, Joe, 74
Fox, Lawrence, 73, 126
France, places
    Amfreville, 59, 65
    Baupte, 80, 81, 82, 83
    Beuzeville, 80
    Bois de Limors Forest, 85
    Caen, 54
    Camp Chicago, 171
    Camp Oklahoma City, 173
    Camp Suippes, 121, 125, 126, 144
    Cauquigny, 69, 77, 78

208 • NEVER A DULL MOMENT

Chef-du-Pont, 59, 64, 66, 71, 72, 73, 74
Cherbourg, 54, 55, 82, 85
Cotentin Penninsula, 59, 77, 79, 81
Dieppe, 57
Douve River, 58, 80, 81, 82, 83
Értienville, 83
Falaise Pocket, 98
Hébert, 86
La Fière Causeway, 63, 65, 66, 68, 69, 71–72, 73, 74, 75, 77, 78
La Haye-du-Puits, 83, 85
Laon, 171
Le Ham, 79
Les Forges, 73
Merderet River, 59, 63, 64, 65, 66, 68, 69, 77, 79, 80
Merville, 55
Neuville-au-Plain, 66, 67, 68
Normandy, 55, 65, 73, 74, 86, 97
Paris, 94, 96, 125, 172
Pas-de-Calais, 54
Pont-l'Abbe, 83
Ravenoville, 55
Rheims, 173
Sainte-Marie-du-Mont, 56
Sainte-Mère-Église, 59, 60, 63, 64, 65, 66, 68, 73, 74, 75, 76, 77, 79, 87, 107, 128
Sainte-Sauveur-le-Vicomte, 57, 58, 59, 81, 82, 83
Sword Beach, 56
Utah Beach, 56, 60, 63, 64, 66, 76, 86
Vindefontaine, 82
French Morocco, places
Casablanca, 29
Ouijda, 30
Fuller, William, 126, 127, 135, 153

Galatzan, Joe S., 16, 46, 47
Gale, Richard, 56

Gates, Jim, 66
Gavin, James
82nd Airborne Division command, 94, 125, 151
Battle of the Bulge and, 126, 128, 136, 137, 138, 139, 140, 144–146
invasion of Germany and 154–155, 159, 163, 164, 165, 170
Occupation of Germany and, 172
Operation *Husky* and, 37, 38, 43, 49, 50
Operation *Overlord* and, 56–57
Operation *Market Garden* and, 101, 103, 106, 113
Operation *Neptune* and, 69, 71, 72, 74, 78
XVIII Airborne Corps, acting commanding general, 126
German Forces
7th Army Sturm Bataillon (assault battalion), 76
3rd Battalion of 1058th Regiment, 67
176th Infantry Division, 98
243rd Infantry Division, 58
709th Infantry Division, 58
719th Infantry Division, 98
91st Luftlande (Air Landing) Division, 58, 59
9th Panzer Division, 98, 107, 114
10th Panzer Division, 98, 107, 114
100th Panzer Replacement Battalion, 69
1057th Regiment, 78, 79
1057th Regiment, 91st Division, 69
1058th Regiment, 76
1st SS Panzer Division, 127, 128, 130
2nd SS Panzer Division, 137, 138, 140, 145
9th SS Panzer Division, 131, 135
10th SS Panzer Division, 106
9th SS Reconnaissance Battalion, 113

INDEX • 209

First Parachute Army, 98
Hermann Göring Division, 37
II SS Panzer Corps, 98
Panzer Abteilung 100 (Tank Task
    Force 100), 59
Germany, places
    Berlin, 164, 172, 173
    Elbe River, 163, 164
    Frankfurt, 169
    Göhlen, 164
    Grabow, 164
    Lövenich, 158
    Ludendorff Bridge, 157–158
    Ludwigslust, 165
    Lülsdorg, 161
    Mödrath, 158
    Neuhof, 153
    Niederkassel, 161
    Oitzendorf, 162–163
    Remagen, 158
    Rheinbach, 162
    Rhine River, 157–158, 159, 160, 161
    Roer River, 154
    Ruhr, 97
    Udenbreth, 153
    Vistula River, 123
    Wöbbelin, 164–65
    Wyler, 105, 108–109, 152
Gliders
    Airspeed Horsa (British), 40, 60, 71,
        89
    advantages of, 21
    carrying capacity, 4, 19, 21, 25, 64,
        89
    construction of, 20, 60
    hazards of, 21, 23, 24, 25, 73, 89
    initial announcement of to 82nd
        Airborne Division, 18
    loading/unloading, 4, 19, 24, 25, 60
    maneuverability of, 89
    nighttime assault, 89
    production of, 26

training, 16, 19, 23, 24, 25, 40, 44
Waco CG-4A, 19, 20, 40, 60, 89
Waco CG-13, 89
Gorham, Arthur, 39–40
Graham, Jay, 131
Grimes, Edward, 115
Gutshall, John, 81

Hall, George, 166
Hannan, Philip, 165
Hansen, Leslie, 118
Harris, William, 105
Harrison, James, 79
Hart, Joseph A. P., 154, 160
Hauptman, William, 82
Heim, Marcus, 69
Hineman, Charles, 109
Hodges, Courtney, 125, 126, 136, 151,
    152, 154
Holland/Netherlands, places
    Arnhem, 96, 97, 106, 112, 113, 114,
        115
    Arnhem Bridge, 98, 108
    Beek, 100, 105, 109
    Eindhoven, 97, 113
    Grave, 97, 106, 112, 116, 118, 165
    Groesbeek, 105, 110, 115, 119, 120,
        165
    Groesbeek Heights, 106, 113
    Horst, 103
    Mook, 103, 104, 105, 109, 130
    Nijmegen, 97, 98, 103, 104, 105,
        106, 107, 108, 109, 111, 112, 113,
        116, 120
    Lower Rhine, 96, 97, 107, 112,
        120
    Reichswald (forest), 103, 111
    Rhine River, 95
    Siegfried Line, 96, 97, 112, 153, 155
    Son Bridge, 113
    Waal River, 106, 107, 112, 114
    Wilhelmina Canal, 113

210 • NEVER A DULL MOMENT

Holliday, Private, 129
Honeycutt, Keith, 81
Hoover, Private, 129
Horrocks, Brian, 96, 112, 114
Hudak, Andy, 120
Hunt, John, 74
Husk, Harold, 81

Ianni, Charles, 31
invasion of Germany
  80th Airborne Anti-Aircraft Battalion
    and, 152, 153, 154, 155, 157, 158,
    159, 161, 162, 163, 164, 165, 171
  82nd Airborne Division and, 151,
    152, 153, 154, 155, 157, 158, 159,
    161, 162, 163, 164, 169
  101st Airborne Division, 158, 159
  307th Airborne Engineer Battalion,
    154
  9th Armored Division and, 158
  12th Army Group and, 152, 153,
    154, 157, 158
  21st Army Group and, 154, 155,
    158, 163
  1-325th Glider Infantry Regiment,
    154
  325th Glider Infantry Regiment,
    153, 159
  2-401st Glider Infantry Regiment,
    153, 154
  1st Infantry Division, "Big Red
    One", 152, 153
  99th Infantry Division and, 154
  504th Parachute Infantry Regiment,
    153, 154, 159, 163
  505th Parachute Infantry Regiment,
    153, 154, 155, 159, 161, 162, 163,
    164, 165
  508th Parachute Infantry Regiment,
    153, 155
  British 6th Airborne Division, 163

Gavin, James and, 159, 163, 164,
  165, 172
Huebner, Clarence and, 154
Miliken, John and, 157, 158
Pratt, William and, 162
SHAEF and, 158, 159, 162–63, 170
Simpson, William and, 154
Singleton, Raymond and, 155, 165
Surrender of German Forces, 165,
  170
Swift, Ira and, 162
U.S. 7th Armored Division, 163
U.S. 8th Infantry Division, 163
U.S. First Army, 152, 154, 157
U.S. III Corps and, 157
U.S. Ninth Army and, 154, 155
U.S. V Corps and, 152, 154, 155
XVIII Airborne Corps and, 152, 163
Ireland, Al, 60, 87
Ison, James, 47
Issacs, Jack, 135
Italy, invasion of. *See* Operation
  Giant II; Operation *Avalanche*
Italy, places
  Battipaglia, 48
  Capo d'Orso, 46
  Castellammare, 47
  Chiunzi Pass, 46
  Maiori, 46, 47
  Minori, 47
  Naples, 46, 48
  Paestum, 46, 47
  Rome, 45, 47
  Salerno, 45, 46, 47, 50, 73
  Tremonte, 47

Jack, Whitfield
  80th Airborne Anti-Aircraft Artillery
    Battalion, command of, 16, 17, 30
  80th Airborne Anti-Aircraft Artillery
    Battalion, Division Anti-Aircraft
    officer, 30

INDEX • 211

82nd Airborne Division staff, G-3
  operations officer, 30–31
Disciplinary philosophy of, 31–32
Jacks, Daniel, 118
Jacobsen, Herald F., 16, 30, 31
Jaeger, Anthony, 120
Jensen, Peter, 136
Johnson, Samuel, 119
Jones, Claire, 149
jump boots. *See* 80th Airborne Anti-
  Aircraft Battalion/Footwear

Karshenbaum, Morris, 126, 132
Kaufman, Glenn, 112, 141
Keith, Warren C., 16, 30
Kellam, Frederick Caesar, 68, 69
Kelly, Harold, 129
Kibbe, Richard, 139
Kish, Jim, 139
Knollwood Maneuvers, 42
Koch, Oscar, 124
Koch, Stuart, 99
Koprowski, Harry, 129
Krause, Ed, 65, 66, 67
Kroos, Arthur, 17, 30, 32, 82–83, 104,
  144, 165–170
Kubas, Stanley, 74

Lebenson, Leonard, 20
Lee, William
  101st Airborne Division, command
    of, 9
  proposes creation of American
    airborne division, 9, 13
  provisional test platoon for parachutist
    training, 12
  Provisional Parachute Group,
    command of, 12
Leh, John, 138
Leigh-Mallory, Sir Trafford, 56, 59
Lettieri, Paul, 119
Leuck, Paul, 110

Lewis, Harry, 37, 77
Lindquist, Roy, 141
Linke, Michael, 83
Littlejohn, Robert F., 17
Luftwaffe, 57–58

MacLean, Edward, 115
Majoros, Joe, 120
March, Francis, 155
Marshall, George C., 32, 33, 41, 55
Matsko, Andrew, 141
McCormick, John, 141
McFadden, John, 64, 109
McLean, Edward, 48
McNair, Lesley, 9, 42
McNeill, Neil, 130, 139, 161
McNeill, Samuel, 119
Middleton, Troy, 85
Miller, Carl, 120
Montgomery, Bernard Law, 34, 55–56,
  94, 95, 96, 115, 138, 141, 150, 153,
  157, 163
Morgan, F. E., 54
Morrissey, Edward, 173
Mullenax, Raynmond, 119
Morris, Estell, 149

Neel, Malcolm, 125, 135, 136, 139
Nelson, Norman, 34, 64, 132
Neuman, Raymond, 79
Neumann, Al, 146
Never A Dull Moment poster, 19
Newman, Ray, 109
North Africa, invasion of. *See* Operation
  Torch
Northern Ireland, places
  Belfast, 50
  Kilrea, 50

O'Leary, Charles, 109
Operation *Avalanche,* 45–48

80th Airborne Anti-Aircraft Battalion
and, 45, 46, 50, 73
82nd Airborne Division and, 45, 47
325th Glider Infantry and, 48
36th Infantry Division and, 46
504th Parachute Infantry Regiment
and, 48
505th Parachute Infantry Regiment
and, 48
Armstice and, 47
Battipaglia, 48
Capo d'Orso, 46
Castellammare, 47
Chiunzi Pass, 46
Maiori, 46, 47
Minori, 47
Naples, 46, 48
Paestum, 46, 47
Rome, 45, 47
Salerno, 45, 46, 47, 50, 73
Task Force Ranger and, 46, 47, 50
Tremonte, 47
Operation *Giant II,* 44–45, 47
Operation *Husky,* 36–42, 98
80th Airborne Anti-aircraft Battalion
and, 37, 40, 41, 98
82nd Airborne Division and, 37, 41,
43
325th Glider Infantry Regiment and,
37, 49
1st Infantry Division and, 39
504th Parachute Infantry Regiment
and, 37, 38, 39, 41, 49
505th Parachute Infantry Regiment
and, 37, 38, 39–40, 43, 86
Biazza Ridge, 38, 49
British Glider Regiment and, 40
Ponte Grande, 40
"Swing Board", review of, 42
Operation *Market Garden,* 96, 97, 98,
114, 115, 120, 123, 152

80th Airborne Anti-Aircraft Battalion
and, 95, 98, 99, 100, 104, 105,
108–110, 114, 115, 117, 118, 119,
120, 121
82nd Airborne Division and, 96,
97–98, 101, 103, 104, 105, 106,
108, 110, 112–113, 114, 117, 120,
121
101st Airborne Division and, 96, 97,
98, 106, 113
307th Airborne Engineer Battalion
and, 107
325th Glider Infantry Regiment and,
105, 106, 110, 112, 116, 118, 120
504th Parachute Infantry Regiment
and, 101, 106, 107, 109, 111, 116
505th Parachute Infantry Regiment
and, 101, 103, 104, 105, 106, 107,
109, 110, 120
508th Parachute Infantry Regiment
and, 100, 101, 104, 109, 111, 113,
115
British 1st Airborne Corps, 96
British 1st Airborne Division and, 98,
106, 107, 108, 112, 113–114
British 73rd Anti-Tank Regiment
and, 114, 118
British 340th Anti-Tank Battery and,
119
First Airborne Division and, 97
First Allied Airborne Army and, 98
Frederick Browning and, 151
Irish Guards and, 114
Operation *Garden,* 96, 106, 114
Operation *Market,* 90, 96, 98, 105,
110, 120, 167
Polish 1st Independent Parachute
Brigade and, 96, 107, 108
XXX Corps and, 95, 96, 97, 98,
103, 105, 106, 107, 108, 112,
113–114, 115
Operation *Overlord,* 37, 54, 60, 91, 96

COSSAC plan, 55–56
Eisenhower, Dwight, and, 55
  Operation *Neptune,* 56, 73, 87, 88,
    89, 94, 98, 100, 110, 153
    80th Airborne Anti-aircraft
      Battalion and, 59–60, 63–64,
      68, 69, 71, 73, 74, 75, 76,
      79, 80, 82, 83, 85, 86, 87,
      88, 89–90
    82nd Airborne Division and,
      56, 58, 59, 63, 65, 66,
      68–69, 78, 79, 80, 81, 85,
      85, 86, 88, 89, 90
    101st Airborne Division and,
      56, 59, 80, 89
    307th Airborne Engineer
      Battalion and, 65, 69
    782nd Airborne Ordnance
      Company, 85
    319th Glider Field Artillery
      Battalion and, 81
    325th Glider Infantry and, 77,
      78, 79, 80, 82, 83, 93
    8th Infantry Division and, 85,
      86
    79th Infantry Division and, 85
    90th Infantry Division and, 78,
      79, 80, 85
    505th Parachute Infantry
      Regiment and, 58, 59, 60,
      65, 66–67, 68, 71, 74, 75,
      76, 77, 78, 79, 82, 85
    507th Parachute Infantry
      Regiment and, 58, 65, 68,
      71, 72, 77, 78, 79, 80, 81,
      82
    508th Parachute Infantry
      Regiment and, 58, 65, 68,
      77, 78, 79, 80, 81, 82, 83
    505th Regimental Combat
      Team, 85
    Bradley, Omar and, 56, 57, 59

    British 6th Airborne Division
      and, 56
    Chef-du-Pont, 59, 64, 66,
      71–72, 73, 74
    Gavin, James and, 56, 57, 71,
      72, 74, 78
    German Forces and, 58–59,
      67–68
    plan for initial assault, 56
    Ireland, Al and, 60, 87
    Kellam's Bridge, 69
    La Fière Causeway, 65, 66, 68,
      69, 71–72, 73, 74, 75, 77,
      78
    Mission *Detroit,* 59, 60, 65, 69,
      73, 74
    Mission *Elmira,* 59, 71
    Montgomery, Bernard Law
      and, 55, 56
    Ridgway, Matthew and, 60, 66,
      77, 78, 79, 83, 86, 89
    Sainte-Marie-du-Mont, 56
    Sainte-Mère-Église, 59, 60,
      63–66, 68, 74, 75, 76, 77,
      79
    Sainte-Sauveur-le-Vicomte, 57,
      59, 81
    Singleton, Raymond and, 60,
      63, 64, 65
    Sword Beach, 56
    Utah Beach, 56, 59, 60, 63, 64,
      66, 76, 86
    VII Corps and, 85
    U.S. VIII Corps and, 80, 81,
      85, 86
Operation *Plunder,* 157
Operation *Torch*
  509th Parachute Infantry Battalion
    and, 43–44
  Vichy French troops and, 33
Operation *Varsity,* 151, 157

214 • NEVER A DULL MOMENT

82nd Airborne Division, non-
participation, 151
101st Airborne Division, non-
participation, 151
British 6th Airborne Division and,
151, 157
Canadian 1st Parachute Battalion and,
157
First Allied Airborne Army and, 151,
157
Ridgway, Matthew and, 151
U.S. 17th Airborne Division and,
151, 157
XVIII Airborne Corps and, 151, 157

pathfinder concepts and techniques, 43
Patton, George, 41, 124, 142
Peterson, Lenold, 69
Pierce, Wayne, 154
Pike, Emory, 1–3, 8
Polish Forces
1st Independent Parachute Brigade,
96
Pratt, William W., 16, 24, 48, 116, 120,
162

Quandt Family, Arthur Kroos and, 168

Rider, Richard E., 80, 81
Ridgway, Matthew
80th Airborne Anti-aircraft Battalion
reorganization and, 90
82nd Airborne Division, command
of, 18
82nd Infantry Division, assistant
division commander of, 17
82nd Infantry Division, command of,
8-9, 18
Arthur Kroos, aide-de-camp and, 83,
104, 170
Battle of the Bulge, 126, 138, 150,
151

glider aerobatics demonstration, 18
hazardous duty pay, advocate, 86–87
invasion of Germany and, 152
nighttime glider operations, ending
of, 89
Operation *Husky* and, 37, 41
Operation *Giant II* and, 45
Operation *Neptune* and, 60, 66, 77,
78, 79, 83
Operation *Varsity* and, 151
Orientation parachute jump at Fort
Benning, 9, 10–11, 18
U.S. XVIII Corps command and, 94,
125

Richgels, Harold, 81, 117
Rippy, Bayard, 79, 82
Risovich, Fred, 85
Robinson, Harry, 131, 133
Rommel, Erwin, 57, 58
Roosevelt, Franklin, 32, 33, 55, 87, 161
Rose, Maurice, 136, 137
Roydson, Dale, 69
Rucker, Choice R., 16, 30, 79, 80, 82
Rule of LGOPs, 38
Rundstedt, Gerd von, 57
Russell, Nock W., 16, 48, 77
Ryan, Edward, 81

Sanford, Teddy, 77
Schlupp, Paul, 126, 132, 134
Schubert, George Junior, 118
Scott, Richard, 131
Seddon, Ernest, 136
SHAEF (Supreme Headquarters Allied
Expeditionary Forces), 93–94, 126,
150, 153, 158, 159, 162–163, 170
Shenafelt, Ken (Kenneth), 118, 121, 135
Sherman, James C., 16
Shirley, Carson, 155
Sicily, invasion of. *See* Operation *Husky*
Sicily, places
Biazza Ridge, 38, 49

INDEX • 215

Castelvetrano airfield, 47
Palermo, 41
Ponte Grand, 40
Primosole Bridge, 44
Straits of Messina, 41, 45
Simpson, William, 125, 154
Singleton, Raymond E.
   80th Airborne Anti-Aircraft
      Battalion, executive officer, 16,
      17, 30
   80th Airborne Anti-Aircraft
      Battalion, command of, 16, 31,
      172
   155th, command of, 172
   battallion combat deployment,
      analysis of, 49–50
   battalion executive officer, 80th
      Airborne Anti-Aircraft Artillery
      Battalion, 16, 17
   Battle of the Bulge and, 127, 128,
      134, 142
   British Armaments and, 35
   invasion of Germany and, 155, 165
   meeting with British officers with
      tank fighting experience, 34
   Morocco, 1943, anti-tank batteries
      and, 30
   Operation *Husky* and, 40, 44
   Operation *Market Garden* and, 99,
      103, 112, 115, 119
   Operation *Neptune* and, 63, 64, 88,
      89
Skufea, Brank, 82
Sluman, Walter, 117
Smital, Gordon, 105, 131, 133
Smith, C. W., 141
Smurr, William V., 104, 165–167
Snyder, Paul, 81
Snow, Private First Class, 129
Sosabowski, Stanislaw, 98
Stark, Marshall, 77, 110, 117, 118
Stephens, John F., 16

Stevens, William, 73
Swift, Ira, 133, 162
Swing Board. *See* Operation *Husky*:
   "Swing Board", review of
Swing, Joseph, 42

Tanks
   M4 Sherman, 142
   Mark I (British), 3
   Mark III (German), 118, 136
   Mark IV (German), 34, 75, 76, 81,
      117, 144
   Renault (German/Captured French),
      69, 75, 81
   Tiger I Panzer (German), 34
Taylor, Maxwell, 45, 56
Taylor, Stokes, 131, 132, 133, 134
Telford, Worthington S., 17, 158
Thacker, Samuel, 117
Timmes, Charles, 77
Tucker, Reuben, 37, 128
Tunisia, places
   Bizerte, 45, 47
   Kairouan, 30
   Mareth Line, 35
   Sousse, 35
Turnbull, Turner T., 66, 67, 68

United States, places
   Camp Edwards, Massachusetts, 29
   Camp Claiborne, Louisiana, 7, 8, 16,
      17, 146
   Fort Benning, Georgia, 9, 12, 18,
      21, 22
   Fort Bragg, North Carolina, 29
   Laurinburg-Maxton Army Airfield,
      North Carolina, 19, 24–25, 26
U.S. 12th Army Group, 94, 125, 150,
   152
U.S. XVIII Corps, 94, 125, 126, 138,
   139, 140, 142, 145, 150, 151, 152,
   157, 163

Uitto, Carl, 76
Urquhart, Roy, 97

Vandervoort, Ben, 65, 66, 67–68, 76,
   107, 130, 131, 132, 133, 144
Vertical Envelopment, U.S.
   British Army and, 12–13
   Eisenhower criticism of, 41
   German success with, 21
   history of, 11–18, 21–22
   McNair criticism of, 42–43
   Operation *Husky* and, 37

Walberg, Gordon, 126, 127, 132

Wales, places
   Cardiff, 62
Weineke, Robert Henry, 119
Werewolves, German, 161
Wertich, Jake, 105, 109, 130, 131, 132,
   133, 134
Williams, David, 48
Willoughby, Darrel, 149
Wilson, Bernard, 81
Wilson, Raynor, 66
Wilson, Walter, 73, 75
Wyman, Cleon, 74

Zimdars, Raymond, 81